D0706656

NATIVE AMERICAN ISSUES

NATIVE AMERICAN ISSUES

PAUL C. ROSIER

Contemporary American Ethnic Issues
Ronald H. Bayor, Series Editor

GREENWOOD PRESS
Westport, Connecticut • London

Library of Congress Cataloging-in-Publication Data

Rosier, Paul C.
Native American issues / Paul C. Rosier.
p. cm.—(Contemporary American ethnic issues, ISSN 1543–219X)
Includes bibliographical references and index.
ISBN 0–313–32002–0 (alk. paper)
1. Indians of North America—Government relations—1934– 2. Indians of North America—Legal status, laws, etc. 3. Indians of North America—Economic conditions. I. Title. II. Series.
E93.R83 2003
323.1′197—dc21 2002044844

British Library Cataloging-in-Publication Data is available.

Library of Congress Catalog Card Number: 2002044844
ISBN: 0–313–32002–0
ISSN: 1543–219X

First published in 2003

Greenwood Press, 88 Post Road West, Westport, CT 06881
An imprint of Greenwood Publishing Group, Inc.
www.greenwood.com

Printed in the United States of America

The paper used in this book complies with the Permanent Paper Standard issued by the National Information Standards Organization (Z39.48–1984).

10 9 8 7 6 5 4 3 2 1

For my mother and father, Kay and Jim Rosier

CONTENTS

SERIES FOREWORD

Northern Ireland, the Middle East, and South Asia are just some of the places where ethnic/racial issues have divided communities and countries. The United States too has a long history of such division which often has erupted into violent conflict. In America, a nation of immigrants with many ethnic and racial groups, it is particularly important to understand the issues that separate us from one another. Nothing could be more damaging to our nation of nations than the misconception of other's opinions on controversial topics.

The purpose of this series is to provide the means by which students particularly, but also teachers and general readers, can comprehend the contentious issues of our times. The diverse groups chosen for inclusion are the country's main ethnic/racial minorities. Therefore, the groups covered are African Americans, Native Americans, Asian Americans, Latino Americans, Jewish Americans and Muslim Americans. Each book is written by an expert on that group; a scholar able to explain and discuss clearly in a narrative style what are the points of friction within the minority and between the minority and majority.

Each volume begins with the historical background of a contemporary issue, including court decisions and legislative action, that provides context. This introduction is followed by the pros and cons of the debate, various viewpoints, the opinion of notables, questions for discussion or paper topics, and recommended reading. Readers of this series will become conversant with such topics as affirmative action and reparations, Indians names and images in sports, undocumented immigrants and border control, intermarriage, separation of church and state, old world ties and assimilation and racial profiling. Knowledge about such concerns will help limit conflict, encourage discussion and clarify the opinions of those who disagree with majority views. It is important, especially for students, to recognize the value of a different point of view.

Also of importance is to realize that some issues transcend ethnic/racial boundaries. Stereotypical images are concerns of both Native Americans and Asian Americans, affirmative action and reparations are more than black-white controversies, separation of church and state affects Muslim as well as Jewish Americans. These subjects are perennial ones in American history and serve to illustrate that they need to be discussed in a way that brings attention to various views.

This type of series would have served a useful purpose during earlier eras when Americans searched for answers and clarification for complex issues tied to race and ethnicity. In a nation that has now become more diversified and during a period once again of extensive immigration, it is time to look at our disputes and calmly appraise and discuss.

Ronald H. Bayor
Georgia Tech

INTRODUCTION

The summer 2002 Hollywood movie *Windtalkers* brought attention to the Navajo codetalkers who were instrumental in fighting Japanese forces during World War II. It may have come as a surprise to many Americans that Native Americans were then and still are deeply patriotic. That patriotism became clear after the terrorist attacks on New York City and Washington, D.C., on September 11, 2001. As an editorial in *Native American Times* put it, "American Indians love this country like no other.... Today we are all New Yorkers."[1] American Indians backed up that sentiment by sending people and money to New York. The Lakota Sioux (South Dakota) sent police officers and emergency medical personnel of the Pine Ridge Ambulance Service to New York, a contribution from one of the poorest communities in the country to one of the wealthiest. All told, American Indian communities contributed several million dollars to various relief funds. President George W. Bush noted Native Americans' contributions during wartime and after September 11 in proclaiming November as Native American Heritage Month. Bush also promised that his administration would "protect and honor tribal sovereignty and help to stimulate economic development" as well as "preserve their freedoms, as they practice their religion and culture."[2] Many Native Americans value their allegiance to America but also express the need for America to respect their own cultural and tribal identities. As U.S. Army Sergeant First Class Leonard Gouge of the Oklahoma Muscogee Creek community put it shortly after the attacks of September 11, "By supporting the American way of life, I am preserving the Indian way of life."[3]

Throughout the twentieth century, Native Americans faced the difficult tasks of protecting tribal sovereignty, stimulating economic development,

Willie B. Underwood, a Seminole-Chickasaw Native American Indian and veteran of the Vietnam War (survivor of the Tet Offensive), bows his head during the playing of taps at a Veterans Day ceremony in 2002 at the 45th Infantry Division Museum in Oklahoma City. (AP/Wide World Photos)

and fighting to preserve cultural and religious freedoms. Beginning in the 1960s, during the so-called Red Power era, American Indian activists helped spur Congress to adopt legislation that granted new sovereign powers to Native Americans or restored to them old powers codified in treaties. Backed by a series of U.S. Supreme Court decisions upholding those sovereign rights, tribal groups recognized by the federal government as being authentic enjoyed a unique political status. "Federally recognized tribes" maintain individual sovereignty over tribal members unless that sovereignty has been abridged by federal court or legislative action. They maintain their own courts to prosecute crimes, with the exception of the so-called Major Crimes—rape, arson, and murder. Indians living on their reservations generally do not need to obey state regulations like hunting and fishing game laws and do not pay state income or excise taxes (though they are liable for federal income taxes). Indians also do not have to permit non-Indians living within reservation boundaries to participate in tribal decision making. This expansion of sovereignty created an anti-Indian backlash against tribal rights that either abridged the rights of non-Indians living on the reservation or extended to Indians certain rights not available to non-Indians off the reservation. Thus, the fight to preserve the right to live an "Indian way of life," of self-determination, continues in the twenty-first century.

At its June 2002 convention, the Native American Journalists Association issued a report criticizing how its non-Indian peers cover affairs of Native Americans across the country, contending that large newspapers focus on Indian gaming and mascot controversies at the expense of other issues. Newspapers like the *New York Times, USA Today,* and the *Los Angeles Times* also mostly cover the events of the Sioux and the Navajo nations, two of the largest Native groups in the country. Additionally, the authors of the study were critical of the language used in such articles, which typically contain words and phrases like *chief* and *circling the wagons.* According to association president Mary Annette Pember, "If we really want to effectively change this, we have to work at it.... Covering Indian country, it's extremely complex."[4] Reporters also tend to marginalize Indian communities. As wildfires were devastating parts of the American West during the summer of 2002, Charlie LeDuff noted in a front-page article in the *New York Times* that "while national attention is focused on the threat Arizona's wildfires pose to Show Low, the [white] resort town, the blaze has already brought widespread and lasting economic damage to Apache country.... Few reporters have come to the reservation. Little emergency aid has been sent to White River, the seat of tribal government, though 1,500 Apaches have been evacuated from their homes."[5]

Such limited coverage has led to stereotypical views of Native Americans as living in extremes: either wealthy from gambling or mired in poverty and alcoholism. Between those extremes lies the complex world of Indian country, one that involves more than 550 separate Indian nations, 4.1 million people who identify themselves as Native Americans, and a myriad of different customs, traditions, and views on Indian life and on association with America at large.[6]

This volume is intended to inform readers of the varied cultural, political, social, and economic dimensions of contemporary Native America as well as to prompt them to consider the complexity and complications of ethnic and cultural diversity in the United States. Each chapter is designed to facilitate an understanding of the debates that have arisen within Indian communities and between Indians and non-Indians on critical issues such as economic development, representations of culture, and treaty rights. The presentation of each issue begins with an introduction that outlines the important historical events, legal decisions, and congressional legislation that frame the debate that follows. To represent fairly both sides of these six debates I examined a great variety of newspaper articles, journal essays, scholarly papers, national magazines like *Time* and *Newsweek,* and books devoted to the subject. A number of the writings came from Native American newspapers and journals, the number of which has been steadily rising since the 1980s. I have emphasized the use of the voices of those involved in these debates, both those of Native Americans and of non–Native Americans. Students will argue for or against a position on the basis of what these voices have to say as well as on their consideration of the historical and cultural forces that inspire them.

Chapter 1, "Sports Mascots, Names, and Images," addresses a fundamental issue for Native Americans: how they are represented in everyday life through public sporting events. More than a thousand high school and college sports teams currently employ Indian names, mascots, or images, as do professional teams like the Cleveland Indians, Atlanta Braves, Kansas City Chiefs, and Washington Redskins. Supporters of the use of Indian-themed mascots and names contend that they celebrate Native Americans and their customs and can thus educate students and fans about Native American culture. Native Americans argue that images of them in the sporting world perpetuate stereotypical representations of Indian life that emerged from the end of the Plains wars of the late nineteenth century and thus preclude an accurate understanding of the literal and figurative face of contemporary Native America. This particular issue has been especially contentious, largely because debates on it have taken place in so many communities across the country as well as on a national level, but also because many Native Americans believe that if such images can persist in public spaces, then respect for contemporary Indian culture and for their political rights will be difficult to secure.

Chapters 2, 3, and 4 address Native Americans' efforts to restore rights guaranteed in nineteenth-century treaties, claim lands they believe were unfairly or illegally taken from them, and repatriate or restore ownership of ancestral remains and sacred objects that were taken by government agents, grave robbers, and scientists. In both treaty rights and land claims cases, the U.S. Supreme Court has ruled in favor of Indian litigants. In the process, however, the expansion of Native American sovereignty has been challenged in a series of lawsuits and by public protests. Non-Indian residents of the territory claimed by or the lands reserved for Indians object that Native Americans are given rights denied other Americans as well as argue that they should not be penalized for events that took place more than a hundred years ago. The efforts of activists to reclaim ancestral remains and cultural artifacts from private and public museums have been less publicly contentious but no less divisive among scientists, tribal officials, and museum administrators.

Chapters 5 and 6 address Native Americans' efforts to build reservation economies that can ameliorate the poverty that clings to a number of reservation communities. Chapter 5 focuses on the controversies generated by the great expansion of Native American gaming enterprises, which operate in more than 30 states today. Gaming enterprises have created jobs and revenues for tribal communities in need of both, but their proliferation has also created grounds for debate on the economic impact of gaming on non-Indian businesses, the political right of Native Americans to operate gaming businesses off limits to other Americans, and gambling's potential social costs for both Indians and non-Indians. Chapter 6 examines the evolving debate between supporters of reservation development that involves the extraction of natural resources from or the storage of hazardous and nuclear wastes on reservation lands and those who oppose such development on the grounds that it damages the earth and its inhabitants. These mining and waste storage projects have divided members of communities in need of revenue and jobs as well as politicians in western states targeted by federal negotiators and private businesses for the dumping of nuclear waste.

As readers will see, these issues have created divisions both within Native American communities and between Indian and non-Indian communities. American Indians are a decidedly heterogeneous ethnic group, divided by geography, politics, traditions, aspirations, and even by what they want to be called—American Indian or Native American. Most Native Americans prefer to be identified by their tribal name, such as Blackfeet, Lakota, or Zuni. They are unified, however, by the goal of protecting their right to be Blackfeet, Lakota, or Zuni, even as they may celebrate their connections to American society and the values it represents.

NOTES

1. Editorial, *Native American Times,* 12 September 2001, <www.okit.com/opinion/2001/augsept/hope.html> (accessed September 2002).
2. President, proclamation, "National American Indian Heritage Month," *The White House,* 19 November 2001, <www.whitehouse.gov/news/releases/2001/11/20011112-4.html> (accessed September 2002).
3. "Honor Spurs Muscogee (Creek) Leonard Gouge to His Country's Defense," *Cherokee News Path,* 28 September 2001.
4. Chet Barfield, "Indians at Convention Take on Media Issues," *San Diego Union Tribune,* 20 June 2002.
5. Charlie LeDuff, "Away from the TV Cameras, Fire Consumes Apache Land," *New York Times,* 27 June 2002.
6. *U.S. Census Bureau,* <www.census.gov> (accessed September 2002).

RESOURCE GUIDE

Suggested Readings

Berkhofer, Robert F., Jr. *The White Man's Indian: Images of the American Indian from Columbus to the Present.* New York: Vintage Books, 1979.

Bordewich, Fergus. *Killing the White Man's Indian; Reinventing Native Americans at the End of the Twentieth Century.* New York: Doubleday, 1996.

Eagle/Walking Turtle. *Indian America: A Traveler's Companion.* Sante Fe: John Muir, 1993.

Frantz, Klaus. *Indian Reservations in the United States.* Chicago: University of Chicago Press, 1993.

Hoxie, Fred, and Peter Iverson. *Indians in American History: An Introduction.* Wheeling, Ill.: Harlan Davidson, 1998.

Iverson, Peter. *"We Are Still Here": American Indians in the Twentieth Century.* Wheeling, Ill.: Harlan Davidson, 1998.

Jaimes, M. Annette. *The State of Native America: Genocide, Colonization, and Resistance.* Boston: South End Press, 1992.

Josephy, Alvin M., Jr., Joane Nagel, and Troy Johnson, eds. *Red Power: The American Indians' Fight for Freedom.* 2d ed. Lincoln: University of Nebraska Press, 1999.

Nagel, Joane. *American Indian Ethnic Renewal: Red Power and the Resurgence of Identity and Culture.* New York: Oxford University Press, 1996.

Parman, Donald. *Indians and the American West in the Twentieth Century.* Bloomington: Indiana University Press, 1994.

Pevar, Stephen. *The Rights of Indians and Tribes: The Basic ACLU Guide to Indian and Tribal Rights.* Carbondale: Southern Illinois University Press, 1992.

1

SPORTS MASCOTS, NAMES, AND IMAGES

It is difficult to travel anywhere in the United States without stumbling on a town, a product, a vehicle, a street sign, or a sports team with an Indian-themed name. On the American road and in America's sky one can see Jeep Cherokees, Pontiacs, Winnebago motor homes, Piper Cherokee airplanes, and, thankfully less visibly, Apache attack helicopters. In American homes and schools, Oneida flatware adorns many tables, while Big Chief writing tablets occupy many desks. Red Man chewing tobacco and Native American Spirits cigarettes are available to adults. Perhaps the most visible arena of this cultural expression is American sports, where one finds professional teams such as the Kansas City Chiefs, Washington Redskins, Golden State Warriors, Atlanta Braves, and Cleveland Indians; one also finds such expression at small-town high schools and big university campuses alike. Since the 1970s thousands of schools have debated whether their mascots are racist, sexist, or just plain offensive. While schools such as Auburn University, the University of Alabama-Birmingham, and the University of Massachusetts have fought over their non-Indian mascots, the majority of battles have been about Native American images and names.

AB 2115

In May 2002, the California state assembly debated Assembly Bill 2115, sponsored by assemblywoman Jackie Goldberg of Los Angeles. AB 2115 proposed banning the use of names such as Braves, Chiefs, Apaches, Redskins, Indians, and Warriors for teams or mascots in elementary, middle, and high schools; community colleges; and schools of the California State University system (private schools were excluded); the original bill would have banned team names that discriminated against any race, ethnicity, or nationality as well as Native American groups. Telling her colleagues in the legislature that AB 2115 was a "simple bill of civil rights,"[1] Goldberg argued that public schools' Indian-themed names and mascots offend California's Indian groups, members of which are both embarrassed and angered by the use of such mascots at pep rallies and sports contests. Native Americans testified in favor of the bill, contending that war chants like "Scalp the Indians" pained them, as did seeing ceremonial objects like eagle feathers and clothing used in inauthentic dances. One father testified that he and his son were disturbed to see a banner that read "Slaughter the Indians," making it difficult to enjoy a sporting contest; a mother claimed her daughter had plastic surgery on her nose because her school's cartoonlike logo featured a "big-nosed" Native American. The issue was important in California because the state's tribal groups had become vocal and important players in legislative affairs, in part because gambling operations have provided revenue and helped them gain political savvy.

The bill was supported by a California group called the Alliance against Racial Mascots, which had been struggling for years to get California public schools to drop Indian-related names and mascots. But in the year 2002, roughly sixty California schools still used names such as the Redskins (Calaveras High School, Colusa High School), the Chiefs (Bardin Elementary School, Harvest Park Middle School), and the Indians (Jefferson High School, Napa High School), as well as tribal names like the Apaches and the Cherokees. In the United States, well over a thousand schools used such names. Across the country, California's case was closely watched by other people interested in the issue.

AB 2115 passed through two assembly committees, triggering a full assembly vote. On May 28, the assembly voted 35 to 29 to reject the bill. Opponents argued that Indian names honored Native Americans rather than ridiculed them and contended that local school districts should have the power to choose their own names. Democrat Jerome Horton, who abstained from voting, said mascots are "a source of pride, a source of honor."[2] Republican Dennis Mountjoy called AB 2115 the "silly bill of the century."[3]

The California legislative debate brought out the two sides of the issue quite clearly. One group thought the use of names of tribal groups or words such as *Indians* or *Redskins* offended and denigrated Native Americans, and made it hard for them to enjoy an educational experience as equals with white students and other racial and ethnic minorities; the other group argued that legislation such as AB 2115 would force schools to abandon traditional names and mascots that honored Native American attributes and believed that such a bill infringed on local communities' right to make such decisions. In this chapter, we explore the two sides and consider the merits of their respective arguments by looking at how scholars, Native Americans, legislators, and students themselves conceive of this important issue. As an editorial in a California paper put it, "Decades of intermittent debate over the issue of Native American names and symbols being used for school mascots is back on the front burner.... Who's right? Who's wrong? Whose feelings take precedence?"[4] Before we turn to the arguments and attempt to answer these questions, let us consider the historical background of the controversy by reviewing some important developments in the decades-long debate.

HISTORICAL BACKGROUND

As American high schools and colleges grew in number in the twentieth century, they began to adopt a name, a mascot, and sometimes a logo for their burgeoning sports programs. In some cases the team's name reflected that of a local Indian tribe, such as the Ute in the case of the Running Utes of Utah or the Illini in the case of the Fighting Illini of the University of Illinois. It didn't matter whether the tribe still existed, as it did not in the case of the Illini. In some cases, teams selected names that took on characteristics of Indianness. For example, the St. John's Redmen were initially named that because of the color of their jerseys. But fans eventually associated the name *Redmen* with Indianness and constructed an identity for the team based on Native American imagery. In all cases, however, students, fans, and alumni incorporated images, stereotypical or not, of American Indians into their entertainment matrix of sports, thus transposing American Indianness into a specific and constructed cultural context. By this I mean that white athletes and their supporters could "play Indian" both by naming themselves the Warriors, the Cherokees, or the Redskins and by including in the event itself representations of Indians, thus objectifying the team name.

The battle over schools' use of Indian-derived names and mascots began in the late 1960s, a time of great strife over issues of civil rights for many racial and ethnic minorities in the United States. African Americans had waged a sustained campaign for civil rights starting in the 1940s, and after nearly two decades of marches, petitions, and, unfortunately, casualties, Congress passed important legislation—the Civil Rights Act of 1964 and the Voting Rights Act of 1965—prohibiting racial discrimination in the workplace, at the polls, and in the schools. Native Americans, as noted in the introduction to the book, began more and more to assert their political power, mirroring in some ways the tactics and strategies of African American activists.

The campaign against offensive mascots and team names was initially inspired by the National Congress of American Indians (NCAI), which in 1968 began to address the general problem of how Native Americans were represented in print, film, and sporting events, which perpetuated images of Indians as savage, conquered, violent, and ignorant. The sports mascot issue was thus part of a larger problem of how Americans conceived of Indians as citizens and as people. But it was an especially important issue because sporting events are so public. They attract millions of spectators each year, and, more important, the widespread use of Indian-related names and mascots in the public school systems meant that American children of all races and ethnicities, including Indian children themselves, were literally growing up with such symbols of a complex and diverse group of people as a main source of information. In addition to such names as Warriors, Indians, Redskins, Chiefs, Braves, Cherokees, Fighting Sioux, and Redmen, some schools in the 1960s were using names like Brown Indians, Brown Squaws, and even Savages. The names of the mascots selected to represent teams at pep rallies and sporting events like football and basketball games ranged from Florida State's Chief Wampumstompum to Chief Wahoo of the Cleveland Indians professional baseball team. These mascots performed a variety of dances, flips, and war cries while wearing "traditional" Native American clothing—a headdress, deerskin pants, jewelry—as well as "war paint."

In 1969 protests against some school names and mascots began. Students at the University of North Dakota petitioned the school to change the name of its Fighting Sioux. Native Americans attacked the use of *Indians* to describe the athletic teams of Dartmouth College, which soon dropped Indians in favor of the Big Green. In 1970, the University of Oklahoma retired Little Red, a mascot that had represented athletic teams for nearly 30 years; the following year, Marquette University in Wisconsin, a Jesuit university with a long history of relations with native groups, dropped its Willie Wampum mascot. Professional teams were also targeted by the American Indian Movement (AIM). In 1970 and 1971, AIM members, including Dennis Banks and Russell Means, lodged protests against the Cleveland Indians mascot Chief Wahoo and met with Washington Redskins owner William Bennett, who refused to change that team's name.

These first protests were significant, but they were not high-profile cases and they chiefly involved the abandonment of mascots, not team names. But in 1972 Stanford University of California responded to student petitions and changed its team name from the Indians to the Cardinal. North Dakota, a state that experienced great racial conflict between whites and native groups, especially the Sioux, was the site of another important case. Dickinson State University dropped perhaps the most racist name of all, the Savages, replacing it with the Blue Hawks. These two cases, one at a prominent university and the other at a regional institution in a racially divided state, heralded the beginning of a broad but diffuse national movement for changing normal practices in naming sports teams and their mascots.

THE STANFORD CASE

The Stanford case is particularly instructive and deserves extra attention here, in part because the issue, decided in 1972, has not completely gone away. The team name *Indians* had been first used on November 25, 1930, in a pivotal football game with arch rival University of California, the Golden Bears. Students composed a war chant for the occasion, which went: "Stanford Indian, Scalp the Bear; Scalp the Golden Bear, Take the Axe; To his Lair, Scalp the Bear, Stanford Indian." The use of *Indians* thus became a long-standing tradition, one especially associated with important showdowns. The symbol of Stanford teams was a caricature of a Native American wearing feathers, whose prominent physical feature was a big nose; and the Stanford mascot was Prince Lightfoot, represented by a "full-blooded" California Yurok Indian named Timm Williams, whose antics accompanied Stanford's sporting events beginning in 1952.

Politicized by protest activities of the American Indian Movement, a number of Stanford's American Indian students began to protest Prince Lightfoot's performances, which they thought mocked traditional native religious ceremonies; they called Williams "an Uncle Tom Tom." The activities of these students led to the formation of Stanford's first Native American student group, the Stanford American Indian Organization, which pressed the issue with Stanford's dean of students and its president. In 1972, all 55 of Stanford's American Indian students petitioned the university's ombuds(wo)man, Lois Amsterdam, to drop the mascot, symbols, and name. The petition argued that the use of such mascots demeaned Native Americans because a race of people should not be presented as "entertainment." If Stanford prohibited the use of Indian names and symbols, then it would be "renouncing a grotesque ignorance" and thus showing a "progressive concern" for all American Indians. As a result of pressure from students and staff, both Indian and non-Indian, university president Richard Lyman announced that "any and all Stanford University use of the Indian Symbol should be immediately disavowed and permanently stopped," a decision that the Stanford Student Senate supported by a vote of 18 to 4.[5] It was an important victory, particularly considering that a small portion of the student body had engineered it. The mascot controversy also led to Stanford's Native American students organizing a powwow in 1971 to present a more positive image of native dancers than Prince Lightfoot's; these powwows continue to this day, and they are used to help celebrate the end of Stanford's Indian images and mascots.

After Stanford changed its sports image, other schools did as well, but change came slowly, and it came in bunches. For example, in 1979 Syracuse University, located in a part of New York State that contained a sizable Indian population, retired its Saltine Warrior mascot. St. Bonaventure University eliminated both the men's team name, the Brown Indians, and the women's name, the Brown Squaws. A year later, Southern Oregon ended a 30-year tradition by abandoning the use of Indian chiefs as mascots or logos during its games, though it retained its Red Raiders name.

A real push for reform, however, came in the late 1980s when administrators associated with state organizations rather than private institutions began to consider the effects of using Indian names for school and sports teams. In May 1988, the State Board of Education of Minnesota, a state with a large Native American population, issued a resolution stating that "the use of Indian (and similar designations) mascots, emblems, or symbols depicting the American Indian in Minnesota schools is offensive to people of American Indian culture and American Indian religious traditions, and such depiction perpetuates negative racial stereotypes of the American Indian."[6] Besides condemning the practice, the Board of Education called on Minnesota schools to "immediately commence or proceed to remove such mascots, emblems, or symbols from the public education system." Minnesota's actions had a ripple effect. In October 1988, the Michigan State Civil Rights Commission released a report titled "Use of Nicknames, Logos, and Mascots Depicting Native American People in Michigan Education Institutions," which concluded that "any use of Indian names, logos and mascots should be discontinued because racial stereotyping of Native Americans is prevalent and destructive."[7] The report called on all schools employing Indian mascots, logos, or names to form study committees to consider the report and to include Native American groups in a discussion of how to address the issue. Public schools in neighboring Wisconsin, another state with a large Indian population, began to change the practice of using Indian-related logos, nicknames, and mascots. It was this kind of official organizational publicity about the issue in the late 1980s that helped generate national press and intensify an ongoing debate that picked up speed in the early 1990s.

Several events heralded this new phase. First, nationally recognized publications such as the *New York Times, Newsweek,* and *Sports Illustrated* began to cover protests about the use of Indian mascots on both the college and the professional level. *Sports Illustrated* writer Frank Lidz provided coverage of an emerging controversy on the campus of the University of Illinois (UI), a case that eventually garnered the most attention of any mascot case in the 1990s. Charlene Teters, a Native American graduate student, attended UI basketball games with her children only to discover that the team's mascot, Chief Illiniwek, performed what she considered to be offensive dances in inauthentic dress. She also took offense at the ubiquity of Illiniwek merchandise; the image of the Chief was found on license plate holders, stationery, mugs, shot glasses, plates, garbage cans, diaper covers, navy blue silk panties, toilet seat covers, and, most egregiously, on toilet paper. In addition, the Chief's image adorned local businesses and bars. Concerned about Illiniwek's impact on her children, Teters began a campaign against the use of Indian mascots and logos that persists today. Lidz's 1990 article on Teters's efforts, titled "Not a Very Sporting Symbol: Indians Have Ceased to Be Appropriate Team Mascots," helped to bring the issue of mascots in general to a national audience.

Publicity about the mascot issue intensified in 1991 and 1992 when professional sports became the target. Major League Baseball's 1991 World

Series featured the Atlanta Braves and the Minnesota Twins. The presence of the Braves in Minneapolis, where the American Indian Movement began and where a sizable Indian population lived, galvanized opponents of Indian imagery and names. A group called Concerned American Indian Parents had been battling mascots for several years. Their protests, fueled by the Braves fans' "tomahawk chop," received national press attention. Both ABC and NBC aired stories about the protests. The media coverage exposed to Native Americans across the country the tomahawk chop, the name *Atlanta Braves*, and the sight of other Native Americans who were offended by them. The National Football League's 1992 Super Bowl was also held in Minneapolis, which saw new protests over the name of one of the teams, the Washington Redskins; the Redskins had been in Washington, D.C. since 1937, but the team had been named the Redskins in 1933 when it was based in Boston. Between three thousand and five thousand opponents of the Redskins name and logo marched in protest, perhaps the largest Native American protest since the Wounded Knee occupation of 1973 and the largest ever assembled at a sporting event. The 1992 Super Bowl protests intensified the national media's coverage of the mascot controversy as the most prominent sports journalists in the country began writing columns opposed to mascots, logos, and names such as the Redskins. When the 1995 World Series featured the Cleveland Indians and the Atlanta Braves, these writers took the offensive by condemning both teams for their nicknames. This national coverage filtered down to the university and high school level, providing new ammunition to opponents of Indian-oriented sports team names but, at the same time, causing their defenders to dig in their heels.

FRAMING THE ISSUE

Before considering the various viewpoints for and against the use of Indian-themed nicknames, logos, and mascots, let us first return to the Stanford University case. In presenting the Stanford students' petition to Richard Lyman, the university president, ombuds(wo)man Lois Amsterdam contended that "Stanford's use of the Indian symbol in the 1970s brings up to visibility a painful lack of sensitivity and awareness on the part of the University. All of us have in some way, by action or inaction, accepted and supported the use of the Indian symbol on campus. We did not do so with malice, or with intent to defile a racial group. Rather, it was a reflection of our society's retarded understanding, dulled perception and clouded vision. Sensitivity and awareness do not come easily when childish misrepresentations in games, history books and motion pictures make up a large part of our experience."[8] Amsterdam's argument is interesting for a number of reasons. It illustrates nicely one theme of the mascot debate—that it speaks to American society's collective treatment of minority groups in one of the most visible public forums, sports. Amsterdam noted that by permitting derogatory images to be publicly accessible, all members of the Stanford University community were, to some degree, responsible. And yet, rather than focus on blaming members of the community, she argued that the use of images and names reflected a broader problem—society's failure to present a positive image of all its citizens. Stanford would no longer be "childish" when it changed its image and its mascot to one that did not insult members of its community, regardless of their numbers or their political influence.

Despite the apparent persuasiveness of Amsterdam's argument and the support of student organizations and the university administration, the issue did not die. Various campaigns to reinstate the mascot or to create a "noble" image of an Indian rather than the big-nosed original have been waged since 1972. In 1994, the *Stanford Review,* a conservative student newspaper, began calling for the return of the mascot and the team name, while running images of that original big-nosed caricature and advertising merchandise featuring it. Some alumni persisted in wearing old Stanford Indians T-shirts or building teepees in parking lots before games. And as late as September 2001, letters to the editor of the *Stanford Magazine,* Stanford's alumni publication, supported the historical accuracy of Prince Lightfoot's dance routines as well as his cultural integrity; his nephew wrote that "everything was authentic, down to his passion for his Indian heritage."[9] The persistence of student and alumni support for the name *Indians* and for Prince Lightfoot speaks to the emotional nature of this particular issue and helps to explain why more than a thousand schools have not abandoned their traditional school names, mascots, or images.

SUPPORTERS OF INDIAN MASCOTS

Professional sports teams recently have been lightning rods for debate over the use of Indian-related names and symbols. The Cleveland Indians professional baseball team has faced impassioned protests against both its name and its logo, Chief Wahoo, a cartoon picture of a Native American's smiling face. This logo is emblazoned at the ballpark, on car license plates, on children's clothing, and on ice cream as well as on other commercial goods readily available inside and outside the ballpark. The Indians' presence in the 1995 World Series against the Atlanta Braves inspired a new level of protest amongst journalists, activists, and supporters of bans on racially oriented sports images and names. The Indians' ball club has vigorously defended both the name of the team and its principal image, Chief Wahoo. As important, the greater Cleveland community has also resisted efforts to force the team to change its name or abandon Chief Wahoo. Legislative, judicial, and police actions have provided a defense against such efforts. The Indians' defense rests on its assertion that the team was named in honor of Louis Francis Sockalexis, a Penobscot Indian who signed with the Cleveland Spiders in 1897. As the Cleveland Indians' official history relates, in 1914 the Cleveland team was named the Naps, after the popular Napoleon Lajoie. After he was traded, the team held a contest to select a new name. According to *The 1999 Cleveland Indians Media Guide,* the winning entry signaled that the name *Indians* "would be a testament to the game's first American Indian." And the city of Cleveland has since grown up with that name, suffering through good seasons and bad. Historians' investigations of this naming process indicate that soon after Cleveland hired Sockalexis, sportswriters began referring to the ball club as the "Indian's team," and eventually they began calling the team the "Indians."[10] The Cleveland Indians ball club today uses the word *legend* in its claim that its original name was established in honor of an Indian ballplayer. Whether the claim is historically accurate is not important to Indians' fans, because their argument for the retention of the name and of the team's logo, Chief Wahoo, is that by keeping them they honor two traditions—that of the Cleveland baseball team and that of American Indians like Louis Francis Sockalexis.

The Washington Redskins football team also has been forced to defend its name against an increasing number of complaints and lawsuits. In a claim similar to that of the Cleveland Indians, the Redskins argue that the club's original owner, George Preston Marshall, adopted the name because his head coach was a Native American and had recruited Native American players to the team in the 1930s. Speaking after a federal decision denied patent protection for the Redskins' seven trademarks, including their name and logo, a spokesman for the team remarked in 1999 that the Redskins were dignified and did not use offensive caricatures. Director of public relations Mike McCall said that "the Redskins believe its name honors native Americans and has for the past 67 years."[11] After the 1991 World Series protests, an Atlanta Braves fan contended, "It's our tradition. We've had it for fifty years.... And, I'll be damned if you're going to take...this away."[12] Braves owner Ted Turner defended the team's name by arguing that he was a big supporter of Native Americans; his Turner Network ran several series on Native Americans in the 1990s.

The theme of honoring Native Americans by using team names such as Indians, Redskins, and Braves, as well as Warriors, Cherokees, Red Raiders, Apaches, and Fighting Illini, is central to the argument for maintaining Indian-related names, logos, and mascots. Editorial writers, private citizens, students attending schools using Indian-related names, and some Native Americans have expressed such sentiments. An editorial in the *Athens (Ga.) Daily News* asserted, "The American Indian represented the pure American who was noble and brave while the white-eyes were greedy, money-hungry land grabbers." Claiming that his "hero Indians" were Crazy Horse and Chief Joseph, the editorial writer condemned the pressure applied to teams to discontinue their names and symbols of an Indian past, which he believed enlivened the present.[13] As the mascot controversy became heated in Maryland, Myron Beckenstein, an editor at the *Baltimore Sun,* argued in August

2001 that "the names are not meant to mock Indians, but to honor them. Sports teams want identities that bolster the players, not demean them—ones that make them feel good about themselves and project a favorable image to the fans.... It is this respect...that is now offered in choosing Indian names and symbols as ones that bestow virtue and power on the recipients."[14]

Students also reacted negatively to the efforts to change mascots or team names, in part because they had grown up with a certain tradition; some wanted to graduate as Indians or Warriors just as their brothers or sisters had. A student from Fairfield's Armijo High School in California, hoping to make his high school football team, commented on AB 2115, California's proposed legislation banning Indian names: "It's just bull. It's like taking away the history of the school. I want to play for the Indians. I don't want to play for the Anteaters."[15] AB 2115 engendered fierce opposition to a name change at Colusa High School. Administrators were not happy that a change would cost nearly $85,000, and students wanted continuity. One student asserted, "It's been a tradition for a long time. I want to graduate as a Redskin, not a Mosquito or a Yellowjacket."[16] And some parents weighed in, making the argument that they wanted their children to have the same team name as they had had.

Supporters of Indian names, including representatives of the Cleveland Indians, the Atlanta Braves, and the Washington Redskins, thus made two related arguments: one, that the use of the name originated in the spirit of honoring a fierce and strong people, and two, that the decades-long use of that name had created a tradition of its own that was just as important as any Native American tradition.

Whose tradition, then, takes precedence? The strength of resistance to changing mascots or team names has been based in part on who is challenging the use of Indian-related themes. In the 1990s and into the early 2000s, defenders of mascots claimed that Native American activists and even white college students were "politically correct," were outsiders meddling in local community concerns, and should "lighten up."

Politically Correct?

A March 2002 *Honolulu Star-Bulletin* editorial claimed that Stanford University dropped its *Indians* name in 1972 "in a fit of political correctness."[17] Matt Kaufman, a University of Illinois alumnus, contended that Chief Illiniwek was "an object of honor" and that the defense of Illiniwek was "a reflection of something healthy. People should have a strong affectionate regard for their traditions; they shouldn't be willing to jettison their heritage as soon as it's deemed offensive by the forces of political correctness."[18] Kaufman's use of the word *heritage* is interesting, stressing that Chief Illiniwek's 75-year history represents an emotional component of the university's identity. In writing about the Chief Illiniwek controversy, *Chicago Sun-Times* columnist Neil Steinberg defended the Illinois mascot, writing, "The time has come to note that being offended has become overdone. We who are not touchy zealots must not sit by while our cultural pleasures are hacked away."[19] The battle over California's Assembly Bill 2115 engendered protests from opponents who thought that it was driven by "activists skilled in the art of detecting the pea of insensitivity under 20 mattresses." Republican assemblyman Dennis Hollingsworth of Temecula called the bill "political correctness in its ugliest form."[20]

AB 2115 opponents also argued that the state government and outside activists should not get involved in resolving local community issues. Mike Heffernan, chairman of the California Association for Health, Physical Education, Recreation, and Dance, complained that "it's basically the central government of the state telling local authorities they can't do it. That should be left up to the local schools to decide."[21] The school board representing John Burroughs High School in Burbank, California, resisted outside efforts to force a vote on its use of an Indian mascot. Board president Elena Hubbell argued that "we alone are responsible to decide on this issue. My constituents elected me to represent them, and just because a few people want something, doesn't make it necessary."[22] John J. Miller, a writer for the conservative *National Review*, opposed AB 2115, but wrote, "If a tribe opposes a team name at a local school and the sentiment comes from the grass-roots, rather than a handful of self-appointed and outspoken national 'leaders,'—it may make sense to switch.... What no state needs, however, is a sweeping rule that serves to only antagonize tribes and schools that ought to find a way of working together."[23] University of Illinois supporters of Chief Illiniwek derided efforts by "out-of-state foreigners" to force the university to change its ways. Lee Bockhorn, associate editor of the *Weekly Standard* newspaper, argued that the "notion that the state must take action to prevent *anyone* from *ever* feeling 'uncomfortable' is something we've become much too fond of in recent decades.... Government efforts to resolve those conflicts by arbitrarily legislating them out of existence, such as the mascot bill in California, are invariably ham-handed."[24]

A related argument is made that Native American activists are expending energy on a minor issue, that they should direct their attention to more pressing concerns. Bockhorn concluded his article in the *Weekly Standard* by writing that "you'd think state legislators would have better things to worry about than high school mascots."[25] In his August 2001 article "Forget about Team Names: Fight for Indians' Quality of Life," *Baltimore Sun* editor Myron Beckenstein contended, "One thing is wrong with the attempt by some Indian groups to have Indian names removed from sports teams: It is the wrong battle.... To do their cause more good, the forces flexing their muscles against the use of Indian names should redirect their efforts to doing something about a truly dishonorable situation—the conditions that prevail for those forced to live on reservations.... Social, health and education problems abound."[26]

Supporters of Indian-related mascots point to their educational value. Bockhorn wrote his article in part because his alma mater, Arcadia High School, whose teams used the name *Apache,* would have been affected by AB 2115. Bockhorn defended Arcadia's use of Apache by mentioning that school officials had invited Apache representatives to discuss Apache life and culture with Arcadia students, had replaced a cartoonish "Apache Joe" logo with a more authentic Apache image, and had sent its well-regarded band to perform on the Apache reservation. He concluded that both the Apache and Arcadia benefited from the relationship because "as the Arcadia example shows, the use of Indian mascots has often given students the opportunity to learn more about Indian tribes' history and culture," while suggesting that the Apache people themselves found nothing offensive about Arcadia's use of the Apache name and image.[27] In another example, students at Colorado's Arapahoe High School, nicknamed the Warriors, learn about Arapaho culture from representatives of the Arapaho Nation in Wyoming on "Arapahoe Day."

Other commentators have argued that the banning of all mascots will eliminate an opportunity for students to learn about Native Americans. Commenting on AB 2115, a parent of a child attending a school with an Indian-related mascot argued that the school's mascot made students more knowledgeable about as well as respectful of American Indian cultures. *Chicago Sun-Times* columnist Neil Steinberg wrote that "the central mistake that activists make is the belief that the vacuum created by eliminating flawed depictions would be filled with genuine ones. [People will] just forget. The last irony is, should all these symbols be wiped away, the activists would take one look at the new landscape, barren of a single feather or dab of warpaint, no matter how fake, and immediately start lobbying to bring them all back. Better to be remembered in caricature than forgotten altogether."[28] Steinberg suggests that mascots provide a frame of reference for many students and that eliminating that frame would be detrimental. Chief Illiniwek's supporters make a similar argument: in "Let the Chief Live," an editorial writer contends that "the Chief's removal from [University of Illinois] athletic events will benefit no one. It would sever an emotional link between today's Illinoisans and those of 74 years ago, and those of centuries earlier. It would be a lost opportunity to honor and remember the people who lived here before us.... Let us remember the American Indians with dignity."[29]

Native Americans' Views

The arguments presented in the preceding section typically include mention of a favorite theme of pro–Indian mascot forces—that not all Native Americans support the banning of Indian-related sports names. Some supporters of Indian mascots look to poll results published in a March 4, 2002, *Sports Illustrated* article, "The Indian Wars." According to the Peter Harris Research Group, of 351 Native Americans (217 on reservations; 134 living off reservations), 81 percent said high school and college teams should not stop using Indian nicknames, and 83 percent said pro sports teams should not discontinue their use of symbols and names. Asked if team names and mascots contribute to discrimination, 75 percent said no. Despite critics' contention that the polling sample was not large enough to justify such conclusions, *Sports Illustrated* writer S. L. Price wrote, "Although Native American activists are virtually united in opposition to the use of Indian nicknames and mascots, the Native American population sees the issue far differently."[30] Although a poll conducted by *Indian Country Today* found that most Native American leaders were opposed to Indian-themed mascots, respondent Mark Thornton, a Cherokee, took the minority viewpoint, writing, "It is my opinion that mascot and other uses of Native American tribe names, terms, etc.... causes the world to acknowledge and respect us. The use of these Native American names for our weapon systems, mascots, and products brings honor and recognition to Native Americans."[31] David "Bad Eagle" Yeagley, a Comanche educator, said Native Americans benefit from such mascots and should want more of them. "If there's an educational element involved, I see mascots as an opportunity for Indians to gain more respect. Removing them removes our opportunity."[32]

Native Americans have opposed change in specific cases, in part for the reasons mentioned in the previous paragraph. When AB 2115 went to a vote, representatives of some of California's gaming tribes indicated that they would prefer that legislators spend time on such issues as economic development and health care. Their opinions apparently swayed the votes of several democrats. The debate over AB 2115 clearly divided California's Indian population. Gloria Grimes, vice chairwoman of the Band of Miwuk Indians of Calaveras, had mixed feelings about the intent of the legislation. But she said that she and other members of the tribe were not offended by the Calaveras High School's *Redskins* name or mascot. "I went to high school there, my kids went to high school there, I've got grandkids there and I hope more of them go there. The Redskins were our mascot. I never felt that was being discriminatory in any way."[33] In another California case, tribal elders of the Pala Indian reservation opposed the bill, supporting local Fallbrook Union High School's use of the *Warrior* mascot, which a tribal elder had introduced in 1936. Several tribal elders felt honored by the use of the mascot and thought more pressing concerns should be addressed. In Oregon, when a group of University of Oregon students petitioned their school to refuse to play against teams with Indian names or mascots in April 2002, the university's athletic director, Bill Moos, who is part Lakota Sioux, argued that Indian names and mascots were honorable and saw them on a par with Notre Dame's Fighting Irish and the Boston Celtics. He mentioned those names "because they are intended to be a compliment to what I believe are the strength and fierce nature of a certain people, and being partly Native American myself that's how I look at names like the Fighting Illini and Fighting Sioux. Personally, I think it's more honoring those people and their strength."[34] Interestingly, the proposed ban was aimed in part at one of Oregon's rivals, the Running Utes of the University of Utah. The Ute Indians of Utah have permitted Utah officials to use the name and the logo, which comprises a drum and two eagle feathers, provided that they are not used in an offensive manner.

In Florida as well, in a highly publicized case, a tribal group apparently sanctioned the use of a mascot and name. The Florida State University (FSU) Seminoles use both the name of the Seminole, a tribe of long-standing in the state, and a mascot named after Chief Osceola, a great leader of the Seminole who fought to protect the tribe's interests in Florida during the so-called Removal period of the 1830s. FSU students selected *Seminoles* in a naming competition, assisted by the apparent ballot-box stuffing activities of football players who especially liked the name. Finding a suitable mascot was more difficult. Sammy Seminole was replaced in the 1960s by Chief Fullabull, both of them, but especially Fullabull, acting as clownish cheerleaders doing acrobatic stunts. Criticized by Native American students, Chief Fullabull became Chief Wampumstompum, but he too was deemed offensive and was replaced by Yahola, a more spiritual mascot; he in turn was supplanted by the current mascot, Chief Osceola, in 1978. The logo went through a similar process. Originally an axe-wielding "Indian" nicknamed Savage Sam, the logo was dropped in the 1970s in favor of a Native American figure in silhouette.

As criticism of Indian-related mascots and logos intensified in the 1980s, FSU began to build a defense of its practices, doing so by forging an apparent relationship with the Seminole tribe of Florida, led by James Billie. Billie lent his support to the mascot, logo, and name, providing the FSU athletic program with a degree of legitimacy and its mascot's practices with a brand of authenticity. President Dale W. Lick wrote in 1993 that "over the years we have worked closely with the Seminole Tribe of Florida to ensure the dignity and propriety of the various Seminole symbols we use.... Our good relationship with the Seminole Tribe of Florida is one we have cultivated carefully and one we hope to maintain, to the benefit of both the Seminoles of our state and university."[35] In the end, Lick quotes James Billie as saying that the Florida Seminole are proud of the FSU Seminoles. Not all Seminole citizens approved of FSU's actions; and the tribe as a political entity actually signed a general statement condemning Indian mascots. But there were many FSU alumni in the state legislature who could smile on Seminole tribal interests, which by the time the controversy became especially heated had grown to include economic ventures, including casino operations.

The reasons for resistance to changing names are varied, as the preceding examples suggest. One additional reason, money, is central to the debate. Some schools, such as the University of Illinois, fear the loss of donations from bitter alumni who cherish the school's mascot, Chief Illiniwek, and who also resent what they call "out-of-state foreigners" dictating what their traditions should be. Professional teams would lose millions in revenue from the sale of merchandise bearing the cherished names and symbols of the home

Chief Illiniwek, the controversial University of Illinois mascot, performs during halftime at the Big Ten semifinal game between Illinois and Indiana in Chicago in 2001. (AP/Wide World Photos)

team. And high schools compelled to adopt new names and images would be forced to locate new funds to begin again.

The success of resistance campaigns also is quite varied. As the Florida State University and California AB 2115 cases indicate, the involvement of Native American actors in the debate provides a legitimacy to the campaigns of resistance on the high school, university, and professional level to the protests against Indian-derived sports mascots, images, and names. Some campaigns to rid schools of mascots succeeded only to be reversed by an angry community. In Michigan, when Marquette High School lost its logo of a stoic Chief by order of the school board, 1,200 people, including members of Marquette's Native American community, protested the decision. In Boiceville, New York, the Oneora High School teams were forced to abandon the name *Indians* and their tomahawk-wielding mascot by a vote of the school board. In the next election, many of the school board members were replaced, and the school's name, the Indians, and their mascot were restored. Given that well over a thousand schools with Indian-related mascots and names remain, one can expect this kind of resistance to continue.

OPPONENTS OF INDIAN-THEMED MASCOTS

Since the late 1960s, a diverse group of Americans have protested against the use of Indian mascots, names, and images. They range from Native American activists, educators, and high school and college students to religious and community leaders, African American figures like Hank Aaron, who criticized his old team the Atlanta Braves, and big-city mayors like Cleveland mayor Michael R. White, who condemned the Cleveland Indians' logo, Chief Wahoo, as a racist caricature. Their reasons for protesting are varied. For some critics, the use of mascots represents an expression of power, a re-creation of a frontier dynamic in which white Americans assumed ownership of Native Americans' land, culture, and future; Laurel Davis, in a gendered analysis, argued that fierce Indian images were used by sports teams to inspire athletic prowess, and that the anti-mascot movement has created a crisis of "masculinity and American Identity." And for other critics it is simple: Native American activist Dennis Banks, who has struggled for decades to improve Native Americans' cultural autonomy and political power, summarizes the issue of Indian mascots in one word, racism. But all agree that Indian mascots like Illinois's Chief Illiniwek, logos like Chief Wahoo, and names like the Washington Redskins should be put out of business in the interests of creating a more tolerant and more just America.

The Importance of Image

A January 7, 2002, article in the *Los Angeles Times* by Steve Lopez, titled "A War on Words Loses Sight of What Matters," argued that the mascot issue was less important than others pressing down on Native American communities. His argument has been made by other commentators opposed to changing Indian-related mascots and names, who generally think the issues involved are insignificant and driven by the impulse to be politically correct. Several readers responded to Lopez's essay, criticizing his treatment of the issue. One letter in particular nicely summarizes a fundamental theme of anti–Indian mascot activists, that change in other areas of Native American life will begin with the rehabilitation of Native Americans' image in public and in the press. Christine Rose told Lopez: "There is no question that when I have gone to reservations, I am overwhelmed at the problems so many people face. I always feel a little silly when I tell Native people on reservations that I am involved in the mascot issue. They look at me like I am fighting invisible dragons when stark reality is staring me in the face. But in my heart I know that if the dominant culture can't, or won't, understand the mascot issue, how will they ever pay attention to the bigger issues? To me the mascot issue has always been the tip of the iceberg, a place to begin to bring understanding to the many issues that face Native people. Once I can get people to understand the mascot issue, it's easier for them to understand other problems."[36]

For Native Americans like Christine Rose and countless others, the daily parading of Indian-related mascots, names, and images, from grade schools up to the professional level, provides all Americans with a limited, distorted, and anachronistic perspective on who Native Americans are in the twenty-first century. Given that many of the team names and images are selected because of an association with nineteenth-century Indian wars, and that many of the mascots and logos reflect a theme of violence with tomahawks or axes, Native Americans are, publicly and repeatedly, both relegated to a historical role as actors in a drama of American history reenacted by children in cowboys and Indian games at an early age and presented as demonstrating characteristics such as violence, fierceness, and cunning. This isn't to say that Native Americans have not been violent, fierce, or cunning. They have, in the past. But this perpetuation of images and stereotypes of the past has blinded most Americans to the realities of the present. Which is why Christine Rose called the mascot issue the "tip of the iceberg." Below it, less visible, are the realities of life for many Native Americans, both off the reservation and on it.

Some Native Americans have made a point of declaring that they are not opposed to all Indian mascots and images, just those that are stereotypical, racist, inauthentic, or used without the knowledge or permission of the tribal community being represented. In a poll conducted by *Indian Country Today,* 81 percent of "American Indian opinion leaders" indicated that "use of American Indian names, symbols and mascots are predominantly offensive and deeply disparaging to Native Americans."[37] While some championed the abolition of all mascots, others like Dan Webster noted that if schools used mascots and symbols in an authentic manner and got "the permission and/or advice in the use of the symbols of the tribes involved," then he "didn't think it would create a hostile educational environment for Native students."[38] Native American educator Cornel Pewewardy, who has written widely on the subject, has noted, "I'm not totally against all Native mascots. I am against negative Native mascots. I think people have to define that. It's negative if it is a caricature—big nose, big teeth. Something like that shouldn't be in the schools."[39]

Many Native Americans clearly believe that the majority of sports mascots and images do not honor them but objectify and humiliate them. And they also do not represent authentic Indian traditions or rituals, as pro–Indian mascot forces claim, largely because sacred objects such as eagle feathers are highly regulated in terms of what ceremonies they can be used for and for what audiences. Most of the dances and clothing of sports mascots have nothing to do with the Native Americans of that particular region and feed off a basic stereotype that lingers from the nineteenth century. Laura Baxter, a Pitt River Indian law student, lamented that "it hurts to see my people in my community or another Indian community portrayed as a red person with a big nose and feathers stuck in their head."[40] Beyond these stereotypical images, most mascots either use counterfeit or constructed attire and behaviors such as the "tomahawk chop," drumbeating, and war chants or simply re-create the image of the Plains Indian—deerskin clothing, headdresses, and feathers—what many Americans think all Indians look like. This Plains Indian image was even used in Washington State, whose Native American citizens have cultural traditions and dress distinctly different from those of the Plains.

In any case, critics contend, mascots appropriate images to use in their culture's game rather than recreating Native American ceremonies and traditions in the spirit of honoring Native Americans or educating whites about them. The novelist Sherman Alexie, whose fiction was the basis of the critically acclaimed film *Smoke Signals*, told a CBSNews.com interviewer in March 2001, "Don't think about [the mascot issue] in terms of race. Think about it in terms of religion. Those are our religious imagery up there. Feather, the paint, the sun, that's our religious imagery. You couldn't have a Catholic priest running around the floor with a basketball throwing communion wafers. You couldn't have a rabbi running around."[41] Barry Landeros-Thomas, an Eastern Band Cherokee living in Ohio, addressed this religious issue by noting, "We have the Saints but you don't see mascots dressed up like Jesus carrying a big Styrofoam cross doing the sign of the cross every time a touchdown is made. That's the parallel with the eagle's feather, which is sacred to many nations and traditions. They don't understand the sacredness of the feathers."[42] Landeros-Thomas, whose daughter was humiliated by fellow students because of her Indian heritage, believes that mascot supporters think of Native Americans only in the past tense. Other critics use the image of a toy or a trophy to condemn the use of mascots. Amber Machamer of the Chumash Nation has vivid memories of attending high school pep rallies at which students waved signs reading "Scalp the Indians" and "Better Dead Than Red." These signs and related images, she said, send a particular message—that "you guys are our toys. We can use your culture and religion for our entertainment. And there's nothing you can do about it."[43]

Native Americans are discriminated against in part because they are associated with these images and the behavior of sports-related mascots, names, and logos. As Bill Means of the International Indian Treaty Council put it in discussing the Atlanta Braves, "You have to look at it as giving respect to the Indian people.... If we can't get white America to understand the basic issue of human dignity, how can we get them to understand the more substantive issues like sovereignty, treaty rights, and water rights."[44] Critics of mascots thus point to the deeper impact of the maintenance of "Indian" stereotypes on problems that afflict native communities. As a TV commercial once put it, "You don't get a second chance to make a first impression." For many Americans, sporting events, either seen in person or on television, are the main source from which they develop their impressions of who Native Americans are.

The other side of the coin, critics contend, is that Native Americans, especially young children, are injured psychologically by the prevalence of Indian-themed mascots in the school systems. It isn't just hurt feelings. In addition to Native American activists, it has been educators who have most influenced anti-mascot campaigns. Beginning in 1988, states such as Michigan, Minnesota, and Wisconsin began evaluating the place of some mascots in schools. As noted in the introduction, the State Board of Education of Minnesota argued that Indian mascots were "offensive to people of American Indian culture and American Indian religious traditions, and such depiction perpetuates negative racial stereotypes of the American Indian." In December 1992, the National Education Association passed a resolution discouraging "the continued use of prejudicial and derogatory names and symbols of ethnic groups for school, sporting teams, and mascots," spurring other city and state educational organizations to study the impact of mascots in their respective schools.[45] Such resolutions have had a direct impact on school debates about keeping or resigning mascots. In September 1997, the Los Angeles City Board of Education prohibited the use of American Indian mascots and names by arguing that their use in schools "evokes negative images that become deeply imbedded in the minds of students, depicting American Indians in inaccurate, stereotypic, and often violent manners.... The cause and effect in the inappropriate and insensitive use of American Indian names and images violates the culture and traditions of American Indians and may prevent American Indian children from developing a strong positive self-image."[46]

Impact of Indian-Themed Mascots on Native American and Non–Native American Students

Anti-mascot resolutions have been influenced by the work of educators such as Dr. Cornel Pewewardy of the University of Kansas, who has studied the impact of Indian mascots on Native American children and found disturbing results. Pewewardy, of Comanche and Kiowa heritage, knows of what he speaks because as a boy growing up he was humiliated when his team played opponents with Indian mascots. In his influential article, "Why Educators Can't Ignore Mascots," Pewewardy argues that "so-called Indian mascots reduce hundreds of indigenous tribes to generic cartoons. These 'Wild West' figments of the white imagination distort both Indigenous and non-Indigenous children's attitudes toward an oppressed—and diverse—minority." In addition to distorting cultural realities, mascots mock Native American sacred practices, and as a result cause many Native Americans to "feel shame about who they are as a cultural being." Pewewardy cites a statement issued by the American Indian Mental Health Association of Minnesota that concludes that the use of Indian-related mascots and images "is damaging to the self-identity, self-concept, and self-esteem" of Native Americans. In the end, schools should be, he writes, "places where students unlearn the stereotypes such mascots represent" rather than places where they are reinforced.[47]

Non–Native American students have indicated the extent to which they are affected by the presence of such mascots. A white student responded to a local mascot controversy by writing, "I would like to see my brother, sister, and cousins go to a school that shows respect and tolerance for other cultures. I don't want them to feel the confusion that I have felt going to this school. It has taken me a couple of years to come to understand Native American stereotypes and their effects on me. By keeping [this Indian] mascot the principal lesson the students, staff, and community learn is how to tolerate stereotypes." This student believed that retiring the mascot would exemplify the school's emphasis on "respect, responsibility, compassion, . . . and tolerance." This theme echoes throughout the halls of schools that have decided to drop Indian mascots or names. In many cases, it has been teachers or the students themselves, and not "outsider activists," who have precipitated the change. In Cheyenne, Wyoming, teachers and administrators led the charge to change the school's name of Redskins. As assistant principal Marcia Graham explained, "You teach by example. We want our students to be leaders in the community in a real global culture."[48] Some students and educators consider *Redskins* to be the most offensive Indian-related name, the name originating from the bloody scalps of Indians killed for bounties by colonial Americans. Students from Neshaminy High School in suburban Philadelphia justified a name change on this basis alone, arguing that the dictionary defined *redskin* as an "offensive term for Native Americans." By retaining Redskins as their school's name, students and the community were "promoting tolerance and acceptance of atrocities committed years ago" and were not honoring Indians but appropriating their objects and traditions for "another culture's game."[49]

Native American educators have been paying careful attention to the negative effects of Indian mascots on all students, but other national and regional professional and civic organizations have also weighed in on the controversy. In addition to the National Education Association, the National Organization for Women and the Governing Council of the American Counseling Association, the world's largest association representing professional counselors, have opposed the use of stereotypical Native American images as symbols or mascots of sports teams. At its annual convention in April 1999, the National Association for the Advancement of Colored People (NAACP) resolved to ask its members to boycott sports products bearing Native American names and logos and support efforts to rid all sports teams of them. The NAACP argued that the "use of Native American people, images, symbols, and cultural and religious traditions [in sports] perpetuates racist stereotypes and undermines the self-determination and dignity of Indian people."[50] The anti–Indian mascot campaign has also earned the support of Christian and Jewish religious organizations, which find the use of stereotypes morally offensive and a violation of civil rights.

A Matter of Civil Rights

The recent campaign against Indian-related mascots has been helped by a statement the U.S. Commission on Civil Rights made in April 2001. Rather than breaking new ground, it summarized neatly the arguments that Native Americans, educators, students, parents, and other civil rights activists had been making for more than three decades. The commission argued that more than 30 years since the country had dealt with "overtly derogatory symbols and images offensive to African-Americans," the time had come for schools (and professional teams) to abandon the use of Native American names, images, and mascots largely because schools were "places where diverse groups of people come together to learn not only the 'Three Rs,' but also how to interact respectfully with people from different cultures." The continued use of mascots and images helped "create a racially hostile educational environment" that could both intimidate Native American students and exacerbate a problem of low self-esteem that contributed to low graduation rates. The commission's statement also touched on the theme of historical inaccuracy. Most mascots and images, it contended, "are romantic stereotypes that give a distorted view of the past" and thus "prevent non–Native Americans from understanding the true historical and cultural experiences of American Indians. Sadly, they also encourage biases and prejudices that have a negative effect on contemporary Indian people."[51] Here, then, is part of the danger of Indian mascots—not only are they inaccurate, offensive, and damaging to Native American children's self-esteem, but they are also injurious to Native Americans' overall campaign for civil rights and social justice.

And here, as well, is what is truly at stake for all involved in resolving this contentious issue. As the Commission on Civil Rights put it, "the elimination of Native American nicknames and images as sports mascots will benefit not only Native Americans, but all Americans. The elimination of stereotypes will make room for education about real Indian people, current Native American issues, and the rich variety of American Indian cultures in our country."[52] American Indians were granted citizenship in 1924. To be truly included in the body politic, they need to be respected, not objectified. Some American citizens have taken this attitude to heart in agreeing to drop mascots and images deemed offensive by Native Americans. One alumnus of a high school debating whether to drop the name *Apache*, reasoned that if Native Americans didn't feel honored by the name, that was justification enough for the change. "We thought of the mascot as being strong, a winner. But if it offends Native Americans, we should change it."[53]

It isn't so simple at some schools, in particular, at the University of Illinois at Champaign-Urbana. The ongoing and bitter case of Chief Illiniwek, the sports mascot of the Fighting Illini of UI, is the most controversial fight of the past decade. As noted earlier in the chapter, a Native American graduate student named Charlene Teters began a one-woman campaign to force UI to discontinue the use of the Chief, whose attire, behavior, and presence she found demeaning to all Native Americans. Her basic argument was that "we are not mascots or fetishes to be worn by the dominant society. We are human beings."[54] Her campaign engendered a visceral and vicious backlash against anyone opposing the Chief. It prompted one person to put on their RV a bumper sticker that read "Save the Chief, Kill the Indians!" During the 1990s, students and faculty began to support her campaign, petitioning the administration to drop Chief Illiniwek. The Department of Anthropology told the UI Board of Trustees that Chief Illiniwek's routine, from clothes to dances, was culturally inauthentic, that the controversy affected its ability to recruit top scholars, and that the Chief's presence on campus "undercuts our goals as educators to foster cross-cultural understanding."[55] The UI Department of History and the Center for African Studies followed suit with their own protests, as did the Illinois Student Government. So far the efforts have been unsuccessful, as a vocal body of alumni, which includes many state politicians, has threatened to cut off donations if Illiniwek is punted. But some changes have resulted. The Chief was banned from homecoming parades and floats, and opposing schools in the athletic conference have prevented the Chief from performing on their turf. And the case has drawn outside attention, as when a UI alumnus from Amnesty International asked the UI Board of Trustees to "show some moral leadership" and "Get Rid of the Chief."[56]

Ultimately, it is a personal decision whether to support or to condemn Indian-related mascots. As one school board member, challenging the label of political correctness applied to those who opposed her school's Indian mascots, said, "This is not a political choice for me; it is a moral choice for me."[57] With more than a thousand schools retaining Indian names, mascots, and images, many future decisions will come down to individuals making this distinction between politics and morality and deciding whether the issue is important for Native Americans alone or for all Americans with a stake in creating a society based on respect for all its citizens.

NOTES

1. Jim Sanders, "Assembly Rejects Indian-Mascot Ban," *Sacramento Bee,* 29 May 2002.

2. Michael Gardner, untitled, *San Diego Union-Tribune,* 29 May 2002.

3. Sanders, "Assembly Rejects Indian-Mascot Ban."

4. "Take a Look at Vallejo's Mascot," *Times-Herald Online,* 17 March 2002, <www.timesheraldonline.com> (accessed June 2002).

5. Denni Woodward, "Stanford's Mascot," *Coming Voice,* 30 September 1996, <seas.stanford.edu/diso/articles/indian.html> (accessed June 2002).

6. Minnesota State Board of Education, "Urging the Elimination of the Use of Racially Derogatory Mascots, Symbols, or Emblems in Schools throughout the State of Minnesota," 10 May 1988, <earnestman.tripod.com/more_educators_resources_on_nati.htm> (accessed June 2002).

7. Michigan Civil Rights Commission, "Report on Use of Nicknames, Logos, and Mascots Depicting Native American People in Michigan Education Institutions," October 1988, <earnestman.tripod.com/more_educators_resources_on_nati.htm> (accessed June 2002).

8. Woodward, "Stanford's Mascot."

9. "In Praise of Prince Lightfoot," *Stanford Magazine,* October 2000.

10. Ellen J. Staurowsky, "An Act of Honor or Exploitation?: The Cleveland Indians' Use of the Louis Francis Sockalexis Story," *Sociology of Sport Journal* 15 (1998): 299–316.

11. Brooke A. Masters, "Redskins Are Denied Trademarks," *Washington Post,* 3 April 1999.

12. Laurel Davis, "Protest against the Use of Native American Mascots: A Challenge to Traditional American Identity," *Journal of Sport and Social Issues* 17, no. 1 (1993): 15.

13. Budge Williams, "Here's a Solution for All Our Mascot Names," *Athens Daily News,* 28 April 2001.

14. Myron Beckenstein, "Forget about Team Names: Fight for Indians' Quality of Life," *Baltimore Sun,* 23 August 2001.

15. Kelly St. John, "Tribes Take Their Fight to Ban Demeaning Team Names to Sacramento: Legislature Urged to Outlaw Use of Indian-Theme Mascots," *San Francisco Chronicle,* 14 May 2002.

16. Jim Sanders, "Taking Offense over Sports Mascots," *Sacramento Bee,* 31 March 2002.

17. Editorial, *Honolulu Star-Bulletin,* 3 March 2002.

18. Matt Kaufman, "Of Mascots and Malcontents," *Boundless,* <www.boundless.org/2001/regulars/Kaufman/a0000594.html> (accessed June 2002).

19. Neil Steinberg, "The Name Blame Game," *Chicago Sun-Times,* 15 April 2001.

20. Michael Gardner, untitled, *San Diego Union-Tribune,* 29 May 2002.

21. Sean Scully, "California Set to Ban Indian Mascot Names," *Washington Times,* 5 May 2002.

22. Gary Moskowitz, untitled, *Los Angeles Times,* 21 July 2001.

23. John J. Miller, "A Ban on Tribal Team Names Shows Disrespect," *Las Vegas Review-Journal,* 5 May 2002.

24. Lee Bockhorn, "Apache Pride: The California State Assembly Wants to Do Away with 'Offensive' High School Mascots," *Weekly Standard,* 3 May 2002, <www.weeklystandard.com> (accessed June 2002).

25. Bockhorn, "Apache Pride."

26. Beckenstein, "Forget about Team Names."

27. Bockhorn, "Apache Pride."

28. Steinberg, "The Name Blame Game."

29. "Let the Chief Live," *News-Gazette,* 26 October 2000.

30. S.L. Price, "The Indian Wars," *Sports Illustrated,* 4 March 2002, 68.

31. "American Indian Opinion Leaders: American Indian Mascots; Respectful Gesture or Negative Stereotype," *Indian Country Today* (*Lakota Times*), 8 August 2001.

32. Sanders, "Taking Offense."

33. Francis Garland, "A Mascot by Any Other Name," *Stockton (Calif.) Record*, 17 March 2002.

34. Greg Bolt, "University of Oregon Students Lead Campaign to End Native American Mascots," *Eugene (Ore.) Register-Guard*, 17 April 2002.

35. C. Richard King and Charles Fruehling Springwood, "The Best Offense... Dissociation, Desire, and the Defense of the Florida State University Seminoles," in *Team Spirits: The Native American Mascots Controversy* (Lincoln: University of Nebraska Press, 2001), 145.

36. Christine Rose to Steve Lopez, undated, <www.bluecorncomics.com/stype211.htm> (accessed June 2002).

37. "American Indian Opinion Leaders."

38. "American Indian Opinion Leaders."

39. Cornel Pewewardy, untitled, *Indian Country Today,* 15 March 2000.

40. Bolt, "University of Oregon Students Lead Campaign."

41. Interview with CBSNews.com, 20 March 2001, <www.bluecorncomics.com/mascots/htm> (accessed June 2002).

42. Megan Kuhn, "Native Americans Face Stereotypes," *The Post* (Ohio University), 1 November 2001.

43. Sanders, "Taking Offense."

44. Tim Giago, "I Hope the Redskins Lose," *Newsweek,* 27 January 1992, 8.

45. National Education Association, "Memorandum," 9 December 1992, <www.aistm.org/nea_resolution.htm> (accessed June 2002).

46. Los Angeles City Board of Education, "Motions/Resolutions Presented to the Los Angeles City Board of Education for Consideration," 2 September 1997, <www.geocities.com/CapitalHill/Lobby/4828/ailausd.htm> (accessed June 2002).

47. Cornel D. Pewewardy, "Why Educators Can't Ignore Mascots," *American Indian Cultural Support,* undated, <www.aics.org/mascot/cornel.html> (accessed June 2002).

48. Coleman Cornelius, "Redskins Out as School Mascot," *Denver Post,* 9 May 2002.

49. Staff of the Playwickian, "Symbol of Oppression Shouldn't Be Team Name," *Philadelphia Inquirer,* 23 April 2001.

50. National Association for the Advancement of Colored People, "1999 NAACP Resolution in Opposition to Native American Mascots," 28 April 1999, <www.aistm.org/naacp_1999_resolution.htm> (accessed June 2002).

51. United States Commission on Civil Rights, "Statement of the U.S. Commission on Civil Rights on the Use of Native American Images and Nicknames as Sports Symbols," 13 April 2001, <www.usccr.gov/whatsnew/2001/ntamstmt.htm> (accessed June 2002).

52. U.S. Commission on Civil Rights, "Statement."

53. "Take a Look at Vallejo's Mascot."

54. David Prochaska, "At Home in Illinois: Presence of Chief Illiniwek, Absence of Native Americans," in King and Springwood, *Team Spirits,* 170.

55. Members of the Anthropology Department Faculty to the Members of the Board of Trustees, University of Illinois, 17 February 1998, <www.uiuc.edu/providers/senate/eq9704_b.html> (accessed June 2002).

56. Morton Winston to Chair, Board of Trustees, University of Illinois, 16 July 1997, quoted in University of Illinois Urbana-Champaign Senate, Committee on Equal Opportunity, "EQ.97.04, Resolution to Retire Chief Illiniwek," 9 March 1998, <www.uiuc.edu/providers/senate/eq9704.html> (accessed June 2002).

57. Catherine Hawley, "Issaquah High to Retire Indian—New Policy Requires Nonoffensive Mascots, Logos," *East Side Journal,* 16 May 2002.

QUESTIONS

1) What do halftime performances involving mascots tell us about American culture?
2) What do halftime performances involving mascots tell us about the place of American Indians in American culture?
3) What are the best arguments against the use of some mascots, names, or logos?
4) What are the best arguments against banning some mascots, names, or logos?
5) Why did the mascot controversy cross racial lines to include African Americans?
6) To what extent does the mascot controversy become an issue of national civil rights?
7) Would your local community permit a team named the Jews, the Wops, or the Negroes? If not, what is the difference between those names and Redskins?
8) Discuss the various ways in which Native Americans view the mascot controversy.
9) What are the factors behind schools' use of mascots; why did they become so prevalent in the first place?
10) In what ways could the association of Native American mascots with violent games like football be considered negative?
11) In what ways could the use of a Native American mascot be considered inauthentic, in that it does or does not represent an actual cultural ritual practiced by a contemporary Indian group?
12) How can the Atlanta Braves fans' "tomahawk chop" be read historically, given the history of the Cherokee Indians in the state of Georgia? Research Georgia's treatment of Native Americans. Situate the tomahawk in this history.
13) To what extent should a local community control the fate of its school's mascot and team name?
14) Can a distinction be made between the names *Redskins* and *Warriors*? In other words, might both be offensive?
15) To what extent could the use of stereotypical images affect the self-esteem of young Native Americans?
16) Consider your racial or ethnic heritage. How would you feel if an image from your people's history were to be represented as your school's team mascot?
17) Does it matter that no harm or insult was intended by the use of a mascot or name?
18) How should a school or any organization respond to students or citizens who feel offended by public displays, traditions, or behavior?
19) Do Native Americans and non–Native Americans look at the mascot issue differently? Is there common ground?

RESOURCE GUIDE

Suggested Readings

"American Indian Opinion Leaders: American Indian Mascots; Respectful Gesture or Negative Stereotype?" *Indian Country Today* (*Lakota Times*), 8 August 2001.

Banks, Dennis J. "Tribal Names and Mascots in Sports." *Journal of Sport and Social Issues* 17, no. 1 (1993).

Beckenstein, Myron. "Forget about Team Names: Fight for Indians' Quality of Life." *Baltimore Sun,* 23 August 2001.

Berkhofer, Robert F., Jr. *The White Man's Indian: Images of the American Indian.* New York: Knopf, 1978.

Bird, S. Elizabeth, ed. *Dressing in Feathers: The Construction of the Indian in American Popular Culture.* Boulder, Colo.: Westview Press, 1996.

Bockhorn, Lee. "Apache Pride: The California State Assembly Wants to Do Away with 'Offensive' High School Mascots." *Weekly Standard,* 3 May 2002. <www.weeklystandard.com> (accessed June 2002).

Bolt, Greg. "University of Oregon Students Lead Campaign to End Native American Mascots." *Eugene (Ore.) Register-Guard* , 17 April 2002.

Caldwell-Wood, Naomi. *"I" Is Not for Indian: The Portrayal of Indians in Books for Young People.* American Indian Library Association, <www.nativeculture.com> 1991.

Claussen, Cathryn. "Ethnic Team Names and Logos—Is There a Legal Solution?" *Marquette Sports Law Journal* 6, no. 409 (1996).

Davis, Laurel. "Protest against the Use of Native American Mascots: A Challenge to Traditional American Identity." *Journal of Sport and Social Issues* 17, no. 1 (1993).

Deloria, Phillip. *Playing Indian.* New Haven: Yale University Press, 1998.

Frazier, Jane. "Tomahawkin' the Redskins: 'Indian' Images in Sports and Commerce." In *American Indian Studies: An Interdisciplinary Approach to Contemporary Issues,* edited by Dane Morrison. New York: Peter Lang, 1997.

Giago, Tim. "I Hope the Redskins Lose." *Newsweek,* 27 January 1992.

Gildea, William. "Redskins: A History of Washington's Team." Washington Post Books. <www.washingtonpost.com/wp-srv/sports/redskins/longterm/book/skinbook.htm> (accessed June 2002).

Gursky, Daniel. "Schools Reconsider Indian Mascots in the Wake of World Series Furor." *Education Week,* 4 December 1991.

Hawley, Catherine. "Issaquah High to Retire Indian—New Policy Requires Non-offensive Mascots, Logos." *East Side Journal,* 16 May 2002.

Hirshfelder, Arlene B. *American Indian Stereotypes in the World of Children.* Metuchen, N.J.: Scarecrow Press, 1993.

King, C. Richard, and Charles Fruehling Springwood. "The Best Offense... Dissociation, Desire, and the Defense of the Florida State University Seminoles." In *Team Spirits: The Native American Mascots Controversy.* Lincoln: University of Nebraska Press, 2001.

Kuhn, Megan. "Native Americans Face Stereotypes." *The Post* (Ohio University), 1 November 2001. <http://news.excite.com/news/uw/011101/university-41> (accessed June 2002).

Lidz, Frank. "Not a Very Sporting Symbol: Indians Have Ceased to Be Appropriate Team Mascots." *Sports Illustrated,* 17 September 1990.

Lopez, Steve. "A War on Words Loses Sight of What Matters." *Los Angeles Times,* 7 January 2002, and reader responses: <www.bluecorncomics.com/stype211.htm> (accessed June 2002).

Loving, Paul E. "Native American Team Names in Athletics: It's Time to Trade These Marks." *Loyola of Los Angeles Entertainment Law Journal* 13, no. 1 (1992).

Masters, Brooke A. "Redskins Are Denied Trademarks." *Washington Post,* 3 April 1999.

McKinley, James C. "Schools Urged to Stop Using Indian Names; Mascots Called Improper but Are Not Prohibited." *New York Times,* 6 April 2001.

"Members of the Anthropology Department Faculty to the Members of the Board of Trustees." University of Illinois. 17 February 1998. <www.uiuc.edu/providers/senate/eq9704_b.html> (accessed June 2002).

Michigan Civil Rights Commission. "Report on Use of Nicknames, Logos, and Mascots Depicting Native American People in Michigan Education Institutions." October 1988. <earnestman.tripod.com/more_educators_resources_on_nati.htm> (accessed June 2002).

Mihesuah, Devon. *American Indians: Stereotypes and Realities.* Clarity Press, Atlanta, GA 1996.

"Mind Your Own Mascot: For Years, Native American Mascots Have Been under Siege—but Their Fans Are Beginning to Fight Back." *Newsweek,* 27 November 2000.

Minnesota State Board of Education. "Urging the Elimination of the Use of Racially Derogatory Mascots, Symbols, or Emblems in Schools throughout the State of Minnesota." 10 May 1988. <earnestman.tripod.com/more_educators_resources_on_nati.htm> (accessed June 2002).

Palmer, Barbara. " 'Destroying Stereotypes': Powwow Continues Mission to Share Cultures: Annual Native American Event Draws Thousands While Celebrating End to Demeaning University Mascot." *Stanford Report,* 15 May 2002. <news-service.stanford.edu/news/may15/powwow-515.html> (accessed June 2002).

Pearce, Roy Harvey. *Savagism and Civilization: A Study of the Indian and the American Mind.* Berkeley: University of California Press, 1988.

Pewewardy, Cornel D. "The Deculturalization of Indigenous Mascots in U.S. Sports Culture." *The Educational Forum* 63 (summer 1999).

———. "Native American Mascots: Continuing the Struggle of Unlearning 'Indian' Stereotypes." *News from Indian Country,* 15 October 1991.

———. "Why Educators Can't Ignore Mascots." Undated. <www.aics.org/mascot/cornel.html> (accessed June 2002).

Plummer, Roger. "Seeking a Compromise—Chief Illiniwek: A Report by Trustee Roger Plummer to the University of Illinois Board of Trustees." 13–14 March 2002. <www.uillinois/edu/trustees/plmmerreport/> (accessed June 2002).

Price, S. L. "The Indian Wars." *Sports Illustrated,* 4 March 2002.

Prochaska, David. "At Home in Illinois: Presence of Chief Illiniwek, Absence of Native Americans." In *Team Spirits: The Native American Mascots Controversy,* edited by C. Richard King and Charles Springwood. Lincoln: University of Nebraska Press, 2001.

Rodriguez, Roberto. "Plotting the Assassination of Little Red Sambo: Psychologists Join War against Racist Campus Mascots." *Black Issues in Higher Education,* 11 June 1998.

Sanders, Jim. "Taking Offense over Sports Mascots." *Sacramento Bee,* 31 March 2002.

Slowikowski, Synthia Syndnor. "Cultural Performance and Sports Mascots." *Journal of Sport and Social Issues* 17, no. 1 (1993).

Spindel, Carol. *Dancing at Halftime: Sports and the Controversy over American Indian Mascots.* New York: New York University Press, 2000.

Springwood, Charles Fruehling, and C. Richard King. " 'Playing Indian': Why Native American Mascots Must End." *Chronicle of Higher Education,* 9 November 2001.

Staff of the Playwickian. "Symbol of Oppression Shouldn't Be Team Name." *Philadelphia Inquirer,* 23 April 2001.

Staurowsky, Ellen J. "An Act of Honor or Exploitation?: The Cleveland Indians' Use of the Louis Francis Sockalexis Story." *Sociology of Sport Journal* 15 (1998).

United States Commission on Civil Rights. "Statement of the U.S. Commission on Civil Rights on the Use of Native American Images and Nicknames as Sports Symbols." 13 April 2001. <wwwusccr.gov/whatsnew/2001/ntamstmt.htm> (accessed June 2002).

Winston, Morton. "EQ.97.04. Resolution to Retire Chief Illiniwek." To chair, Board of Trustees, University of Illinois. 16 July 1997. <www.uiuc.edu/providers/senate/eq9704.html> (accessed June 2002).

Woodward, Denni. "Stanford's Mascot." *Coming Voice.* 30 September 1996 <seas.stanford.edu/diso/articles/indian.html> (accessed June 2002).

Videos

Foley, Hugh, producer. *Savage Country: Indian Mascots in Oklahoma High School Football, 2000.* Foley is coordinator of the Native American Studies Program at Rogers State University in Claremore, Oklahoma.

People Not Mascots. 30 min. Advertised as "An in-depth look at the use of Native American tribal names and sacred symbols by sports teams in the United States." For information, contact United Church of Christ, 700 Prospect Avenue, Cleveland, OH 44115 (phone: 216-736-2224).

Redskin: A 500 Year Hate Crime. 20 min. *American Comments Magazine.* According to its advertising, the film "graphically shows how the imagery of ridiculing Native Americans and other minorities is entwined in the history of mainstream European American culture." Call 620-241-7240 for more information.

Rosenstein, Jay. *In Whose Honor?* New Day Films (phone: 201-652-6590), 1997. An excellent film, originally shown on PBS, featuring Charlene Teters's campaign to get the University of Illinois to drop Chief Illiniwek.

Music

WithOut Rezervation. Are You Ready for W.O.R.? CR-7035. Phoenix: Canyon Records, 1994. Includes the song "Mascot."

Web Sites

"Academic Institutions Using Native Names/Stereotypes." <nativenet.uthscsa.edu/archive/nl/9406/0105.html>. A list of schools using Indian names.

Alliance against Racial Mascots. <www.allarm.org>.

American Comments Web Magazine. <www.iwchildren.org>. Contains section on mascots.

"American Indian Sports Mascots." <www.main.nc.us/wncceib/IndianMascotIssue.htm>. A good case study of battle in North Carolina.

American Indian Sports Teams Mascots. <earnestman.tripod.com>. An excellent resource for a variety of articles on the issue.

"Cartoons Relating to Native American Indian Sports Team Mascots." <earnestman.tripod.com/cartoons.htm>. Good images of offensive stereotypes.

Find Another Name. <www.findanothername.com>.

Grand Rapids Institute for Information Democracy. <www.griid.org/mediaracism.shtml>. Media and racism.

Indian Mascots and Logos: What's the Big Deal? <people.ku.edu/~tyeeme/fightinwhities.html>. An excellent source of articles and information.

National Coalition on Racism in Sports and Media. <www.aimovement.org/ncrsm/index.html>.

Native News Search. <ishgooda.nativeweb.org/racial/mascot.htm>. Search engine for news items on mascots issue.

North Carolina Educators for the Elimination of Racist Mascots. <nceerm.home.att.net>.

"November 2001: Native American Heritage." *PBS TeacherSource.* <www.pbs.org/teachersource/thismonth/nov01/index.shtm>. PBS site about the controversy.

"Redskins: A History of Washington's Team." *Washingtonpost.com.* <www.washingtonpost.com/wp-srv/sports/redskins/longterm/book/skinbook.htm>. Provides a history of the Washington Redskins.

Students and Teachers against Racism (STAR). <www.turtletrack.org/STAR/UnderstandingMascots.htm>. See "Understanding the American Indian Mascot Issue," among other articles.

Tennessee Chapter of the National Coalition of Indigenous Cultures. <home.att.net/~tcs4peace/mascot001.htm>.

2

NATIVE AMERICAN TREATY RIGHTS

THE TRAIL OF BROKEN TREATIES

In the fall of 1972, Native Americans fed up with conditions in their communities set out on a protest march that began in communities on the West Coast and proceeded to Washington, D.C. They called it the Trail of Broken Treaties. The caravan of activists grew larger as it visited Indian reservations and picked up new recruits before arriving in Washington in November, where the caravan's leaders intended to present a position paper titled "The Twenty Points" to federal officials on the eve of the country's presidential elections. "The Twenty Points" articulated grievances Native Americans wanted the government to address, many of which related to the issue of treaty rights. The fourth point, for example, demanded that the federal government establish a presidential commission "to review domestic treaty commitments and complaints of chronic violations and to recommend or act for corrective action."[1] The authors of "The Twenty Points" noted that Indian nations had been forced to spend nearly $40 million between 1962 and 1972 fighting against treaty violations in court, an expensive and frustrating process that drained Indian communities of precious resources. A related point, number seven, asked the federal government to provide "mandatory relief," or injunctions against state agencies or governments accused of violating treaty rights, thus shifting the burden of proof from Native American litigants to the states. The Trail of Broken Treaties ended with the occupation of the Bureau of Indian Affairs headquarters when activists grew restless and feared a confrontation with riot police who had assembled outside the building. The tense standoff prevented the caravan's leaders from mounting an effective campaign with "The Twenty Points," and the demonstration failed to accomplish its goals. But the incident provides us with an important context in which to evaluate the issue of treaty rights. In 1972 many Native Americans saw treaties as sacred documents that state and federal authorities had ignored for nearly a century. As demands for expanded sovereignty emanated from across Native America, the fight over treaty rights became an important cause in the search for self-determination.

HISTORICAL BACKGROUND

Between 1778, when a very young American nation began negotiating treaties with Indian nations, and 1868, when Congress approved a treaty with the Nez Perce, the United States government ratified 373 treaties. A number of the treaties were signed with an Indian nation after the government determined that the terms of an original treaty were inadequate because of increased settlement or the discovery of a valuable natural resource such as gold. Importantly, when Congress decided to stop making new treaties in 1871, it explicitly accepted the continued legality of the old treaties, stipulating that "nothing herein contained shall be construed to invalidate or impair the obligation of any treaty heretofore lawfully made and ratified with any such Indian nation or tribe."[2]

The majority of the treaties involved the sale of an Indian nation's territory in exchange for a restricted reservation, cash annuities for educational and economic programs, and specific land use rights. It is important to note two legal aspects of the treaties, which were essentially contracts between two sovereign powers, albeit one with leverage and one without. One is *ownership* of property. Native Americans ceded—or sold—millions of acres to the federal government, which then either incorporated that land into state or territorial jurisdictions or retained control of it. The next chapter, "Native American Land Claims," considers the extent to which the title to Native Americans' land was improperly taken or not properly compensated. This chapter, however, focuses on a second legal aspect of treaties, the legal right of using land that was ceded in the treaties, which entails what are known as *usufruct rights.* Treaties usually contained a clause defining the rights of tribal members to use the sold territory, especially "traditional" hunting and fishing sites.

Two early series of treaties bear detailing, as they will be referenced on several occasions later in this chapter. The federal government negotiated a series of treaties with Indian nations in the Wisconsin Territory, including the Chippewa Nation (also known as the Ojibwe or Anishinabe) in 1837, 1842, and 1854. Article V of the 1837 treaty stipulated, "The privilege of hunting, fishing and gathering the wild rice, upon the lands, the rivers, and the lakes included in the territory ceded, is guarantied [sic] to the Indians, during the pleasure of the President of the United States."[3] The 1842 and 1854 treaties contained similar clauses, ensuring that until the president of the United States, or the U.S. Congress, acted to deny Indians the "privilege" of hunting, fishing, or doing anything else related to the use of natural resources on their former lands, that privilege was a federally protected right. In another important case, the superintendent of the Washington and Oregon territories, Isaac Stevens, negotiated treaties (known as the Stevens Treaties) in 1854 and 1855 restricting some forty-two thousand Native Americans to small reservations in exchange for certain privileges or rights, which included "the right of taking fish at all usual and accustomed places in common with citizens of the Territory."[4] One of the treaties involved the Makah tribe of Neah Bay, Washington, who were granted the continued right to hunt whales in return for most of their land. Thus, even though the federal, state, or territorial government took ownership of Indian land, tribal members were legally entitled to make use of the land's natural resources, enabling them to sustain their cultural and economic traditions.

As the non-Indian population expanded in the Washington Territory at the end of the nineteenth century, challenges to Indians' usufruct rights arose. The first occurred in 1887 when a homesteader built a fence around his property, blocking the Yakima Indians' access to their traditional fishing site on the Columbia River. The resulting lawsuit ended up in the Supreme Court of the Washington Territory, which decided in favor of the Yakima. In 1905, the U.S. Supreme Court heard a similar case, and in *U.S. v. Winans* recognized the Yakima Nation's treaty rights. However, the Court also set the precedent of allowing the state to regulate Indian fishing in terms of the methods used to catch fish (for example, nets versus hooks). In the end, the Court ruled that treaties secured Native Americans' right to access traditional sites but not necessarily the right to continue traditional fishing practices that clash with state regulations. That distinction set the stage for a series of state court setbacks for Washington Indians attempting to fish in a traditional manner. The courts repeatedly rejected Indian sovereignty and ignored treaty rights, forcing Washington's Native Americans to fish under the cover of darkness to continue their old ways.

Just as it would take decades for African Americans to secure federal support of civil rights, so too would it take decades of activism by Native Americans to force the federal government to restore their treaty rights. Efforts by various Native American groups to secure federal intervention in treaty disputes began in the 1940s, especially in the Pacific Northwest, where a number of Indian nations depended on salmon for food and for rituals. In March 1942, the U.S. Supreme Court ruled in *Tulee v. Washington* that Indians in Washington State could fish off the reservation without a state fishing license because of the 1854 and 1855 treaties. But it allowed the state to define allowable fishing practices on the basis of "conservation," thus giving state officials a legal tool to deny Native Americans unrestricted fishing access. As the state crafted stringent conservation measures to limit Indian fishing rights, Native Americans mounted legal challenges to them. In 1951, the Makah tribe won a legal victory when the Ninth Circuit Court ruled that Washington State officials could not regulate tribal members' use of nets. But a subsequent case decided by the Washington State Supreme Court failed to articulate what Native Americans' treaty fishing rights were. In that case, Robert Satiacum and James Young of the Puyallup tribe were arrested for violating Washington State fishing regulations by using nets to catch steelhead and salmon in the Puyallup River. The court did uphold a lower court ruling that dismissed the charges against the two men because the state failed to prove that their actions were injurious to its conservation programs. The dismissal emboldened Satiacum and other Native American activists in Oregon and Washington to continue to challenge state fishing regulations.

Just as the sit-ins staged by young African American activists in the early 1960s helped publicize and energize the civil rights movement, so the fish-ins staged by Native American activists helped publicize and galvanize the nascent treaty rights movement. Indeed, young Native American activists associated with the National Indian Youth Council that formed in 1961 had participated in "freedom rides" and other civil rights demonstrations on behalf of African Americans, learning the art of civil disobedience in that similar struggle against racism and discrimination. In the early 1960s and beyond, Native Americans in the Pacific Northwest began to protest the denial of treaty rights by defying state law and fishing Washington's and Oregon's waters, resulting in verbal abuse by non-Indians and harassment and arrests by state officials using tear gas and blackjacks. In turn, though, a series of lawsuits was launched, aimed at forcing government authorities to recognize the validity of treaties signed more than a century earlier. Actors Marlon Brando and Jane Fonda, African American activist and comedian Dick Gregory, and other celebrities supported acts of civil disobedience, traveling to Frank's Landing and other sites of protest in Washington State to lend their presence to the struggle. In perhaps the most famous sit-in of the period, Brando, an Episcopal clergyman, and Robert Satiacum, the leader of the Puyallup tribe, were arrested on March 2, 1964, for fishing for salmon in the Puyallup River without state permits; Satiacum had been challenging state fishing restrictions for at least a decade. Several months later, in another well-publicized incident, Gregory was arrested for participating in a Nisqually tribe fish-in; in protest, he conducted a 39-day hunger strike. During these fish-ins, Native Americans lost boats, nets, fish, and other equipment, and men and women were jailed and fined for engaging in acts of peaceful civil disobedience. It was the Native American version of what African Americans in Birmingham and other southern cities faced. As Birmingham had, the fish-ins elicited support from President Lyndon Johnson, who pledged to back the Puyallup tribe in its lawsuit with Washington State officials.

THE BOLDT DECISION

The protests intensified during the 1950s and the 1960s in part because Washington tribes were getting fewer and fewer fish from the annual salmon runs due to non-Indian commercial fishing operations and the building of numerous dams, which proved damaging to the salmon population. After nearly two decades of individual challenges to restrictive state regulations and of organized fish-ins designed partly to create media attention, various tribes of the Pacific Northwest pooled their resources and moved the fight to the courts. Claiming that state officials had abridged their fishing rights as guaranteed in the Stevens Treaties, 13 tribes (seven other tribes later joined the suit) sued the State of Washington in federal court in 1970. Federal attorneys then joined the suit on behalf of the tribes. In 1974, after three and a half years of studying the issues involved—the treaties, the migratory patterns of the fish, the history of state regulation, among others—Judge George Boldt decided in *United States v. Washington* (known as and hereafter called the Boldt Decision) to uphold the rights of Native Americans in Washington State as well as Oregon to fish off-reservation sites using whatever method they chose, regardless of state laws, and to share equally the commercial catch of fish, or 50 percent of the "harvestable fish"; Boldt's quantification reflected the need to give both state governments and their citizens and tribal governments and their citizens half of the harvest, since the treaty related to two separate sovereign parties. Boldt developed two themes in his decision. First, Indians of the region depended on fish (salmon and steelhead) for sustenance and for cultural traditions, or as Boldt put it, salmon fishing "constituted both the means of economic livelihood and the foundation of native culture." And second, despite the evolution of industrial society and the advance of white settlement, "the mere passage of time has not eroded, and cannot erode, the rights guaranteed by solemn treaties that both sides pledged on their honor to uphold."[5] In a sense, Boldt viewed the treaty in two traditional contexts: one, in the Indian world, fishing is an aspect of culture, and two, in the classic white conception of property rights, a treaty is a contract and thus must be respected.

The right to fish using any method and the guarantee of half of the harvestable fish created a resurgent Indian fishing culture and industry; tribal members returned to reservations with employment opportunities in new businesses like fish processing, fish hatchery management, and other related enterprises. Native Americans caught roughly less than 5 percent of Washington's fish harvest the year of the Boldt Decision; by 1984 that percentage had risen to 49 percent, representing an economic bonanza to tribes hard hit by unemployment and declining federal assistance during the Reagan years. As a result, Washington State's commercial and recreational fishermen appealed the Boldt Decision, and they protested it by refusing to honor its stipulations. Effigies of Judge Boldt were burned, and the Washington Supreme Court refused to uphold Judge Boldt's fisheries allocation system, which granted equal proportions to Indian and non-Indian fishermen, forcing Boldt to step in and manage it himself. Between 1974 and 1978 Native American fishermen (and fisherwomen) were harassed by white citizens as well as by state officials, leading to 35 court cases and a review of the Boldt

Decision by the U.S. Supreme Court. On July 2, 1979, the Court upheld the Boldt Decision in *Washington v. Washington State Commercial Passenger Fishing Vessel Association,* a case brought by a non-Indian commercial fishing operation. The State of Washington also sought a reversal of Boldt's decision, arguing that the enforcement of the original treaties would violate principles of equal protection and equal opportunity. The Supreme Court disagreed. First, it argued that "this Court has already held that these treaties confer enforceable special benefits on signatory Indian tribes, and has repeatedly held that the peculiar semi-sovereign and constitutionally recognized status of Indians justifies special treatment on their behalves when rationally related to the Government's 'unique obligation toward the Indians.' "[6] Second, the Court chastised the Washington State Supreme Court for interfering with a federal court decision, giving state officials further impetus to respect the terms of the Boldt Decision.

A year later, Congress took an additional step to bolster Native American fishing by passing the Salmon and Steelhead Conservation and Enhancement Act, an act designed to ensure the continued success of salmon and steelhead runs in the Pacific Northwest and thus help Indians profit from the Boldt Decision. So not only did the federal government restore to Native Americans the right to fish based on the terms of nineteenth-century treaties, but it tried to ensure that fish continue to exist in sufficient amounts to satisfy those terms and provide Indians with a livelihood.

THE CHIPPEWA IN WISCONSIN

The Boldt Decision and the Supreme Court's rejection of appeals of it provided a legal precedent and inspiration for other tribes facing similar battles. Another important case is worth noting here. The Chippewa of Wisconsin and Minnesota also resisted state fishing and hunting regulations that they believed compromised treaties signed in the 1840s and 1850s that established the Chippewa's usufructuary rights in off-reservation waters and land. As in the Washington State case, Wisconsin state officials slowly eroded the Chippewa's right to hunt and fish in the territory ceded in those treaties. Through the early 1980s, the Chippewa found state courts hostile to their claims of treaty violations. They were especially angry that Wisconsin officials applied their regulations to traditional Chippewa practices like spearfishing both *on reservations* as well as off reservations. In 1959 one band (or tribal group) of the Chippewa declared that "a state of cold war exists between the Bad River Band of Chippewa Indians and the officials of the Wisconsin Department of Conservation, and that such state shall exist until such time as the State of Wisconsin shall recognize Federal treaties and statutes affording immunity to the members of this Band from State control over hunting and fishing *within* [emphasis added] the boundaries of this reservation."[7]

As the state cracked down on Chippewa fishing, particularly off-reservation fishing, tribal elders began to fish at night to avoid prosecution. Such acts of resistance ultimately led to a legal showdown over the issue of Chippewa treaty rights. On March 8, 1974, Fred and Mike Tribble of the Lac Courte Oreilles Chippewa Band were arrested by officials of Wisconsin's Department of Natural Resources (DNR) for spearfishing on Chief Lake in violation of state conservation laws. Their arrest was just one of dozens of cases where Chippewa were detained. But this case was different. Fred Tribble, with a copy of the 1837 treaty in his pocket, told the game warden that he and his brother would be crossing the reservation boundary that night to spear walleye, a prized fish indigenous to northern U.S. lakes. Their arrest triggered a lawsuit by the Lac Court Oreilles Band that claimed that off-reservation spearfishing was permitted under the terms of Chippewa treaties. The suit named as a defendant Lester Voight, the director of Wisconsin's DNR. In what is called the Voight Decision, Judge James Doyle of the U.S. District Court ruled in 1978 against the Chippewa. But in January 1983, a U.S. Court of Appeals overturned the decision, determining, as Judge Boldt had, that nineteenth-century treaties were still valid legal documents. The decision set off a new wave of legal challenges that lasted until 1991, when Judge Barbara Crabb, Doyle's successor, released a Final Judgment that upheld the usufructuary rights of the six bands of Wisconsin Chippewa in land ceded in 1837 and 1842 treaties, thus enabling the Chippewa to establish their own regulations for off-reservation hunting, gathering of wild rice, and fishing for walleye and muskie.

FRAMING THE ISSUE

In the same month that the U.S. Court of Appeals preserved Chippewa treaty rights, President Ronald Reagan promised in a statement on federal Indian policy that his administration would negotiate with tribes on a "government-to-government" basis, reinforcing the federal government's commitment to Native American sovereignty. Importantly, he mentioned the word *treaties* several times in the statement: "When European colonial powers began to explore and colonize this land, they entered into treaties with sovereign Indian nations. Our new nation continued to make treaties and to deal with Indian tribes on a government-government basis."[8] This attitude trickled down to the state level in 1989 when the governor of Washington and the state's 26 tribes signed the Centennial Accord, in which the state recognized the sovereignty of the tribes and agreed to adopt a government-to-government process for solving problems that affected both state and tribal government.

In the end, Reagan explicitly agreed to honor federal responsibilities to Native Americans, saying, "the Constitution, treaties, laws, and court decisions have consistently recognized a unique political relationship between Indian tribes and the United States."[9] Reagan acknowledged that the 1960s and the 1970s had produced a series of laws and court decisions that solidified what he called a "unique political relationship" between Indians and the federal government, and that forcing a change in that relationship would not work. But that didn't stop some non-Indians from trying. All this new sovereignty and federal and state support of treaty rights created problems for some Americans because Indians were, once again, owners of resources that non-Indians either wanted or didn't believe Indians should have exclusive access to.

Despite improved federal and state governmental support of Indian tribes, some state officials and citizens continued to oppose the granting of what they regarded as special privileges to Indians and created an anti-Indian backlash movement against treaty rights and tribal autonomy. Individuals in Washington, Wisconsin, Montana, Minnesota, and Michigan opposed tribal sovereignty because it strengthened Indians' legal jurisdiction and fishing and hunting rights, both on reservations, where many whites lived, and off reservations. In regions where Indians began to fish under newly defined fish and game laws, especially Wisconsin, bumper stickers started to appear that read "Save a Deer, Shoot an Indian" and "Spear an Indian, Save a Muskie." When Indians began fishing in the spring, whites would congregate and throw at them threats, rocks, and racial slurs like "timber niggers." At one demonstration against Indian fishing rights, white protestors carried signs that read "Save a Walleye, Spear a Pregnant Squaw" and "Too Bad Custer Ran Out of Bullets." Another carried a fake Indian head stuck on a spear. Indians' tires were slashed, their boats swamped, and sometimes their lives endangered by snipers firing from the shore. A reporter who witnessed a protest against Chippewa fishing called it a "gauntlet of hate."

The most recent case of violent confrontation occurred in waters off the Makah reservation of Washington. For centuries, two thousand years according to the tribe, the Makah hunted the gray whales that migrated past their home on the Olympic Peninsula. After commercial whalers decimated the gray whale population in the 1920s, the Makah stopped hunting them. But after they were taken off the federal list of endangered species in 1994, tribal members sought permission to resume whale hunts to restore their place in tribal culture. With U.S. support, based on the 1855 Stevens Treaty, international whaling bodies granted the Makah permission to kill 20 whales through 2004. As the Makah began preparations for the first hunt, antiwhaling activists assembled off the Makah reservation in protest, some waving signs like "Save a Whale, Harpoon a Makah." Tribal police arrested four protestors after they landed on reservation territory. A network of local and state anti-treaty groups formed, supported in part by anti-treaty politicians like Representative Jack Metcalf of Washington, a former commercial fisherman.

There is, then, a disjunction between how the federal courts and the president saw Indian rights and how some American citizens and state officials viewed them. The tenacity with which Native Americans fought to resurrect hunting and fishing rights codified more than a century earlier and non-Indians' visceral and violent response to Indians' exercise of those rights demonstrates the importance of this contemporary Native American issue. Although the demonstrations for and against treaty rights have not been as widespread as those regarding Indian mascots and gambling, they are indicative of the principles that underlay those issues—the search for both civil rights and sovereign rights.

OPPONENTS OF NATIVE AMERICAN TREATY RIGHTS

Anti-Indian-treaty-rights groups (also referred to as anti-Indian groups by scholars and Native Americans) started forming in the mid-1970s as part of what has been called a "citizen backlash movement," which developed not so much in reaction to the militancy of Red Power movements, which declined after the Wounded Knee occupation of 1973, but because court cases supported tribal jurisdiction over that of non-Indians within reservation boundaries and because many Indians, like those in Washington and Wisconsin, were given the legal right to fish outside reservation boundaries. In short, arguments against Indians' treaty-derived rights have been based on political, economic, and environmental considerations.

The Political Argument

As tribal sovereignty expanded in Washington, Wisconsin, Minnesota, and elsewhere, non-Indians, most of them whites living on or near Indian reservations, began to organize politically to challenge Native Americans' new-found treaty rights. They formed names like All Citizens Equal; Totally Equal Americans; Property Owners' Association; Citizens Rights Organization; the North Dakota Committee for Equality; and Enough Is Enough, a Michigan group that protested Indian hunting and fishing practices protected by treaties. These groups formed on the local community level, the state level, and eventually the national level as the larger state groups formed a coalition in search of expanded political influence. The common denominator of the groups, as one can surmise from their names, is that they all believed to varying degrees that Native Americans should not possess privileges that non-Indians did not have and that what was at stake was not only "equality" of access and opportunity but also economic issues such as fishing yields and property rights. Many anti-treaty activists consider treaty rights to be a form of federal welfare, available only to Indians. Fundamentally, they believed that granting Indians "special treatment" violates the civil rights of whites, creating an unequal playing field and what one anti-treaty protestor called a "Red Apartheid." Anti-treaty pamphlets carried titles like "200 Million Custers" and "Are We Giving America Back to the Indians?"—reflecting opponents' belief that Native Americans were taking over parts of America with the use of treaty rights.

The Boldt Decision proved to be a major impetus to the formation of these groups, spurring the creation of the first to affect the backlash movement, the Interstate Congress for Equal Rights and Responsibilities (ICERR). Although the name of the organization signified a regional or national reach, members of ICERR were non-Indian sport fishermen and commercial fishing groups from Washington. They believed that state and local laws should apply to reservations, that constitutional rights should take precedence over treaty rights, and that non-Indians should not have to face tribal laws. Some members owned property on Indian reservations such as Quinault and Port Madison, and they feared that the expansion of Indian sovereignty threatened their property rights. Commercial fishermen in particular were angered that the Boldt Decision allocated 50 percent of the salmon and steelhead harvest to Indians on the basis of documents signed more than a century earlier. It affected their livelihood. Although it took Indian fishermen 10 years to secure the 50 percent allocation, over that period the number of non-Indian fishing fleets declined.

Although ICERR was a local organization, its lobbying campaign found expression in Congress in 1977 and 1978 when a freshman congressman named John E. Cunningham introduced legislation to abrogate Indian treaties, break up tribal holdings, and end the policy of giving Indians special consideration. Cunningham had campaigned on this issue, attacking treaty-based Indian fishing rights by arguing, "While we encourage diversity in this country, we must not have two classes of citizens, whether black or white, immigrant American or Native American. It is for this reason that Congress must act to end the confusion caused by judicial interpretations of treaties and Executive Orders."[10] Fellow Washington state representative Lloyd Meeds introduced similar measures that would have severely curtailed Indian sovereignty. But Congress did not act on these proposals, and ICEER's influence waned. A second group formed in 1983, the Steelhead and Salmon Protections Action for Washington Now (S/Spawn). S/Spawn took direct action by organizing in 1983 a public ballot initiative for Washington voters, which failed. But a year later Washington voters narrowly approved a second measure, Initiative 456, which called for the end of special rights for Indians. State officials refused to enforce the measure, however, largely because the 1979 Supreme Court's affirmation of the Boldt Decision had made it clear that a failure to enforce treaty terms was a violation of federal law. S/Spawn treaty rights opponents then organized United Property Owners of Washington in 1989 to fight against Indian shellfish operations protected by treaties.

Similar resentment surfaced in Wisconsin when federal court decisions supported Chippewa Indians' right to hunt and fish on territory they once owned but ceded in the nineteenth century. As noted earlier in the chapter, Wisconsin state officials opposed the granting of treaty rights but ultimately agreed to honor the legal decisions supporting them. Non-Indian opponents were less accommodating, claiming that the treaty rights would destroy deer and fish populations. A Wisconsin group called Protect Americans' Rights and Resources (PARR) formed in 1987 and attempted to organize a national opposition; its first conference attracted roughly five hundred people from several states. Members of PARR, founded by paper mill foreman Larry Peterson, wanted the federal government to abrogate Indian treaties and dissolve Indian reservations. The principle reason, according to PARR's executive director, was that "the [liberal] courts have expanded on [Indian] rights—giving one group of people special privileges other Americans don't have," such as special hunting and fishing rights.[11] PARR's founder presented a states' rights argument, noting that federal courts were "writing new laws with their treaty interpretations, laws that discriminate and run contrary to the constitutions of the states."[12] Pizza parlor owner Dean Crist helped found another Wisconsin anti-treaty group called Stop Treaty Abuse (STA). Crist complained that treaty rights established two sets of rules and laws, which was discriminatory. STA has been criticized for its militancy. After a Chippewa tribe sued STA for violating its members' civil rights, a court fined the group and gave the Indians injunctive relief against further protests. STA lawyer Fred Hatch did not openly advocate violence but remarked that Wisconsin "is not far from becoming a Northern Ireland."[13]

The group with the broadest constituency is the Citizen Equal Rights Alliance (CERA), formed in 1988 in Montana, another hotbed of anti-treaty activity. CERA was led by officers who were also leaders of ICERR, S/Spawn, and PARR and represented members from at least 13 states. Still based in Montana, CERA has sent representatives to Washington to lobby Congress to abrogate Indian treaties; its leaders also participate in the so-called Wise Use Movement. One of CERA's founders is William Covey, a Montana resident who left government service to live on the Flathead reservation. Covey became upset when he learned that he could be prosecuted in tribal courts for violating tribal laws while on the reservation. First he joined Montanans Opposing Discrimination (MOD), which then became All Citizens Equal (ACE). As president of ACE, he met backlash leaders from Wisconsin groups such as PARR and STA and helped form CERA.

Like other anti-treaty groups, CERA wants legal reform in Indian-white affairs, specifically the termination of Indian sovereignty. Its main argument is that "federal policies currently deny millions of people living on or near Indian reservations their full constitutional rights."[14] A related group called Proper Economic Resource Management (PERM), which opposed treaty rights of Minnesota and Wisconsin Indians, also rejected Indians' right to govern. One PERM newsletter stated, "PERM wishes to thank all the clubs and organizations that have contributed to our efforts to SAVE MINNESOTA in 1995.... They do not want to be controlled by corrupt tribal governments in which we have no voice."[15] In this context, some Native

American activists have campaigned against tribes' sovereign status. Roland Morris, an enrolled member of the Chippewa tribe of Minnesota, has been active in Montana's All Citizens Equal. William Lawrence, also a Chippewa, has used his newspaper *Ojibwe News* to attack tribal governments, which he believes have violated his civil rights. Both Morris and Lawrence have testified in favor of federal anti-sovereignty legislation filed by senators Slade Gordon of Washington and Conrad Burns of Montana.

The Economic Argument

Covey, Crist, Lawrence, and others in the anti-treaty movement resent the political status of Indians; they feel betrayed by the Boldt Decision, by Reagan's recognition of Indian tribal governments, and by state acquiescence in these matters. Covey, Peterson, and Crist were not commercial fishermen but recreational hunters and fishing enthusiasts who objected to Indians' ability to set the terms of their use of natural resources. Members of their organizations, however, opposed treaty-based fishing and hunting rights because Wisconsin and other Upper Midwest states have tourism based on sport fishing and hunting. A reallocation of fish according to quotas threatens that industry, opponents say, because Chippewa usually spear fertile fish during their spawning season; as a result, the Wisconsin Department of Natural Resources reduced catch limits from five fish to two during the non-Indian fishing season. A 1997 court decision restoring Minnesota Chippewa's treaty-based hunting and fishing rights angered sportsmen and business owners in the popular Lake Mille Lacs area of Minnesota. Eddy Lyback, president of the Mille Lacs Lake Advisory Association and the owner of a local resort, hoped that legal appeals would continue. The main concern of his group, which comprises about seventy property and business owners, was "how this will affect the sport-fishing, tourism and the economy of the area. Basically, what it boils down to is, everyone gets a smaller piece of the pie. How many anglers will be willing to accept that smaller piece of the pie and come to this lake to fish?"[16] As noted earlier, the economic argument was first made by Washington State commercial fishermen who felt threatened by the Boldt Decision of 1974. Some non-Indians fished in spite of the new laws, either for economic or political reasons, in a sense mirroring the behavior of pre–Boldt Decision Indian fishermen by fishing at night in an effort to elude law enforcement officers. Illegal fishing became commonplace in Washington waters as fishermen protested the new economics of salmon fishing. Sympathetic lower courts generally dismissed citations given to non-Indians caught fishing illegally.

The Environmental Argument

The fight against treaty rights has also found support from American environmental and wildlife groups, which oppose Native Americans' asserted right to hunt all species on reservation land. A distinction should be made here, however. A number of mainstream environmental groups like the Environmental Defense Fund and Defenders of Wildlife are not necessarily opposed to all Indian treaty rights, just those that relate to the protection of endangered species, specifically bald eagles and Florida panthers, and to species of limited population like the gray whale; at the same time, organizations such as Ocean Defense International have used language similar to that of groups like PARR and STA in opposing Indians' exercise of treaty rights to hunt whales, suggesting a general opposition to Indian sovereignty.

On June 11, 1986, the U.S. Supreme Court overturned a circuit court ruling that threw out the conviction of a Yankton Sioux man who had killed four bald eagles while on reservation land on the basis of an 1858 treaty granting the Sioux the right to hunt for "non-commercial purposes." Justice Thurgood Marshall argued, however, that federal action to protect bald eagles "reflected an unmistakable and explicit legislative policy choice that Indian hunting of the bald eagle . . . is inconsistent with the need to preserve those species. We therefore read that [1962] statute as having abrogated that [Indian] treaty right."[17] The Court did not deny Indians the right to hunt on their land but did restrict, to a limited degree, what they could or could not kill on the basis of a 1962 congressional statute called the Bald and Golden Eagle Act (and not, explicitly, the Endangered Species Act). John Fitzgerald of Defenders of Wildlife made this distinction in hailing the Supreme Court judgment: "This decision is very important because the best habitat for several endangered species is on Indian land. Indians have not lost their right to hunt but they have lost the right to hunt protected species."[18] Indeed, the following year the U.S. Department of Justice filed charges against James Billie, the leader of Florida's Seminole Nation, for killing a Florida panther, an endangered species.

The most vocal debate between defenders of wildlife and Native Americans asserting treaty rights to hunt them has come from the fight over Makah whaling of migratory gray whales. A variety of U.S. antiwhaling groups, as well as some from Europe, New Zealand, and Canada, have fought the Makah's right to hunt whales, in part because they fear that other indigenous groups will try to find the authority to resume their whaling traditions, either for cultural or economic reasons. Activist Ben White noted that he respects Native American rights and the idea of reinvigorating the culture, but opposes the Makah's killing of whales because of its potential impact on whale populations around the world. White sees his actions in religious terms. He is a cofounder of the Church of the Earth, which believes that the Holy Spirit lives in all creatures. "I don't believe all traditions should be respected. If they don't need the meat, then why don't they just go out and touch the whale? If this need is truly spiritual, then why should the remedy be nutritional? . . . . A lot of us consider whales sacred, and it is simply wrong to kill them."[19] The Sea Shepherd Conservation Society, one of the main groups fighting the Makah hunt, is opposed to all whaling, not just Makah whaling. Its leader, Paul Watson, a founder of Greenpeace, pledged to interfere with the hunt using the group's 173-foot boat and its six-ton submarine. Watson argued that Makah leaders have played a "culture card" by focusing on the whales' significance to Makah life. "They have effectively created an atmosphere in which concern for the welfare of whales is now perceived as a de facto attack on native rights and the cultural heritage of an oppressed minority." Watson believed that the Makah's ancestors "hunted to survive" rather than because of a "cultural or traditional impulse," and thus the hunt was "an act of make-believe, an empty gesture toward a vanished past."[20] Although whaling opponents are mostly non-Indians, some Makah elders agreed with Watson, arguing that the hunt was not based on spiritual considerations and that the tradition of using whale meat and blubber had died out years ago; one elder claimed she lost her job for holding such views. Another dimension of the fight over Makah whaling is economic. Hundreds of whale-watching boats follow gray whales and orcas off the Washington State coast. Although the Makah had no plans to kill five whales per year, boat operators fear that the killing of one gray whale could induce a behavioral change in other whales, making them more suspicious of whale-watching boats.

After the Makah killed a whale in May 1999, activists sought injunctions against further hunts. Lawsuits filed in February 2000 and June 2002, supported by anti-treaty politicians and groups such as the Fund for Animals and the Humane Society of the United States, accuse the federal government of failing to consider public safety and environmental risks associated with the whale hunts, contending that whale watchers and sea kayakers could be injured in the future. The Makah whale hunts will continue to generate vociferous opposition, given that they are the only tribe granted the right to hunt whales on the basis of a treaty. And opponents of other treaty-based hunting and fishing rights will, no doubt, continue to search for legislative and legal means to attenuate or end Indian sovereignty in the years to come.

PROPONENTS OF NATIVE AMERICAN TREATY RIGHTS

Treaty rights defenders, both Indian and non-Indian, have had their hands full countering the citizen backlash movement in its various forms. They have done so by pointing up the right-wing tendencies and environmental deficiencies of its main groups. Leaders of the backlash movement may be connected to antigovernment militia, some analysts claim; the agendas of groups like PARR, STA, and CERA mirror those of antigovernment groups, which oppose federal or state officials' interference in their lives, but are focused particularly on Indian rights. Dan Thurman of the Center for Democratic Renewal pointed out that Milwaukee skinheads of the White Patriots League attended rallies staged by PARR. In 1990, the *Wisconsin State Journal* quoted STA's founder Dean Crist arguing that "David Duke [white supremacist from Louisiana] is saying the same stuff we have been saying, like he might have been reading it from STA literature."[21] Other treaty defenders argue that some Americans simply don't like the idea of Indians having power—power to hold attractive property and power to decide how whites will use that property. For example, William Covey of CERA began his crusade against Indian sovereignty because he rejected the Flathead Nation's right to impose fishing and hunting regulations on non-Indians, like him, living on the reservation. Hilary Waukau of Wisconsin's Menominee Nation argued that by signing a treaty, a "sacred document," the Menominee "gave up our land in return for certain things. Now they [whites] say we have too much. But these are inborn rights that can't be taken away because we are the native people of this country. Many people are jealous."[22]

At the least, according to many Native Americans, the anti-treaty movement is clearly driven by racism. Critics of the anti-treaty groups point to the slogans and images PARR, STA, and others use. Gilbert Chapman, a Chippewa spearfisherman who witnessed violent anti-treaty demonstrations, called the Wisconsin community of Minoqua, where several anti-treaty leaders lived, "another Selma [Alabama]. They call us 'sand niggers,' 'timber niggers,' every bad name they can think of."[23] Ken Toole, the director of the Montana Human Rights Network, has studied the evolution of the anti-treaty movement in Montana, which has seen the birth of groups such as Montanans Opposing Discrimination and All Citizens Equal. In his report "Drumming Up Resentment: The Anti-Indian Movement in Montana," Toole addressed the issue of racism, contending, "Even if we set aside the racial epithets and affiliations with white supremacist groups which plague anti-Indian groups across the country, the movement is racist at its core. Taken at face value, the anti-Indian movement is a systematic effort to deny legally established rights to a group of people who are identified on the basis of their shared culture, history, religion and tradition. That makes it racist by definition."[24] Some anti-treaty protestors don't mince their words. The animosity extends to some state officials. In the most vitriolic rhetoric, a Washington State prosecutor said, "We had the power and force to exterminate these people from the face of the earth, instead of making treaties with them.... Perhaps we should have. We certainly wouldn't be having all this trouble with them today."[25]

The Centrality of Culture

The racism of the anti-treaty movement has framed Native Americans' defense of their treaty rights, making the issue an essential one for the maintenance of their cultural and political autonomy. Ironically, the attacks on Indians brought the issue of discrimination into the public eye, before the mascot controversy erupted in the late 1980s. Countering opponents' claim that treaty rights were a form of welfare, Harrison Sasche, a former federal attorney, noted that "the real impact [of the treaty rights struggle] is that it shows the lengths that the Indians will go to preserve their culture. It is the opposite of the myths regarding Indians—that they are lazy and don't want to work."[26] Sasche was impressed by Native Americans' willingness to face racist epithets, rocks, and other hazards in championing their treaty rights, a struggle that brought Indian communities together even as it presented a new image to the American public.

Native American advocates of treaty rights point to a major force behind the original protests against state laws restricting Indian fishing and behind the contemporary conservation movement. The object of the hunt, whether it be a walleye for the Chippewa, a salmon for a Lummi from Washington, or a gray whale for the Makah, is first seen as a cultural issue rather than as an economic one. While Washington Native Americans in particular profit from salmon fisheries, their connection to the salmon is one of cultural identity. As Judge Boldt noted in his famous 1974 decision, salmon fishing "constituted both the means of economic livelihood and the foundation of native culture." Anthropologists, historians, and Native American oral history have demonstrated that Pacific Northwest tribes have been fishing for salmon for centuries, using a variety of methods, and have done so for three reasons—ceremony, subsistence, and trade. The arrival of immigrant fishermen in the early twentieth century slowly diminished the tribes' access to salmon runs, making it difficult for them to continue this three-pronged usage of the salmon and thus maintain spiritual, nutritional, and economic health. According to Donald Sampson, the executive director of the Columbia River Inter-Tribal Fish Commission (CRITFC), which coordinates tribal conservation programs in the Pacific Northwest, "We are all salmon people.... Salmon are important to our ecosystem, the water we drink, the health of our bodies, the interconnectedness of all beings and the nourishing of our very existence. It is a message of balance, of give and take.... We all must be conservationists."[27] Sampson is sensitive to both the cultural and scientific issues involved in modern conservation issues, drawing upon his degree in fisheries resource management as well as his appreciation for the place of salmon in Indian culture. In addition to providing food and a livelihood, for Sampson and other Native Americans of the Pacific Northwest the salmon keep their culture alive. CRITFC puts it in stark terms: "Salmon are part of our spiritual and cultural identity.... The annual return of the salmon allows the transfer of traditional values from generation to generation. Without salmon returning to our rivers and streams, we would cease to be Indian people."[28]

The Chippewa of the Great Lakes area have a similar relationship with the walleye, which has met their nutritional needs for centuries. Over half of Chippewa families today consume the fish, while some tribal members earn cash income from fish sales, but only on the basis of strict tribal regulations. Those Chippewa who risked imprisonment, intimidation, or even violence to fish walleye using the tradition methods of gillnetting or spearfishing by torchlight did so because they were continuing a tradition that was older than the treaties of the 1800s. Indeed, French explorers named one band of Chippewa the Lac du Flambeau, or Torch Lake, because they noticed its members fishing for walleye at night with torches. As with Washington Native Americans, the right to fish transcends issues of subsistence and politics for the Chippewa and other Indians of the Great Lakes. Reconnecting with old ways such as spearfishing at night helps to restore a community's spiritual and cultural integrity. Nick Hockings of the Chippewa Wa-Swa-Gon Treaty Association, who used alcohol to fill a spiritual void before kicking the habit, sees culture as an important way to attack high rates of alcoholism. "I think [a solution] lies in going back to traditional ways, to start acting more like our ancestors—very proud, honest, trustworthy. The Indian people don't want to be totally separate, but we need to have a sense of identity. Each person needs to feel complete and a spiritual connection with the earth and the environment. When people feel good about who they are . . . they don't need the crutch of alcohol."[29]

The Importance of Conservation

The rebirth of Native American fishing, especially in Washington State, has brought about economic opportunity, which in turn has engendered social change. As with gambling, tribal salmon fishing operations have created a reason for younger Indians to return to their reservations. Andy Fernando, a former leader of the Upper Skagit Community, addressed this positive development by arguing that the Boldt Decision acted as "a catalyst" to reverse the flow of talented tribal members from the reservation to Pacific Northwest cities. After the decision, "many Indian people returned to their [nations] at first only to fish. But now they stay on because they see renewed activity in their tribal communities. Those people bringing skills have found welcoming tribal councils and communities eager to tap their knowledge and experience." As with gambling, treaty rights have not solved all the problems communities face, but they have provided a more stable foundation. Fernando did not call the Boldt Decision a panacea but noted that "the opportunities created directly or indirectly from the legally secured right to fish are the differences between staying and leaving for many young Indian families. Today, when young Indians leave the reservation for college or to learn a skill, most intend to return and use their knowledge close to home. And many of those young people will return, to stay and build a future."[30]

Some of the young Native Americans return to their reservations with degrees in biology and computer science to help run their tribes' state-of-the-art fisheries. And they have helped to keep important river systems like the Columbia River environmentally sound, benefiting both Indian and non-Indian fishermen. After Boldt reached his decision, fishing tribes of Oregon

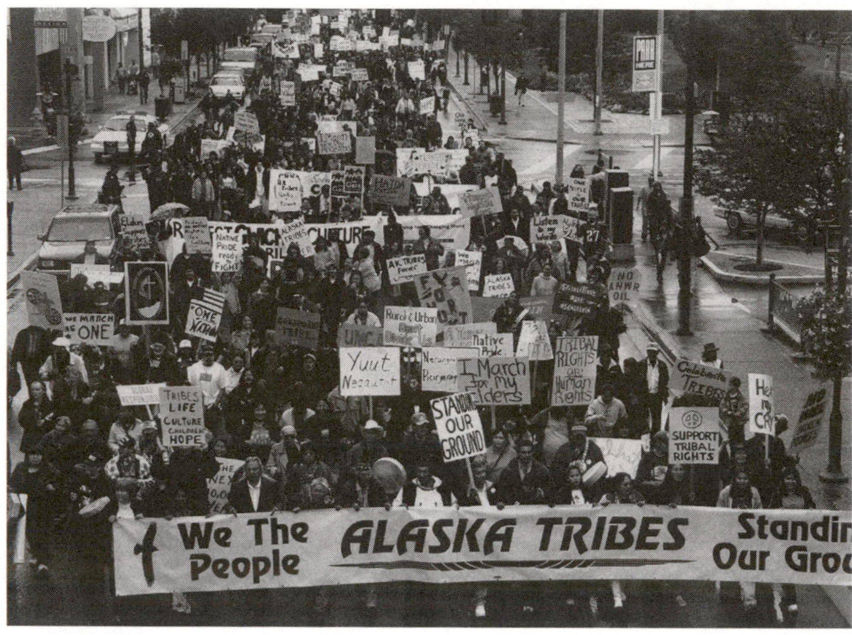

Thousands of Alaska natives, Native Americans, and non–Native Americans march in the rain in a show of unity during the fifth annual We the People march in 2002, in downtown Anchorage. The first rally was called five years ago in response to the U.S. Supreme Court's Venetie decision, which denied sovereignty to Alaska natives. (AP/Wide World Photos)

and Washington organized the Northwest Indian Fisheries Commission (NIFC), which stated that "our fisheries are a basic and important natural resource and of vital concern to the Indians of this state, and that the conservation of this resource is dependent upon effective and progressive management."[31] The NIFC, now the Columbia River Inter-Tribal Fish Commission, acted to preserve the very species Indians fought so hard to win the right to fish. After Chippewa fishing rights were upheld in 1983, 11 Chippewa nations from Wisconsin, Minnesota, and Michigan formed the Great Lakes Indian Fish and Wildlife Commission (GLIFWC). Its agenda, besides defending those rights and educating the public about them, also focuses on conservation. The GLIFWC's constitution states that member nations "recognize that our fish, wildlife, and other renewable resources are important natural resources and of vital concern to the Indian tribes of the Great Lakes region and the conservation of this resource is dependent upon effective and progressive management." Members also stress that their agenda reflects a desire to work "not only for the benefit of our people but for all of the people of the Great Lakes."[32] Native Americans' efforts to create sustainable resources have created better cooperation between Indians and non-Indians and have become an important dimension of treaty rights.

Given this emphasis on conservation programs, Native Americans argue that anti-treaty forces are simply wrong in declaring native fishing injurious to the ecosystem and to the sport fishing and commercial industries. For example, as the Wisconsin dispute over Chippewa spearfishing dragged on, the Chippewa pointed out that they took a small percentage of the gross catch of walleye and muskie. In 1989, the Chippewa took roughly sixteen thousand fish, while non-Indians caught more than six hundred thousand. Addressing the anti-treaty argument that Chippewa spearfishing forced Wisconsin officials to cut limits from five to two, state biologist Michael Hansen noted Chippewa spearfishing has had "more impact in the mind than in reality," in part because most non-Indian anglers never caught five fish in a day.[33] Additionally, a Wisconsin Department of Natural Resources report noted that the "angling bag limit [for non-Indians] would need to be cut to two walleye (from the present five), regardless of spearfishing."[34]

Native Americans argue that the groups opposed to their fishing programs blame them for environmental problems instead of addressing other issues like overdevelopment and pollution, PCBs in particular, which have had an impact on fish populations in Washington, Wisconsin, and Minnesota. The walleye population in Wisconsin has been hurt by the timber and paper industries, which have clogged lakes and rivers with logs, raised their silt levels, and polluted them with chlorine, mercury, and PCBs. As Chippewa journalist Patty Loew put it, "Where was PARR [Protect American Rights and Resources, a Wisconsin-based anti-treaty group] when these issues were debated? Why do its members only involve themselves in issues concerning Indian treaty rights?"[35] PARR did join Chippewa in opposing a nuclear waste dump in Michigan in 1990, and anti-sovereignty activists in South Dakota have worked with members of the Sioux nation in an environmental campaign against mining. These cases of cooperation are rare, however. Native Americans also contend that anti-treaty politicians like Senator Slade Gorton and Representative Jack Metcalf of Washington have terrible environmental records, and that their attacks on Indian fishing rights are, therefore, hypocritical. The Sierra Club and the League of Conservation Voters have criticized the voting records of Gorton and Metcalf as being anti-environment.

Native Americans have also had to defend their right to hunt species considered to be endangered or in decline, such as the Florida panther and the gray whale. The Department of Justice case against Seminole leader James Billie, charged with killing a Florida panther, at the time listed as an endangered species, reflected discriminatory prosecution, according to Billie's lawyer Bruce Rogow. "We find it a bit of an irony that the panther is endangered by the white man's commercial development of the Everglades, and yet Chief Billie is the only person ever to be prosecuted for this offense."[36] Rogow contended that Billie had a right to hunt on his reservation because the federal government had never notified tribal members that they were liable under the Endangered Species Act.

The Case of the Makah

The Makah whale-hunting controversy deserves special attention because it illustrates nicely the various themes of the pro-treaty forces. Makah have been threatened, sued, and insulted by antiwhaling forces, some of which have argued that the Makah are opportunists with no hope of restoring their culture through whaling. The leader of one group shouted at tribal members through a megaphone, "Just because you were born stupid doesn't give you any right to be stupid." In response, a Makah waved a sign reading "Go home eco-colonialist."[37] The Makah, living in an isolated community, have not been pleased that their exercise of treaty rights has engendered so much hostility, which stemmed in part from the televised spectacle of tribal members killing a whale, and the confrontational tactics of their opponents. Some Native Americans found the criticism misplaced. In a letter to the *Seattle Times*, a Native American woman wrote, "Whales were killed almost to extinction by commercial whaling, not by native whalers. Why is it so upsetting to the public to see the Makah taking one whale when it isn't upsetting to them that native people are almost extinct? Where is their 'compassion' while they watch American bombs kill humans in Kosovo? And where is the compassion for victims of American economic policy around the Earth? We wonder if non-native people are upset because natives have survived 507 years of the war against us, and we still resist. Not all native people are alcoholic, casino-loving replicas of the white man. Viva Makah."[38] Not all environmental groups protested against the hunt. While opposed to commercial whaling, Greenpeace and the Sierra Club did not object to "aboriginal whaling." Michael McGinn, chairman of the Sierra Club's Cascade Chapter, stated, "We neither support nor oppose the Makah whaling. Given the unique and limited nature of the hunt and the health of gray whale populations, we didn't feel this was a conservation issue we needed to take a position on."[39]

Makah officials stress their respect for the whale and for the environmental issues involved. Since the first hunt in May 1999, tribal officials have pointed out that the Makah have killed only one whale out of the 20 allotted, in part because of the expense involved. More important, the tribe defends its treaty right by claiming that the hunt is a sacred tradition and that it does not harm the environment. As Makah Whaling Commission president Keith Johnson put it, "We are stewards of our resources."[40] The National Marine Fisheries Service stated that according to its environmental studies, the Makah's hunting of five gray whales a year out of a population of about twenty-six thousand would not pose a threat to the species. In addition to following tribal tradition in hunting the whale, the Makah agreed to follow guidelines codified in the Makah Whaling Management Plan, which tribal officials designed along with the National Marine Fisheries Service.

Although the tribe had not staged a whale hunt for more than 70 years, the gray whale was still a visible part of Makah society. Its image appeared prominently on the high school as well as served as a backdrop during traditional tribal dances and celebrations. Some tribal members hoped the hunt would restore some spiritual equilibrium to the community. According to the tribe's official statement on the hunt, "Many Makahs feel that our health problems result, in some degree, to the loss of our traditional diet of seafood and sea mammal meat. We would like to restore the meat of the whale to our diet. Many of us also believe that problems besetting our young people stem from lack of discipline and pride. We believe that the restoration of whaling will help to restore that discipline and pride."[41] The tribe said that it would follow the traditional protocol in its use of the whale. According to Denise Dailey, a fisheries biologist and the executive director of the Makah Whaling Commission, which oversees all aspects of the whale hunt, "We have a ceremony for everything—for potlatches, for distribution of each cut."[42] Contrary to critics' charges that the Makah would sell the whale meat to Japanese buyers, the Makah signed an agreement with the National Oceanic and Atmospheric Administration to prohibit the commercial sale of whale products, with the exception of traditional handicrafts and artwork made from whalebone. Some of the whale meat would be frozen or smoked, but all of it would be consumed on the reservation, some by Native Americans from other Pacific Northwest Indian tribal communities invited to join in the feast. Lawrence Watters, who teaches coastal-resources law, said, "You shouldn't underestimate the spiritual and cultural significance of whaling to this tribe. It's a basic identity, like baseball or the right to drive cars in America."[43] The day of the hunt, May 17, 1999, Joddie Johnson, the owner of a reservation restaurant in Neah Bay, where tribal members watched the hunt on TV, said the experience was "just overwhelming. I've been telling people, there's no words that can express what's inside. Very full of pride, honor . . . respect of the whale, for the warriors and the warriors' respect for the greatness of the whale."[44]

The first hunt resulted in a resurgence of cultural pride and tribal unity, but it was never seen as a panacea for the tribe's problems. Whaling is no longer managed or funded by the Makah tribal council, which has a different set of priorities, including jobs and infrastructure improvement on land. According to council member David Lawrence, whaling is now the domain of those Makah families interested in whaling, which was the Makah tradition. "It's not so much the whaling; we are securing the treaty right. That is the big difference."[45]

The Makah case demonstrates the various threads that tie together a tribe's fight for treaty rights—cultural, economic, political, and environmental. For many Native Americans, regaining that treaty right is the first step toward securing a foundation for self-determination. An exercise of treaty rights can provide a tribal community with access to a dormant tradition like hunting a whale, fishing for walleye, or netting salmon. With the exception of the whale hunt, non-Indians to a much greater extent than Indians practice all these

Makah Indian tribal members work on the carcass of a gray whale killed in 1999 during the tribe's first successful hunt in 70 years, in Neah Bay, Washington. Members of the community pitched in to help the whaling crew butcher the animal, peeling back an inches-thick layer of blubber to reveal the whale's red meat. Some was cured for a few days in preparation for a big feast for the Makah and visitors. Some was distributed to tribal members, with the blubber rendered into oil for cooking and dipping. (AP/Wide World Photos)

activities; Native Americans simply choose a different ritual than the non-Indian fishermen, but it has greater cultural import. In the case of Wisconsin and Washington Indian nations, the exercise of treaty rights has also brought either increased food supplies or economic opportunity, which in turn has helped to restore demographic stability to isolated communities. In nearly all cases, the hunting or fishing practices are done in accord with both tribal traditions and modern environmental requirements. Native Americans have had to contend with a shrinking natural resource base for more than a century and take seriously the need to manage it properly. While preserving their sovereign rights, Washington fishing tribes, the Chippewa, and the Makah have worked closely with federal or state authorities to produce a workable conservation program. Native communities have married the traditions of the past with the scientific and ecological practices of the present to ensure a long-lasting Native American future, an agenda that reflects a pragmatic understanding of the need to work with non-Indians to preserve the larger ecosystem of which they are part.

The Meaning of the Treaties

When Chippewa journalist Patty Loew asked the chairman of the Lac du Flambeau Nation what his people took from the treaty rights struggle, he answered, "Pride. The Anishinabe [Chippewa] are standing a little taller and walking a little prouder these days." That feeling of pride, generated by the struggle, has fueled what Loew calls a spiritual "renaissance of art and culture."[46] Attendance at powwows rose, cultural centers were opened, and Wisconsin schools began to provide more coverage of Native American history and culture. The struggle, as with Washington tribes and others across the country, has led to a sharpened cultural identity that has helped reservation communities rebuild. Some tribal communities have learned from the legal issues of the struggle to strengthen their sovereignty in other matters, such as protecting themselves from mining companies and state infringement on the operation of reservation businesses.

As the twentieth century came to a close, state and federal courts continued to uphold the validity of treaties of the nineteenth century. A June 1999 editorial in the *Seattle Times,* responding to a Washington State Supreme Court decision on Indian hunting rights, noted that the ruling "restates loudly that a treaty is as good, or better, today as the day it was signed."[47] As the recent fight over Makah whaling indicates, not everyone is willing to accept that judgment. If species such as the bald eagle and gray whale remain embattled, if salmon and steelhead continue to face pressure from encroaching development and its concomitant pollution, and if walleye and muskie populations decline, then the battle over treaty rights will flare anew. Native Americans will be ready to fight for their rights, not only because a piece of paper called a treaty provides a legal justification for it, but because their way of life requires it. In discussing Indians in Kansas and Nebraska, the commissioner of Indian affairs wrote in 1856 that they would survive "if the guarantees and stipulations of their treaties are faithfully fulfilled and enforced, and the federal government discharges its obligations and redeems its pledged faith towards them."[48] In the nineteenth century, federal negotiators recognized that Native Americans had particular cultural needs that had to be met, in part because Native American negotiators demanded that those cultural needs be met. They do so today.

NOTES

1. Quoted in Francis Paul Prucha, *American Indian Treaties: The History of a Political Anomaly* (Berkeley: University of California Press, 1994), 412.

2. Quoted in Francis Paul Prucha, *The Great Father: The United States Government and the American Indian* (Lincoln: University of Nebraska Press, 1984), 165.

3. Quoted in Patty Loew, "Hidden Transcripts in the Chippewa Treaty Rights Struggle," *American Indian Quarterly* 21, no. 4 (fall 1997), 716.

4. Quoted in Starla Kay Roels, "Borrowing Instead of Taking: How the Seemingly Opposite Threads of Indian Treaty Rights and Property Rights Activism Could Inter-

twine to Restore Salmon to the Rivers," *Environmental Law* 28, no. 2 (summer 1998), 375.

5. Francis Paul Prucha, ed., *Documents of United States Indian Policy* (Lincoln: University of Nebraska Press, 2000), 269.

6. Quoted in Fay G. Cohen, *Treaties on Trial: The Continuing Controversy over Northwest Fishing Rights* (Seattle: University of Washington Press, 1986), 112.

7. Quoted in Loew, "Hidden Transcripts," 717.

8. Ronald Reagan, "Indian Policy: Statement of Ronald Reagan," 24 January 1983, in *Public Papers of the Presidents of the United States: Ronald Reagan, 1983* (Washington, D.C.: GPO, 1984), 303.

9. Reagan, "Indian Policy," 303.

10. Quoted in Prucha, *American Indian Treaties*, 423–24.

11. Cheryl Sullivan, "Indian Treaty Rights under Attack," *Christian Science Monitor*, 8 September 1987.

12. Laurence Jolidon, "Battle Builds over Indians' Fishing Rights," *USA Today*, 21 March 1990.

13. Jolidon, "Battle Builds."

14. *Citizens Equal Rights Alliance*, <www.citizensalliance.org/> (accessed July 2002).

15. Doug Grow, "Anti-Indian-Rights Group Gets United Way Money; 'Choice Campaign' Can Be 2-Edged Sword, the King of Charitable Giving Discovers," *Minneapolis Star Tribune*, 15 November 1995.

16. Larry Oakes and Doug Smith, "Judges Affirm Indian Treaty Rights," *Minneapolis Star Tribune*, 27 August 1997.

17. David G. Savage, "Other Threatened Species Could Benefit; High Court Holds Indians May Not Kill Bald Eagles," *Los Angeles Times*, 12 June 1986.

18. Savage, "Other Threatened Species."

19. Christopher Dunagan, "The Hunters Become the Hunted," *Bremerton (Wash.) Sun*, 5 October 1998.

20. Christopher Dunagan, "Activist: Hunt Is 'Empty Gesture,' " *Bremerton (Wash.) Sun*, 5 October 1998.

21. Quoted in Dan Thurman, Center for Democratic Renewal, "Indian Issues and Anti-Indian Organizing," *Native Americans and the Environment*, 1995, <www.indians.org/library/anti.html> (accessed July 2002).

22. Jolidon, "Battle Builds."

23. Jolidon, "Battle Builds."

24. Ken Toole, "Drumming Up Resentment: The Anti-Indian Movement in Montana," *Montana Human Rights Network*, 2000, <www.mhrn.org/news/Drumming.html> (accessed July 2002).

25. Quoted in Clifford E. Trafzer, *As Long As the Grass Shall Grow and Rivers Flow: A History of Native Americans*. New York: Harcourt, 2000, 422.

26. Cohen, *Treaties on Trial*, 179.

27. Donald Sampson, "Message from the Executive Director," *Columbia River Inter-Tribal Fish Commission*, <www.critfc.org/main.html> (accessed July 2002).

28. "The Importance of Salmon to the Tribes," *Columbia River Inter-Tribal Fish Commission*, <www.critfc.org/main.html> (accessed July 2002).

29. Lucia Mouat, "Leader Pushes for Indian Sense of Identity," *Christian Science Monitor*, 9 July 1990.

30. Andy Fernando, introduction to Cohen, *Treaties on Trial*, xxv.

31. Cohen, *Treaties on Trial*, <www.nwifc.wa.gov/aboutus/overview.asp> (accessed July 2002).

32. "Constitution of the Great Lakes Indian Fish and Wildlife Commission," *Great Lakes Indian Fish and Wildlife Commission*, <www.glifwc.org> (accessed July 2002).

33. Jolidon, "Battle Builds."

34. Quoted in Loew, "Hidden Transcripts," 719-20.

35. Loew, "Hidden Transcripts," 719.

36. Philip Shabecoff, "Killing of a Panther: Indian Treaty Rights vs. Law on Wildlife," *New York Times*, 15 April 1987.

37. Lynda V. Mapes, "Standoff at Makah Border Gets Ugly," *Seattle Times*, 1 November 1998.

38. "Readers Write about the Makah Whale Hunt, Other Topics," *Seattle Times*, 20 May 1999

39. Christopher Dunagan, "Bigger Groups Sit It Out, *Bremerton (Wash.) Sun*, 5 October 1998.

40. Elizabeth Murtaugh, "Makah Prepare to Hunt Whales," *Seattle Times*, 29 March 2002.

41. "Makah Whaling: Questions and Answers," *Northwest Indian Fisheries Commission*, undated, <www.makah.com/whales.htm> (accessed July 2002).

42. "Work, Celebration When First Whale Is Landed," *Bremerton (Wash.) Sun*, 29 October 1998.

43. Danny Westneat, "Makahs' Request for Whale Hunt Withdrawn," *Seattle Times*, 27 June 1996

44. Peggy Andersen, "Whale Goes Down," *Bremerton (Wash.) Sun*, 18 May 1999.

45. Lynda V. Mapes, "Makah Leaders Say More Pressing Needs Than Whale Hunts Face Their People," *Seattle Times*, 15 April 2002

46. Loew, "Hidden Transcripts," 724.

47. Editorial, "Court Limits Hunting but Backs Native Rights," *Seattle Times*, 18 June 1999.

48. George W. Manypenny, *Annual Report of the Commissioner of Indian Affairs*, 34th Cong., 3d sess., Senate Executive Document no. 5, serial 875, 571–75, 22 November 1856.

QUESTIONS

1) Should nineteenth-century documents matter when addressing contemporary social issues? Take into consideration even earlier documents, such as the Constitution.
2) Have Native Americans exploited treaties their ancestors signed or simply received what could be called a belated inheritance from them?
3) What are the similarities between the Washington State cases and those in Wisconsin?
4) What are the essential differences between those cases?

5) Do non-Indians have a legitimate complaint that Indians are given special "privileges" that they don't get?
6) Can we distinguish between legitimate and illegitimate arguments against treaty rights?
7) To what extent has racism been a part of the campaign against Indian treaty rights?
8) Can one make a case that not all exercises of treaty rights are appropriate? If so, which ones would you accept and which ones would you reject, and why?
9) What are the most compelling reasons to be adduced in favor of treaty rights?
10) What are the most compelling reasons to be adduced against treaty rights?
11) Do anti-treaty groups appear to be part of a larger antigovernment movement?
12) To what extent is the exercise of treaty rights an economic issue? To what extent is it a cultural issue?
13) Is the hunting of a whale a different matter than the fishing of salmon or the hunting of elk? If so, explain why.
14) To what extent are environmental issues important in the debate over treaty rights? Discuss how each side views these issues.
15) How would you react if a Native American tribe in your community exercised its legitimate treaty rights and changed your ability to hunt or fish?
16) Research the Makah whaling case. What is the status of the hunt? Report on the actions of all sides and then defend a position.

RESOURCE GUIDE

Suggested Readings

Ballew, Wayne. "Native Americans Feel Betrayed Again." *New York Times,* 3 August 1995.

Barsh, Russell L. *The Washington Fishing Rights Controversy: An Economic Critique.* Seattle: University of Washington Press, 1979.

Boxberger, Daniel L. *To Fish in Common: The Ethnohistory of Lummi Indian Salmon Fishing.* Lincoln: University of Nebraska Press, 1989.

Burton, Lloyd. *American Indian Water Rights and the Limits of Law.* Lawrence: University Press of Kansas, 1991.

Cohen, Fay G. *Treaties on Trial: The Continuing Controversy over Northwest Fishing Rights.* Seattle: University of Washington Press, 1986.

Cohen, Fay G., and Vivian L. Bowden. "A Legacy Restored: Another Perspective on the Boldt Decision." *Cultural Survival Quarterly* 12, no. 3 (1988).

Combs, Mariel J. "United States v. Washington: The Boldt Decision Reincarnated." *Environmental Law 29, no. 3* (fall 1999).

Cornell, Stephen. *The Return of the Native: American Indian Political Resurgence.* New York: Oxford Press, 1988.

Deloria, Vine, Jr. *Behind the Trail of Broken Treaties: An Indian Declaration of Independence.* New York: DelaCorte Press, 1974.

Deloria, Vine, Jr., and Clifford Lytle. *The Nations Within: The Past and Future of American Indian Sovereignty.* New York: Pantheon Books, 1984.

Finnigan, Richard A. "Indian Treaty Analysis and Off-Reservation Fishing Rights: A Case Study." *Washington Law Review* 5 (1975).

Great Lakes Indian Fish and Wildlife Commission. *A Guide to Understanding Chippewa Treaty Rights.* Odanah, Wis.: Great Lakes Indian Fish and Wildlife Commission, 1995.

Handrick, Philip. "A Chippewa Case: Resource Control and Self-Determination." *Cultural Survival Quarterly* 11, no. 2 (1987).

Harmon, Alexandra. *Indians in the Making: Ethnic Relations and Indian Identities around Puget Sound.* Berkeley: University of California Press, 1988.

Hundley, Norris, Jr. "The Dark and Bloody Ground of Indian Water Rights: Confusion Elevated to Principle." *Western Historical Quarterly* 9 (October 1978).

Institute for Natural Progress. "In Usual and Accustomed Places: Contemporary American Indian Fishing Rights Struggles." In *The State of Native America: Genocide, Colonization, and Resistance,* edited by M. Annette Jaimes. 1992.

Josephy, Alvin M., Jr. *Now That the Buffalo's Gone.* New York: Knopf, 1982.

Knutson, Peter. "The Unintended Consequences of the Boldt Decision." *Cultural Survival Quarterly* 11, no. 2 (1987).

Krogseng, Kari. "Minnesota v. Mille Lacs Band of Chippewa Indians; Native American Treaty Rights to Hunt and Fish Must Be Allowed within Conservation Standards." *Ecology Law Quarterly* 27 (August 2000).

LaDuke, Winona. "Indian Treaty Rights Are a Critical Environmental Issue." *Utne Reader,* January–February 1990.

Landau, Jack L. "Empty Victories: Indian Treaty Fishing Rights in the Pacific Northwest." *Environmental Law* 10 (1980).

Laurence, R. "The Abrogation of Indian Treaties by Federal Statutes Protective of the Environment." *Natural Resources Journal* 31 (1991).

Loew, Patty. "Hidden Transcripts in the Chippewa Treaty Rights Struggle." *American Indian Quarterly* 21 (fall 1997).

"Makah Whaling: Questions and Answers." <www.makah.com/whales.htm> (accessed July 2002).

McGuire, Thomas R., et al. *Indian Water in the New West.* Tucson: University of Arizona Press, 1994.

Meyers, Gary D. "Different Sides of the Same Coin: A Comparative View of Indian Hunting and Fishing Rights in the United States and Canada." *Journal of Environmental Law* 10 (1991).

Murtaugh, Elizabeth. "Makah Prepare to Hunt Whales." *Seattle Times,* 29 March 2002.

Parman, Donald. *Indians and the American West in the Twentieth Century.* Bloomington: Indiana University Press, 1994.

———. "Inconstant Advocacy: The Erosion of Indian Fishing Rights in the Pacific Northwest, 1933–1956." *Pacific Historical Review* 53, no. 2 (May 1984).

Prucha, Francis Paul. *American Indian Treaties: The History of a Political Anomaly.* Berkeley: University of California Press, 1994.

———. *Documents of United States Indian Policy.* Lincoln: University of Nebraska Press, 2000.

———. *The Great Father: The United States Government and the American Indian.* Lincoln: University of Nebraska Press, 1984.

Roels, Starla Kay. "Borrowing Instead of Taking: How the Seemingly Opposite Threads of Indian Treaty Rights and Property Rights Activism Could Intertwine to Restore Salmon to the Rivers." *Environmental Law* 28, no. 2 (summer 1998).

Ryser, Rudolph. *Anti-Indian Movement on the Tribal Frontier.* Kenmore, Wash.: Center for World Indigenous Studies, 1992.

Satz, Ronald N. *Chippewa Treaty Rights: The Reserved Rights of Wisconsin's Chippewa Indians in Historical Perspective.* Madison: Wisconsin Academy of Science, Arts, and Letters.

"Shellfish Decision in Washington State Fuels the Ire of Property Owners. *Native Americas* 12, no. 12 (1995).

Thurman, Dan. Center for Democratic Renewal. "Indian Issues and Anti-Indian Organizing." *Native Americans and the Environment.* 1995. <www.indians.org/library/anti.html> (accessed July 2002).

Toole, Ken. "Drumming Up Resentment: The Anti-Indian Movement in Montana." *Montana Human Rights Network.* 2000. <www.mhrn.org/news/Drumming.html> (accessed July 2002).

Townsend, Mike. "Congressional Abrogation of Indian Treaties: Reevaluation and Reform." *Yale Law Review* 98 (February 1989).

Watts, Tim J. *American Indian Treaty Rights: A Bibliography.* Monticello, Ill.: Vance Bibliographies, 1991.

Wilkinson, Charles. *American Indians, Time, and the Law: Native Societies in a Modern Constitutional Democracy.* New Haven: Yale University Press, 1987.

———. *Message from Frank's Landing: A Story of Salmon, Treaties, and the Indian Way.* Seattle: University of Washington Press, 2000.

Video

Spring of Discontent. ABC, University of Michigan Media Resource Center, Ann Arbor, 56 min., May 1990.

Web Sites

American Indian Heritage Foundation. <www.indians.org>. Has links to Indian treaty rights sites.

Citizens Equal Rights Alliance. <www.citizensalliance.org>.

Columbia River Inter-Tribal Fish Commission. <www.critfc.org>. Conservation and lobbying organization of four Pacific Northwest fishing tribes.

Great Lakes Indian Fish and Wildlife Commission. <www.glifwc.org>. Includes "A Guide to Understanding Ojibwe Treaty Rights."

Indigenous Environmental Network. <www.ienearth.org>.

Makah.com. <www.makah.com/>. Web site of the Makah Indian nation.

"Makah Whaling Management Plan." <www.nwifc.wa.gov/whaling/whaleplan.html>.

Menominee Treaty Rights and Mining Impacts Office. <www.menominee.com/treaty/home.html>.

Midwest Treaty Network. <www.alphacdc.com/treaty>.

Ocean Defense International. <www.oceandefense.org>. Fights Makah whaling.

Safe Passing. <www.safepassing.org>. Fights Makah whaling.

Sea Shepherd Conservation Society. <www.seashepherd.org>. Fights Makah whaling.

Treaty Rights: Understanding the Conflict. <www.fw.umn.edu/Indigenous/stakhold.htm>. A good general source.

3

NATIVE AMERICAN LAND CLAIMS

In the previous chapter we explored the conflicts that have arisen as a result of the 373 treaties the U.S. Congress ratified between 1778 and 1868. Generally speaking, federal courts have been sympathetic to Native Americans' claims that rights guaranteed in those treaties have been violated, granting to a number of Indian nations the legal authority to continue to hunt, fish, and gather natural resources on land ceded in the original treaties—as Judge George Boldt argued in the pivotal case *United States v. Washington* (1974), "the mere passage of time has not eroded, and cannot erode, the rights guaranteed by solemn treaties that both sides pledged on their honor to uphold."[1] The cases presented in chapter 2 had to do with Native Americans' usufructuary rights—those of land use. In this chapter we consider Native Americans claims to the land itself. In these cases, rather than arguing that they had been denied proper access to natural resources, Native Americans claimed that the land was taken improperly and should be restored, both for spiritual and for economic reasons, to what they considered to be its rightful owners. In return they sought the land, access to sacred sites, monetary compensation, or federal recognition of the tribal community. In doing so, they engendered a storm of protest from non-Indians worried about potential loss of property, multimillion-dollar settlements, and jurisdictional disputes from enhanced tribal sovereignty.

HISTORICAL BACKGROUND

The treaty-making process stripped Native Americans of a vast territory in the United States. This land included sites that were sacred to specific tribal communities, especially the Pueblo Nation's Blue Lake and the Sioux Nation's Black Hills, as well as valuable resources such as gold, oil, coal, and rangeland. In 1887, American Indians occupied roughly 138 million acres. By 1934 that number had shrunk to about 48 million acres, in what some historians have called "the dispossession of the American Indian." The nearly 65 percent reduction of Indian land stemmed from the passage of the General Allotment Act of 1887, which divided much of Native America into 160-acre plots in an attempt to remake Native Americans in the image of the white yeoman farmer. Reservations shrank in size as white settlers snatched up fertile acres in land sales that often defrauded tribal members.

As the allotment program was stripping Indians of land, some tribal communities began to fight back in the courts, claiming that both the goals of the allotment policy and the terms of treaties signed in the eighteenth and nineteenth centuries had not been fulfilled, specifically that they had not been compensated according to the treaty they had signed or that the land they had ceded had been appraised at an insufficient amount. Between 1880 and 1946, Indian nations filed 219 claims in the U.S. Court of Claims, which resulted in 35 cases yielding about $77 million in awards. As the U.S. Court of Claims began to face a backlog of cases, tribal leaders and U.S. officials began calling for the creation of a separate commission to hear just Native American claims. In August 1946, the U.S. Congress established the Indian Claims Commission (ICC) to adjudicate American Indians' claims for more than a century's worth of fraudulent land cessions, treaty violations, and financial mismanagement. The federal government saw the ICC serving several purposes. One, it hoped to use it to fulfill its moral and legal obligations to Indians before "terminating" its special relationship with them. After signing the legislation that created the ICC, President Harry S. Truman remarked, "With the final settlement of outstanding claims which this measure insures, Indians can take their place without special handicaps or special advantages in the economic life of our nation and share fully in its progress."[2] In addition, federal officials wanted to reward Native Americans for their loyalty during World War II as well as to create a record of fairness in dealing with America's minorities as the Cold War expanded. Facing a 1951 deadline, nearly all the 176 federally recognized Indian nations filed at least one claim before the ICC, resulting in 611 separate cases. In most of them, Indian nations claimed the federal government had provided either inadequate compensation or none for land taken from them. Nearly a third claimed that the government had mismanaged tribal resources or trust funds. ICC proceedings were adversarial rather than sympathetic. Faced with the possibility of paying out billions of dollars in claims, government attorneys worked to defeat the claims rather than settle out of court. Both sides hired expert witnesses—historians and anthropologists—to help their case.

Before the ICC was retired in 1978, it resolved 546 cases and awarded compensation of $818,172,606.64; the 342 awards ranged from several hundred dollars to $31.2 million. Those tribes that did win their claim did not receive all of the financial judgment, however. More than $100 million of the $818 million went to attorney fees.[3] Tribal leaders rightly complained that the awards did not include interest and protested "gratuitous offsets," money the government deducted for services it had provided decades earlier. And in some cases the government stipulated how the claimants could spend their awards. Despite these problems and the contentious legal battles, the monetary awards clearly benefited some Native American communities. Another important legacy was that Native Americans gained valuable legal experience while fighting for these claims, which they translated into other legal contexts during the Red Power era of the 1960s and 1970s and the era of self-determination beyond that. But in the end, most Indian nations thought the ICC failed to provide real justice because it did not return an acre of land to any tribe. Two cases stand out from the ICC years, those of the Taos Pueblo and Sioux nations. The ICC granted both nations a legal victory, but the Pueblo and the Sioux rejected monetary awards in the hopes of securing a return of their land, largely because of the sacred nature of the territory involved.

In 1906 President Theodore Roosevelt took 48,000 acres of Taos Pueblo land and incorporated them into the Carson National Forest. Included in the territory was Blue Lake, a sacred site for the Pueblo, who had performed important ceremonies there for centuries. In return for the land, the ICC awarded the Pueblo $10 million. But the Pueblo wanted the land, not the money. They rejected the award and continued to wage a legal battle for its return. In 1970, the Pueblo were rewarded for their persistence when Congress restored their legal title to the land and to Blue Lake. In light of the historic circumstances, President Richard Nixon made a public statement on the case in December 1970: "I can only say that in signing the bill [returning the land] I trust that this will mark one of those periods in American history where, after a very, very long time, and at times a very sad history of injustice, that we started on a new road—a new road which leads us to justice in the treatment of those who were the first Americans, of our working together for the better nation that we want this great and good country of ours to become. . . ."[4] The Pueblo succeeded in part because church groups supported their contention that Blue Lake was essential for the maintenance of the Pueblo's religious and spiritual life; Nixon referred to the Pueblo's religion in his statement.

The Sioux Nation of South Dakota also rejected a monetary award from the ICC in hopes of securing the return of the sacred Black Hills. The Sioux's quest for justice began after the federal government seized the Black Hills in 1877 in violation of the 1868 Fort Laramie Treaty, which guaranteed that the Black Hills would remain in Sioux hands unless the tribe consented to its sale by a vote by three-fourths of its adult males. The gold from the territory earned whites billions of dollars, some of it helping to establish the Hearst fortune. Besides compensation for the land and the gold, the Sioux wanted the Black Hills because they claimed it served as a spiritual center for the tribe. Shortly after losing the land the Sioux began legal challenges to get it back. It was not until 1923 that the federal government considered the Sioux's claim, but it took decades and several court reversals before the ICC rendered its decision to award the Sioux $17.5 million. In 1980, the U.S. Supreme Court rejected the federal government's appeal in *United States v. Sioux Nation of Indians.* Justice Harry Blackmun opined that a "more ripe and rank case of dishonorable dealing will never, in all probability, be found in our history."[5] By the Court's calculation, the Sioux were owed nearly $106 million because of interest charges. Yet the eight separate tribal communities that make up the Sioux Nation, many of them poor, voted to reject the award, claiming that they wanted only the land. But the justice that President Nixon had spoken of in his statement upon the return of Blue Lake did not extend beyond the Taos Pueblo. The Sioux continue to fight for the return of the Black Hills to this day.

The Taos Pueblo and Sioux cases grew out of the work of the Indian Claims Commission. As the ICC neared its retirement, the U.S. Supreme Court ruled unanimously in 1974 that the Oneida Indians of New York State could sue for redress in federal court, a landmark decision that opened the door for other East Coast tribes, from Maine to Florida, to sue in federal court; a related 1985 Supreme Court decision rejected arguments that claims stemming from eighteenth-century land deals could be thrown out because of their long history. Time and space stood still, legally, after the Court ruled that no statute of limitations applied and that territory of the original 13 colonies was fair game.

In one of the first of these cases, three Indian nations from the state of Maine elected to take a monetary judgment rather than hold out for land as the Sioux did. This case is perhaps most instructive for an examination of contemporary land claims because it provided a precedent that other Native Americans could consider to assert land claims of their own, provided the terms of a possible strategy to settle such claims, and demonstrated the contentious and bitter issues involved in their adjudication. Maine Indians' history of injustice went back even further than the Sioux's. When the federal government adopted the Trade and Intercourse Act of 1790, also called the Nonintercourse Act (which was subsequently amended in 1793 to require the presence and approval of a federal Indian commissioner at all treaty signings), it stipulated that all sales of Indian lands needed Congress's stamp of approval. It did so in light of fraudulent land cessions that troubled American politicians like George Washington. Shortly after its passage, Washington explained the Nonintercourse Act to the Seneca Nation of New York State by telling them, "when you find it in your interest to sell any part of your lands, the United States must be present, by their agent, and will be your security that you shall not be defrauded in the bargain you make."[6] Intent on creating peace on the frontier and in settled regions like upstate New York, where a number of tribes were coerced to sell land under suspicious circumstances, Congress asserted control over all Indian affairs. Since no sale of Indian land in Maine had received congressional approval, the Passamaquoddy, Penobscot, and Maliseet Indians filed a claim in 1972 for nearly two-thirds of Maine's territory, which contained nearly 350,000 non-Indians and was valued at nearly $25 billion. At the urging of attorneys affiliated with the Native American Rights Fund, the U.S. Department of Justice joined the suit and convinced the Penobscot and Passamaquoddy to narrow their claim to unpopulated areas of the state. Justice officials had described the original land claim as "potentially the most complex litigation ever brought in the federal courts with social costs and economic impacts without precedent."[7] According to U.S. Assistant Attorney General Peter R. Taft, the grandson of William Howard Taft, "It was in the interest of the tribes to diminish the economic and social impact of their claim. The tribes have to be concerned that if the impact is too great, Congress will impose its own settlement. It wasn't in their interest to bring the state to its knees."[8] The tribes' attorney described the time as "a very nasty and disillusioning period in Maine. Indian children were harassed at school, there was a big run on guns at the sporting-goods stores, and after a number of threats were made against my life I even carried a gun myself for a while."[9]

Rather than face a costly and lengthy legal fight, the state and the tribes accepted a financial settlement to adjudicate the land claim. Congress's passage of the 1980 Maine Indian Settlement Act provided federal recognition of the tribes and $81.5 in compensation for land improperly taken from them (a small portion of the award went to the Houlton Band of Maliseet Indians), which included an opportunity to buy back 300,000 acres. The act noted that the impetus for the settlement came from a fear of a protracted legal fight. "Substantial economic and social hardship to a large number of landowners, citizens, and communities in the State of Maine, and therefore to the economy of the State of Maine as a whole, will result if the aforementioned claims are not resolved promptly.... In the absence of congressional action, these land claims would be pursued through the courts, a process which in all likelihood would consume many years and thereby promote hostility and uncertainty in the State of Maine to the ultimate detriment of the Passamaquoddy Tribe, the Penobscot Nation, the Houlton Band of Maliseet Indians, their members, and all other citizens of the State of Maine."[10] The lengthy quote is included here to illustrate an important theme of the land claims issue—a legal case involving huge tracts of former Indian land represents a potential nightmare for all parties involved. A victory for the tribes would have resulted in legal appeals that would have likely stretched on for years, tying up both state and tribal officials in courts. A final judgment in the tribes' favor could have resulted in economic chaos. Congress also feared that social friction between Maine citizens and tribal members could have resulted in violence. Another theme that the Maine Indians' case brings out is tribal dissension. Not all tribal members supported the settlement; others felt it was a pragmatic solution, the best they could get after two centuries of white settlement. In short, land claims can create bitter divisions between non-Indian and Indian residents of a state, between members of a tribal community, and between state and federal officials.

A similar dynamic has developed in recent cases. Land claims have polarized Indian and non-Indian communities in Washington (Puyallup tribe), South Carolina (Catawba), Connecticut (Paugussett and Pequot), Vermont (Abenaki), Minnesota (White Earth Chippewa), Massachusetts (Gay Head Wampanoag), Texas (Tonkawas), and Nevada (Shoshone). In the case of the Hopi-Navajo land dispute, a land claim involved two Indian nations; the Hopi were awarded part of the Navajo's land in the Navajo-Hopi Land Settlement Act of 1974, though the case has yet to be resolved, as traditional Navajo have continued to claim ancestral rights to the disputed territory. The Navajo also settled another land claim, in March 2000, giving the San Juan Southern Paiute tribe roughly 5,400 acres of land in Arizona. In all of these claims cases much was at stake—Indian sovereignty, hundreds of millions of dollars, a potential revolt by property owners, and, not least, the integrity of federal law. In response, Congress has passed a series of land settlement acts that have clarified the question of aboriginal landownership. Most of the settlements have involved cash and economic development funds, but occasionally they have included the return of land, access to sacred sites, or federal recognition, which accords a tribe sovereign powers and participation in federal Indian programs.

Several examples are worth mentioning. In August 1993 Congress passed the Catawba Land Claim Settlement Act, ending a nearly 13-year battle by the Catawba Indians of South Carolina, who agreed to drop their claim to 144,000 acres of settled land as well as damages for 140 years of lost income. In return, the federal government granted the Catawba the status of a federally recognized Indian nation and compensation of $50 million. Like the Penobscot and Passamaquoddy, the Catawba had claimed a violation of the Trade and Intercourse Act of 1790 as the basis of their claim. Most claims stem from pre–Allotment Act (1887) treaties, but the White Earth Reservation Land Settlement Act of 1985 addressed the improper transfer of 100,000 acres of White Earth Chippewa land in the early 1900s that stemmed from aggressive allotment policies that stripped the Chippewa of prime acreage. Although many White Earth Chippewa were dissatisfied with the settlement, the tribe received 10,000 acres of state-owned land, $500,000 of state funds for technical assistance, and more than $6 million in federal economic development funds.

The case of the Zuni illustrates the place of sacred sites in as well as the complexity of the land claims process. For nearly a century the Zuni tribe of Arizona and New Mexico had fought for the return of land surrounding Zuni Salt Lake and compensation for millions of acres taken during the nineteenth and twentieth centuries. In May 1978 Congress passed Public Law 95-280, which contained two main parts. One, the U.S. government would buy land around the Zuni Salt Lake and restore it to its rightful owner, the Zuni. Two, the act allowed the Zuni to sue for compensation for territory that was taken from them. The Zuni's decision to sue would mean that they would give up their right to all former land, which included a sacred site called *Kolhu/wala:wa,* where Zunis go after death (non-Zunis call it "Zuni Heaven"); every four years Zunis made a pilgrimage to the site. The Zuni decided to file a compensation claim for its aboriginal (original) territory of 14,835,892 acres, except *Kolhu/wala:wa* and the trail that led to it, called the *We:sak'yaya Onnane* (or Barefoot Trail). The Zuni refused to give up their claim to this sacred site and access to it. With the support of Senator Barry Goldwater and other politicians, the Zuni got what they wanted in S. 2201 ("To Convey Certain Lands to the Zuni Indian Tribe for Religious Purposes"), which passed in August 1984. In the end the Zuni settled out of court in November 1990, electing to avoid a costly trial in part because they were satisfied with the negotiated sum. The Zuni case was unusually complex because it involved the return of territory, two states' jurisdictions, and resistance by a non-Indian rancher who opposed the Zuni pilgrimage to the sacred site because it crossed his land. After five years, a lawsuit was settled in favor of the Zuni.

Two cases of the late 1980s highlight a complication of land claims—they cloud land titles and prevent economic development. The 1987 Seminole Land Claims Settlement Act settled a jurisdictional dispute over access to state waters and precluded a potentially expensive lawsuit for Florida citizens. In the Washington Indian Land Claims Settlement Act of 1989, one of the biggest settlements of the twentieth century, the Puyallup Indians settled their claim to 20,000 acres in the Tacoma area, including 120 prime acres of the city's industrial and port sections. The land claim had complicated Tacoma development, preventing city officials from expanding sections of the port and improving traffic bottlenecks on a prime waterway.

In all these settlements, including the Native Claims Settlement Act of 1971, which gave native Alaskans $1 billion in return for 44 million acres, Indian nations agreed to "extinguish" all further claims to what is called *aboriginal title,* or Indian landownership, thus precluding any additional legislative or judicial effort to seek land or compensation. This aspect of the land claims process, the finality of the legislative or judicial decision, helps to explain the energy and passion with which Native Americans pursue their claims. They will have no other opportunity to seek justice, whether it comes in the form of returned land, belated compensation, access to sacred sites, or federal recognition of tribal status.

FRAMING THE ISSUE

In a May 2000 op-ed piece in the *New York Times,* Robert P. Porter, a professor of law and a member of the Seneca Nation, wrote, "It is hard to imagine another issue that forces Americans to confront their sinful past quite like an Indian land claim."[11] The editorial, titled "Apologies to the Iroquois Are Not Enough," addressed ongoing land claims in New York State that have created great tension between Indian and non-Indian communities. Although Indian nations across the country have adjudicated land claims since 1980, many of them ending in legislative settlements, several claims in New York State, a heavily populated state with a long and controversial history of Indian–white relations, have been dragging on in the courts, one of them for more than 20 years. Nations of the old Iroquois Confederacy, which dominated upstate New York before the American Revolution, have asserted claims along the lines of Maine Indians—that their land was taken in violation of the 1790 Trade and Intercourse Act. The Cayuga of western New York lost land in treaties of 1795 and 1807. As the *New York Times* noted in a November 2001 article titled "Justice, 200 Years Later," New York State "has always been vulnerable to the Cayugas' claims because of the patent illegality of the land transfers. The U.S. Constitution... specifically forbade the type of treaties under which the state obtained the Cayuga's land." The author described the 1795 treaty as "a shady deal."[12] The Cayuga, who have sought justice for decades, filed a federal lawsuit against the state of New York in 1980 that continues to this day. In February 2000 a New York State jury declared the treaties illegal and awarded the Cayuga $36.9 million in damages for the loss of 64,000 acres. It was the first time a land claims case had gone to jury trial in New York State, and one of the few times it had happened in the history of land claims. Federal Judge Neal P. McCurn awarded an additional $211 million in interest in October 2001, pushing the total award to nearly a quarter of a billion dollars; McCurn could have awarded as much as $527.5 million but chose to cut the award in the spirit of compromise. At this time, New York State is considering an appeal, keeping the case alive.

The stakes are enormous for state officials. In a time of budget problems, the state faces several other major claims. The Seneca of western New York have filed a claim to 18,000 acres, most of them on Grand Island in the Niagara River; a decision in that case is imminent. A potentially explosive case is that of the Oneida of central New York, who have been seeking redress for 250,000 acres since the 1800s. In addition, the St. Regis Mohawk have laid claim to 15,000 acres near the St. Lawrence River and the Onondogas have been preparing a claim to 70,000 acres, including parts of the city of Syracuse, though they have taken a wait-and-see approach in hopes of securing an out-of-court settlement from the state. Given the precedent of the Cayuga's case—the jury verdict declaring that the treaties were signed in violation of the Trade and Intercourse Act of 1790, the acknowledged history of coercion practiced by New York land speculators, and the $247.9 million awarded the Cayuga—these claims have the potential to be the most costly and contentious cases.

The Oneida's claim deserves some explanation, in part because it has generated the most visceral responses from non-Indians and because it is a complex case that involves three different tribal communities and two different countries—New York Oneida, Wisconsin Oneida, and the Thames Band of Oneida from Ontario; members of the Wisconsin and Thames Band Oneida fled New York State after treaties helped to break up the integrity of the original Oneida Nation. The Oneida, who once owned six million acres in upstate New York, saw their tribal estate shrink to 32 acres in 1919. Even though tribal members had dispersed to new communities in Wisconsin and Ontario, those in New York kept their hopes of justice alive. In 1970 they sued Oneida and Madison counties over the validity of the 1795 treaty, prompting the famous 1974 Supreme Court decision that opened the doors to tribal lawsuits against county or state governments. Although they won an initial court victory in 1985, their larger land claim of 250,000 acres has continued to be fought in the courts, in the press, and on the campaign trail during the 2000 Senate race between Rick Lazio and Hillary Rodham Clinton. In the interim, flush with revenue from the immensely popular Turning Stone casino, the New York Oneida have repurchased 11,000 acres of their original territory, creating stressful relations with non-Indian neighbors, some of whom have organized against the land claim in fear of expanded Oneida sovereignty; upset with New York State's intransigence on the issue, in December 1998 the Oneida added 20,000 property owners to the suit, creating a heightened opposition. The land claim generated such hostility that a group calling itself the United States National Freedom Fighters "threatened to bomb Oneida businesses, to kill one Indian every three days and to shoot at least one white 'traitor' caught frequenting Oneida-owned establishments."[13] The Oneida themselves have not been unified, as different factions have protested the management of the claims. The Oneida case will be particularly difficult to resolve, in part because of the settled nature of the land claimed by the Oneida, the persistence with which the tribal leaders involved have been pursuing their claims, and the resistance on the part of state officials. Said one New Yorker active in landowner groups, "I definitely don't feel upbeat, because knowing what I know about the other land claims, it's not going to be an easy route. No matter who wins the lawsuit, they'll appeal, and appeal, and appeal, and nothing is going to be resolved any time soon."[14] Native Americans have waited decades and in some cases close to two centuries for justice. The Oneida newspaper *Indian Country Today* noted, "The wheels of justice turn slowly, but they do turn. Despite chronic bigotry that has stained this history for more than 200 years, the opportunity is now upon a great state and a great country to do the right thing. The path to honor, peace and reconciliation can only be paved with justice."[15] As all these examples demonstrate, the path each land claim case takes is a complex, controversial, and contested one.

OPPONENTS OF NATIVE AMERICAN LAND CLAIMS

Landownership

One of the most anxious and angered group of opponents of Native American land claims is non-Indian property owners, both commercial and residential, who face the possibility of losing their businesses or their homes, some of which have been in their families for generations. Even if they were compensated fairly for their land or homes, they would not want to leave. This position stems mostly from the argument that the treaties that tribes are using to assert their claims were signed a long time ago and not by the people facing the consequences in the late twentieth or early twenty-first century. One Massachusetts official said in reaction to a tribal claim for his town's land, "We can't be held responsible for what our ancestors did to the Indians more than one hundred years ago."[16] In June 2000 the Miami Indians laid claim to 2.6 million acres of Illinois, which includes land farmed by 98-year-old Rex Walden. His daughter said, "That old man's lived out there for 70 years, and the farm's been in the family for 140."[17] Residents of upstate New York have been particularly concerned about Native American land claims. The Oneida claim 250,000 acres (in Oneida and Madison counties), while the Seneca and the Cayuga claim thousands more. Daniel Gates, a key organizer of Madison [County] Oneida Landowners, Inc. (MOLI), a group of about two thousand residents of the land contested in the Oneida claim, contends that history is on his side because, he says, "I'm the seventh generation of my family on this land. We raised our children here, that's eight generations, and my grandchildren visit me here—that's nine generations."[18] Another local resident talked about her family's land as "something you can't replace. This ground is our burial ground. It's sacred to us."[19]

Judges have not accepted this argument as a legal strategy to adjudicate land claims, but landowners have used it to garner support for their cause. Opponents have been asserting, since the claims began, that the average property owner is an innocent figure in a larger drama. Allan van Gestel, an attorney for Madison and Oneida counties, said at a 1986 symposium on land claims that upstate New Yorkers "are nothing less than hostages in a power struggle between three governments—Federal, state and Indian."[20]

Indian Sovereignty and the Federal Government

Many activists oppose the very nature of the land claims, the idea that a sovereign Indian nation can file suit against their county or state government and do so with the help of the federal government. As with the treaty rights struggle, opponents of land claims see an activist federal government representing someone's interests besides their own. Both citizens and their representatives have made this argument. As the Mashpee Wampanoag case evolved in the mid-1970s, a town selectman lobbied against the tribe, telling his constituents that "you and I are an endangered species" because of the Indian rights movement, which could "destroy the United States of America as we know it now and as it was conceived by our Founding Fathers."[21] After a federal task force began to search for a legislative compromise in the Passamaquoddy and Penobscot case, Maine lawmakers expressed their outrage. One did so by stating that "someone should get a gun and shoot those bastards [task force members]." Another legislator declared that he was going to "invest heavily in Winchesters and Remingtons [rifles]."[22] The land claim became an election issue in which a gubernatorial challenger accused the incumbent governor of giving large portions of the state back to the Indians. State officials face enormous pressure from their constituents and, as the preceding examples indicate, don't hesitate to publicize their position to reassure those voters that they're representing their interests. The New York claims have engendered heavy opposition from state lawmakers, attorneys, and citizens. In fighting the Seneca's claim, an assistant state attorney general of New York described the claim as "an affront to the sovereignty of New York."[23] Peter Sullivan told a federal judge that the Seneca, if successful, would reduce state power and decrease tax revenues. Citizens like Scott Peterman, the president of Upstate Citizens Equality (UCE), have echoed Sullivan's complaint. Peterman argued against Oneida sovereignty by saying, "We are not going to stand with having a foreign country in the middle of Upstate New York. We would like to challenge sovereignty.... It sets up a special class of people in the country."[24]

Upstate New York residents organized a number of anti–land claims groups in the late 1990s to publicize their positions and bring pressure to bear on their political representatives. Besides MOLI and UCE, the Central New York Fair Business Association and the American Land Rights Coalition formed to oppose the claims, especially after the Seneca and the Oneida added property owners to their lawsuits. UCE, the largest and most vocal of the organizations, brought the groups together by staging a 400-person convoy that crossed the New York State Thruway from Buffalo to the state capital in Albany. The protestors, most of whom came from territory affected by the Oneida and Cayuga claims, railed against the expansion of Indian sovereignty and the federal government's role in the claims process. Many of them carried anti-sovereignty signs. One read, "Indian Sovereignty Is the Quiet Conquest of America"; another stated, "Indian Land Claims + Sovereignty = the Fall of the United States." Speakers also criticized the federal government for allowing the expansion of Indian sovereignty. A UCE organizer said the goal of the protest was to "send the message to Congress to get on the stick and do something about these land claims before they take over the state of New York. We're not blaming the Indians for the situation. The federal government is perpetuating it."[25] Peter McMahon, a supervisor for Grand Island, which was contending with the Seneca's claim, told the crowd, "The problem is the federal government. The very people who should be protecting their citizens and taxpayers from these threats are in fact helping those who threaten us."[26] But other UCE members were equally critical of the Oneida. Leon Koziol, the UCE attorney and a driving force behind the group, criticized the Oneida for expanding their casino and related services like hotels, which have affected businesses in central New York. Koziol told the motorcade crowd, "They [the Indians] are trying to create countries within countries, a state within a state. They're calling us trespassers in these various lawsuits."[27]

The activities of these groups, especially the thruway motorcade protest, attracted the attention of New York's politicians, who added fuel to the fire by condemning the Department of Justice for facilitating the claims, even though it was compelled to do so. Governor George Pataki wrote President Clinton in April 2000 to protest the lawsuits' inclusion of property owners and the general issues of the claims, which he claimed held New York citizens "hostage under clouded real estate titles and the constant threat of eviction."[28] But Pataki has come under fire for playing games with the claims process. Critics charge that Pataki has been complicating the adjudication of claims until Indian nations agree to concessions on points like sales tax and casino revenues. A federal judge acknowledged that Pataki's negotiators were linking the land claims with other equally contentious issues and thus delaying a final resolution. And UCE has filed its own suit against Pataki for his support of the Oneida's gambling rights. The question of property rights surfaced during the 2000 Senate race between Rick Lazio and Hillary Rodham Clinton. Ignoring the federal court's recent decision to exclude property owners from the lawsuits, Lazio ran several ads criticizing both President Clinton and candidate Clinton, contending that "the Clinton administration's Justice Department is suing New York homeowners to reclaim hundreds of thousands of acres of land, claimed by an Indian treaty that's more than two hundred years old.... [Hillary Rodham] Clinton refuses to stand up for the rights of upstate New Yorkers."[29] In September 2000 a federal judge excused New York property owners from the claims, ruling that the Oneida could sue state and local governments but not private citizens. But the campaigns against the claims continued because they were about more than just property rights.

The Economics of Land Claims

The economics as well as the politics of land claims stir up vocal opposition. UCE's campaign is driven by both the Oneida land claim and by the Oneida's growing economic power, which is derived from the revenues earned at the Turning Stone casino. The Oneida Nation employs 2,600 people, who contribute more than $5 million in local, school, and county taxes, a small part of nation's estimated $168 million impact on the regional economy. But critics fear that the Oneida will continue to expand by buying property through the land claim or in separate transactions, which will reduce property tax revenues because Native American property and businesses are not taxable on a local or state level. Other citizens oppose the Oneida because the nation's businesses have cut into the profits of white enterprises. UCE members have taken to picketing Oneida businesses and discouraging others from patronizing them. And as Governor Pataki noted, land claims can tie up economic development for years since they "cloud," or leave in doubt, land titles; residential and business owners can have trouble selling their properties if claims are pending, as no one wants to buy land that could revert to new owners by court judgment. In Mashpee, Massachusetts, on Cape Cod, a 1976 land claim by the Wampanoag Indians disrupted development in the area. Paul Brodeur reported that "after the [Wampanoag] filed suit, banks refused to grant mortgages and loans, land development halted, construction came to a virtual standstill, and people found it difficult, if not impossible, to sell their homes."[30] A similar dynamic has occurred in upstate New York and in Connecticut. Residents of Grand Island, which the Seneca claimed ownership of, have feared "ejectment" from the island. Peter McMahon, a Grand Island supervisor, complained that the land claim has brought about economic decline and put homeowners' rights in jeopardy; new housing starts have dropped while neighboring communities' have risen because until the claim is settled, the title to the Grand Island properties could be transferred to the Seneca; although that is unlikely, the possibility of land transfers precludes normal real estate transactions.

Opposition to land claims and Indian sovereignty in Connecticut mirrors that of New York's. Officials of towns that border the Mashuntucket Pequot reservation, which houses its huge casino operations, asked congressional leaders to limit the impact of land claims with new legislation. Although the state of Connecticut recognizes the Paugussett as a "tribe," Connecticut attorney general Richard Blumenthal opposes the Paugussett's pursuit of a land claim and federal status, in part because the claim clouds real estate titles and thus makes it difficult for homeowners to sell their property or get equity loans. A title-insurance company hired a real estate lawyer to defend property owners against the claim, while the Connecticut state legislature has considered bills to protect homeowners during the claims process. Blumenthal also argued before a federal judge that he believed the tribe's claim was designed to win approval for operation of a casino. "The whole effort is driven by gambling," he said.[31] Critics of the Miami's lawsuit against property owners in Illinois echo Blumenthal's complaint, contending that the tribe's claim is designed to leverage support from the state for a gambling agreement. "It's just a pressure thing to get the governor to give them a casino," argued one of the property owners named in the suit.[32]

Native Americans' Opposition to the Management of Land Claims

It is obvious that most Native Americans favor the prosecution of land claims, for reasons that will be made clear presently. But it should be noted that land claims have divided tribal communities for a variety of reasons, including casino-related issues. In some cases, factions of Indian voters have opposed cash justice and continue to hold out for the land. After Congress signed the Maine Indian Settlement Act in 1980, some tribal members felt that their leaders had "sold out" and accepted money over land. The Puyallup of Washington were divided over settling their claim against Tacoma in the late 1980s. They rejected an initial settlement of $111 million before accepting the revised offer of $162 million worth of cash, land, and a marine terminal, on a vote of 319–162. But not all Puyallup were happy with the settlement. Some considered it a buyout of ancestral land and thus a sell-out by other tribal members. Silas Cross, who promised to pursue his own lawsuit, said of the settlement, "All this does is say that the Indian is for sale. You put money on an Indian's head and he'll go for it. That's what is happening here." He thinks the tribe made a mistake by "giving up their greatest asset and their best income source—the city of Tacoma."[33] Although not opposed to the land claim, Oneida traditionalists have criticized Harvard-educated Ray Hilbritter, the Oneida Nation president, for including 20,000 property owners in the land claims lawsuit, facilitating a culture of gambling on the reservation, and suppressing the traditional Iroquois style of decision making by consensus.

In the case of the Sioux, the nation's decision to reject the huge cash settlement for the Black Hills engendered opposition from some younger Sioux citizens, who see the settlement money as having potential for expanding economic opportunity among some of the nation's destitute communities. Other Sioux have complained that their leaders' emphasis on pursuing the land claim comes at the expense of other pressing community issues, including the day-to-day management of the reservation. Some Sioux are pragmatic, believing that the present suffers while other Sioux hope for a future based on the return of land of the past. Although Native Americans have not opposed the filing of land claims, the lawsuits and what it as stake in them have caused internal dissension in some Native American communities, particularly when the cases drag on for years.

PROPONENTS OF LAND CLAIMS

The Moral Foundation of Land Claims

The land claims that have been adjudicated in the past 25 years have been the result of efforts made by two or three generations of tribal activists rather than the product of opportunistic tribal leaders looking to cash in on a trend. Chief Oren Lyons of the Onondaga Nation of New York explained his tribe's land claim by saying, "Our people have been waiting a long time for this. This is not something we just made up."[34] The Sioux Nation, for example, had sought restitution almost immediately after the 1877 land cession that took the Black Hills from them, in what they call the "seize or starve" treaty.

The Zuni had fought for justice since the end of the nineteenth century. The Oneida had waged a campaign for restitution and compensation for well over a hundred years prior to the filing of their 1970 land claim. The Passamaquoddy and Penobscot of Maine, like many Native Americans, passed down stories of when and how their land was taken. Each subsequent generation talked about broken treaties, lost land, and a shrinking cultural identity. When asked when he became aware that his land had been taken, an elderly Penobscot answered, "The elders talked about it all the time. My father's father... told me about it when he first took me muskrat trapping, before the First World War."[35] The case actually started when a Passamaquoddy elder produced an aged copy of the tribe's 1794 treaty, which provided evidence to other tribal members that their land had been unfairly taken from them.

What drove these campaigns and others was the desire for the return of land rather than money. Whether a tribal community decided to seek monetary compensation rather than land had much to do with the nature of the territory involved, the extent to which the land in question was considered sacred, and the prospects of an extended court fight. Many tribal officials have been pragmatic in taking monetary compensation, since the return of land in some heavily populated states could necessitate the uprooting of many non-Indian property owners and thus produce hostile opposition, as in the New York cases. But underlying all of the claims has been a search for justice based on the belief that history doesn't negate the validity of agreements between sovereign nations. The 1974 Boldt Decision that restored Washington Indians' right to an equal salmon harvest rested on the notion that the law of the treaties signed in the nineteenth century remained good law and should be obeyed. The decisions underlying the land claims settled before and since that landmark decision have rested on similar moral and legal ground: what the United States articulated in 1790 and 1793 remains valid in interpreting contracts between Indian nations and individual states. It took perseverance on the part of Native American leaders and ultimately a more activist federal government willing to support them to bring these contracts into federal courts. Proponents of Native American land claims, therefore, include both Indians and non-Indians. Attorneys, judges, politicians, and even juries assembled from territory claimed by Indians have generally agreed that land claims are legitimate. For example, Daan Braverman, dean of the Syracuse University College of Law, commented on the federal judge's decision to award the Cayuga $211 million by saying, "It seems to be a well-reasoned, fair result, well-supported by legal grounds and the factual record before him." Braverman also addressed the fear that such judgments jeopardized private property: "The public needs to understand that other claims have been settled and no one has ever had private land taken away."[36] Where the differences occur in most cases is how to rectify the injustice.

Land claims have offered the United States an opportunity to provide belated justice to a minority group that has suffered grievous losses in land, spiritual health, and self-sufficiency. This argument has been made by private citizens, scholars, politicians, and, of course, Native Americans. After reading about a proposed bill that would bar the federal government from paying for the prosecution of Indian land claims, a professor of government at St. Lawrence University argued in a 1981 letter to the *New York Times,* "the liberties which the states took in appropriating Indian land in the early years of the Republic show that a historical injustice must be rectified. To propose legislation which prevents the Federal Government from exercising its historic 'trust responsibility' to sue on behalf of Indians...is not in the public interest."[37] In March 1987 Senator Bill Bradley of New Jersey introduced a bill restoring to the Sioux 1.3 million acres of land they lost in the 1877 cession and access to the Black Hills to perform ceremonies there. Bradley argued that the bill was an acceptable compromise because it did not require any landowners to give up their property. At a press conference attended by Sioux leaders, Bradley said, "The legislation has a simple purpose: to right a wrong committed by the United States 100 years ago."[38] Congress elected not to act on the bill.

Like Bradley, the Oneida Nation wanted the United States to "right a wrong." Ironically, the Oneida used similar language in petitioning President Jimmy Carter to aid their land claim against New York State. The Oneida had been "petitioning for generations, to no avail." They asked Carter, "May the United States keep its pledged word to us and not forget that our Warriors, and Scouts, and our contributions of grain at Valley Forge, helped sustain the United States in its fight for justice. May the United States observe its own laws and its treaties, which are the supreme law of the land."[39] The Oneida people, who had been loyal to the American colonists' cause during the American Revolution, asked only that the United States live up to the ideals established as a result of the revolution. As the Oneida's attorney put it in 1988, "There really is a very strong moral principle here, and that is whether the United States is good for its word."[40] In a successful case, the Ho-Chunk Nation of Wisconsin reacquired 1,200 acres of land it held before being forcibly removed by American soldiers in 1840. State representative DuWayne Johnsrud called the agreement a big deal not only for Wisconsin and the Ho-Chunk but for America as well. U.S. senator Russell Feingold agreed, saying, "We are finally able to say to the people of the Kickapoo Valley that the federal government can act to improve their lives and correct a situation that has long been a symbol, to many in the area, of a broken promise."[41]

Importantly, Indian nations have been sensitive to claims that they plan on evicting landowners out of revenge for past wrongs, arguing instead that their intent is to secure belated justice for past injustices and a better future for new generations of tribal members. Oneida leaders added local property owners to their suit in December 1998 only after New York State ignored their efforts to reach a cash settlement. And they assert that the Oneida

Nation provides jobs and investment to the area, pumping millions of dollars into a neglected part of New York. Indian activists also object to arguments that whites have owned the land for generations. Said Joyce Mitchell, a New York Mohawk, "No matter if they had it in their family for two hundred years. We had it in our family for two thousand years."[42] Cliff Halftown, a prominent Cayuga official, is sympathetic to the questions of land cessions because of his people's experience with them. "I understand when people say, 'My family has lived here for generations.' We don't want to do to them what they have done to us. The other side of it is, whose land was it before they moved in? We lived there for generations upon generations upon generations, until we were forced out."[43]

Federal Recognition and Economic Development

Recognition by the federal government confers upon Indian nations a unique political status that grants them individual sovereignty over tribal members (unless that sovereignty has been abridged by federal court or legislative action), the right to maintain their own courts (with the exception of major crimes like rape, arson, and murder), immunity from state regulations and taxes, and access to federal Indian programs. For a number of tribes the land claims have opened the door to federal recognition and the benefits that it offers. In 1987 the Aquinnah (formerly Gay Head) Wampanoag of Massachusetts' Martha's Vineyard were accorded recognition and awarded 400 acres of undeveloped land as part of the Rhode Island Indian Claims Settlement Act; however, the Mashpee Wampanoag of Cape Cod were denied federal recognition in a jury trial in 1977, thus preventing them from filing a claim for thousands of acres. Only one other Massachusetts Indian community has been granted federal recognition. In January 2001 federal officials formally recognized the Hassanamisco Band of the Nipmuc, while denying that status to the Chaubunagungamaug Band of Nipmuck. The Hassanamisco have announced plans to file a land claim, as well as to explore the possibility of establishing a casino enterprise. In Connecticut, the Mashantucket Pequot received federal recognition and 1,400 acres in a 1983 settlement, setting the stage for their successful gambling operation and inspiring other tribes to file land claims in search of both federal recognition as a tribal entity and a land base from which to launch a casino. The Pequot parlayed their 1983 land claim into enormous casino profits that have enabled the tribe to reconstitute itself, expand its land base, and build a museum celebrating its centuries-old culture.

The prospects of starting a casino have added a wrinkle to the land claims process. Several tribes have filed land claims with the intent of establishing casino operations; for example, the Golden Hill Paugussett's lawsuit has yet to be settled in Connecticut. Others have filed claims for other reasons while indicating an interest in using casino gambling to further economic development. And these claims have found backing from unlikely sources. Donald Trump, who opposed casino-type gambling in Connecticut in the late 1980s, has offered his assistance to the Paucatauk Eastern Pequot in their efforts to secure federal recognition and thus the right to compete with the Mashantucket Pequot for New England's gambling dollars. In Texas, a non-Indian investment group led by former Dallas Cowboys general manager Tex Schramm backed a claim filed by the Tonkawa Indians of Oklahoma, who filed suit against Texas for failing to provide the tribe with 4,428 acres of land for service to Texas during various wars. Although tribal officials have not said they would definitely start a casino, they haven't ruled it out either. Tonkawa president Virginia Combrink says, "The state of Texas still owes us. We're not trying to put anybody out of their homes. We wouldn't do that to anybody, even though we were put of our homes. We just want our land." Although Schramm said that he was not motivated by the casino possibilities, he acknowledged, "If they're successful, then we may see if we can also participate after that."[44] Economic development in the form of casinos has proved to be both a by-product of the claims process and an impetus to initiate it. In either case, proponents of land claims argue that the standards that the federal government employs to recognize a tribal community are very high and that federal recognition is accorded only after a lengthy period, if at all.

The Puyallup case offers two other economic reasons for supporting the settlement of a land claim. For one, it cleared up the clouds hanging over the aboriginal title that the Puyallup claimed, a reason some Washington residents cited in opposing the Puyallup. The claim had slowed the development of the Tacoma port. Further development of the area likely would have stopped if the case had not been settled. And two, the settlement provided to the struggling Puyallup people $162 million in the form of cash, job training, land, and a $51 million deepwater marine terminal on the Puget Sound. The tribe's administrative manager said, "With this settlement we can protect our culture and our river system. Our people should know they will always have a future."[45] As with the restoration of salmon fishing rights in the Boldt Decision, the land claim enabled the Puyallup to take control of their fishing operation. The settlement also granted the Puyallup the right to enforce environmental laws. Within five years of the settlement, the tribe had finished construction of a profitable venture, the $4 million Chinook Landing Marina. The tribe was also busy with other projects, including a 79-acre industrial park. The settlement, then, has allowed the Puyallup tribe to restore its cultural roots while building toward a modern future. Other tribes have used land claim settlements to good cause, investing the money in profitable businesses and thus working toward weaning their members from dependency on state and federal welfare programs. The Passamaquoddy of Maine used money from their settlement to buy the Dragon Cement Company in 1983 for $25.5 million. They sold it six years later for $81.3 million. The tribe also bought a blueberry farm that had employed its members. A number of white residents of territory claimed in tribal lawsuits have been supportive of Indians because of this economic dimension. For example, a supervisor of Hamilton, New York, commented on the Oneida's claim by noting that if a monetary settlement could be reached, then "some of this money will be tied into economic development. It will help the Indian nation . . . and what helps the Indian nation helps us locally."[46]

Tribal Identity and Sacred Sites

Many tribal communities who have filed land claims have been discouraged by their failure to achieve any progress toward a resolution of decades-long or even century-long claims. The effect of the claims process has been to politicize tribal members. Even when land claims fail, as in the case of the Mashpee Wampanoag, the process can sharpen tribal identity. Because the assertion of land claims requires the assembling of historical knowledge of tribal affairs and chronologies of Indian–white relations, the cases can enliven a tribal community's sense of itself. Ramona Peters, whose father was the Wampanoag medicine man, told a journalist, "There's a great rejuvenation going on here. It's what Indians call preparing for Purification Time. By practicing rituals such as burning tobacco, offering thanks for all living things, and attending the naming ceremonies, we can protect our Indian identity. . . ." A fellow Wampanoag noted, "The main thing is that there has been a new awakening among us. A new awareness of our heritage. . . . Soon our people will wake up to the fact that we still have a lot of land here and many other resources."[47]

A complex relationship with the land has been the foundation of the Native Americans' experience. Land has provided sustenance and sites of enormous spiritual and cultural importance. For example, New York Indians cite the sacredness of the land. The Oneida's claim includes Big Spring, a sacred site that contains Oneida burial ground. Brian Patterson, an Oneida who has worked tirelessly to restore the ancestral lands of his "homeland," explained his assiduous efforts by saying, "Knowing this land has embraced the dust of our ancestors from time immemorial and we're powerless to protect it, that's hard for us as a people."[48] The question of sacred sites and land claims has overlapped in several important cases. In 1980 the Sioux rejected the Supreme Court–ordered compensation of $106 million and have fought a battle ever since for the return of the Black Hills, which they say is "the heart of everything that is." According to Gerald Clifford, the coordinator of the Black Hills Steering Committee, "The Lakota see the earth as mother. It provides both spiritual and material needs."[49] The Black Hills in particular are important to the Sioux. As Gerald Big Crow put it to a United Nations Working Group on Indigenous Populations, "The taking of the sacred Black Hills was the same as taking our spiritual altar. It would have the same impact if all churches and synagogues were closed."[50] To get that land they need a congressional act. Until that happens, their claim award, now more than $500 million, will continue to gather interest. Edward Lazarus, a legal expert on the Sioux claim, has argued that a solution to the stalemate could involve using the claims award to purchase private property in the Black Hills and "returning specifically identified sacred sites within the Hills to the tribe...." Although such measures would not solve all the Sioux's problems, "it would be a further step in healing a wound that has crippled the tribe for generations. And neither proposal would cost the government a dime. It would just be a triumph for the ever elusive principle of doing the right thing."[51] Despite the poverty that visits the communities of the Sioux, and the frustration from waging a legal battle for more than a century, the Sioux's resistance to the monetary settlement and persistence in pursuing their claim to the Black Hills has fostered a revival of Sioux cultural identity.

A similar dynamic emerged in the Zuni's land claim. One of the byproducts of the claim process was the sharpened sense of Zuni identity that came to some of the participants; the ordeal brought the tribe closer together and reinforced in some Zuni the meaning of their tribal affiliation. For example, Edmund Ladd served as an interpreter during the Zuni claims process. As a result he became intimately familiar with his people's history through the testimony of tribal elders. He also witnessed elders performing a War Ceremony of the Galaxy Society during the trial. He described the experience by saying, "That was one of the most awesome things because I'd only heard of these things before, and then I was actually a part of them."[52] The settlement of August 1984 gave the Zuni 12,000 acres, which included the rights to their most sacred site, *Kolhu/wala:wa,* and the trail that led to it, the *We:sak'yaya Onnane*. The advantages of the claim were economic as well as spiritual. In 1987 the tribe was awarded a $25 million judgment, most of which the tribe used to improve the quality of tribal land. With the help of the federal government, tribal officials established the Zuni Resource Development Plan, which emphasized rehabilitating tribal watersheds, developing renewable natural resources, and training Zuni to help implement and manage the plan. In addition, the tribe elected to spend $1.7 million to complete the construction of the Zuni Elementary School. All the money from the land claim went to further tribal economic, environmental, and educational programs rather than to individuals in the form of per capita payments. As Zuni project leader James Enote put it, "We are faced with the enormous challenge of moving into the next century maintaining our traditions and values, yet needing the modern technical capability to deal with the environment and development issues that confront us."[53]

Enote's statement captures the sentiments of many tribal communities struggling with environmental, economic, and cultural issues in the twenty-first century. For many Native Americans, the opportunity to expand their communities' land base, access development funds, and feel a sense of victory and accomplishment after decades of defeats has improved the spiritual ecology of their reservations. The Zuni and other tribes involved in the claims process have emerged from their battles with a painful past with both a strengthened cultural identity and economic situation, which has served to inspire a sense of hope for the future.

NOTES

1. Francis Paul Prucha, ed., *Documents of United States Indian Policy* (Lincoln: University of Nebraska Press, 2000), p. 269.

2. Quoted in Peter Iverson, "*We Are Still Here*": *American Indians in the Twentieth Century* (Wheeling, Ill.: Harlan Davidson, 1998), p. 116.

3. Paul C. Rosier, "Indian Claims Commission," in *Dictionary of American History* 4. Ed. Stanley L. Kutler. (New York: Charles Scribner's Sons, 2003), pp. 265–66.

4. Richard M. Nixon, "Remarks of President Richard M. Nixon, December 15, 1970," in *Public Papers of the President of the United States: Richard Nixon, 1970* (Washington, D.C.: GPO, 1970), pp. 1131–32.

5. Fergus M. Bordewich, *Killing the White Man's Indian: Reinventing Native Americans at the End of the Twentieth Century* (New York: Anchor Books, 1996), p. 230.

6. Quoted in Paul Brodeur, *Restitution: The Land Claims of the Mashpee, Passamaquoddy, and Penobscot Indians of New England* (Boston, Northeastern University Press, 1985), p. 4.

7. Diana Scully, Maine Indian Tribal-State Commission, "Maine Indian Land Claims Case," *Passamaquoddy Tribe at Pleasant Point,* 14 February 1995, <www.wabanaki.com/land%20Claims%Settlement.htm> (accessed July 2002).

8. William Chapman, "Taft Key in U.S. Backing of Indians' Land Claims," *Washington Post,* 9 April 1977.

9. Brodeur, *Restitution,* p. 109.

10. *Maine Indians Claims Settlement Act, U.S. Statutes at Large* 94 (1980): 1785–89, 1793–95.

11. Robert B. Porter, "Apologies to the Iroquois Are Not Enough," *New York Times,* 27 May 2000.

12. Bob Berbert, "Justice, 200 Years Later," *New York Times,* 26 November 2001.

13. Beverly Gage, "Indian Country, NY," *The Nation,* 27 November 2000.

14. David W. Chen, "Battle over Iroquois Land Claims Escalates," *New York Times,* 16 May 2000.

15. "New York Cayuga Land Claim Gets Measure of Justice," *Indian Country Today,* 17 October 2001.

16. Brodeur, *Restitution,* p. 6.

17. Deirdre Shesgreen, "Illinoisans Say Suit Seeks Their Land So Indians Can Build Casino; Miami Tribe Insists Treaties, Injustices Give Right to Property," *St. Louis Post-Dispatch,* 10 August 2000.

18. Meg Schneider, "Roots in Land Go Deep," *Utica Observer-Dispatch,* 28 March 1999.

19. Ibid.

20. "Land Claims by Indians in New York Are Aired at Symposium," *New York Times,* 13 April 1986.

21. Brodeur, *Restitution,* p. 6.

22. Quoted in Brodeur, *Restitution,* p. 107.

23. Agnes Palazetti, "Decision on Indians' Claim to Ownership of Grand Island Is Put Off until March," *Buffalo News,* 21 February 1998.

24. James Odato, "Tribe Plays High-Stakes Game with Landowners," *timesunion.com,* 25 October 1999, <www.timesunion.com> (accessed July 2002).

25. Mary Pasciak, "Motorcade to Albany Aims for Attention," *Buffalo News,* 29 April 1999.

26. Tom Precious, "Homeowners Drive Home Protest of Indian Land Claims," *Buffalo News,* 2 May 1999.

27. Pasciak, "Motorcade to Albany."

28. Chen, "Battle over Iroquois."

29. Jim Adams, "Critical State Races: Clinton vs. Lazio," *Indian Country Today,* 1 November 2000.

30. Quoted in Brodeur, *Restitution,* p. 6.

31. Edmund Mahony, "Indians Ask Court to Reverse Land Ruling," *Hartford Courant,* 19 February 1994.

32. Shesgreen, "Illinoisans."

33. Timothy Egan, "Indian Tribe Agrees to Drop Claim to Tacoma Land for $165 Million," *New York Times,* 29 August 1988.

34. Chen, "Battle over Iroquois."

35. Brodeur, *Restitution,* p. 138.

36. David L. Shaw, "Settlement Urged in Cayuga Claim: The Interest of All Parties Will Be Served If State Doesn't Appeal, Some Experts Say," *Cayuga-Syracuse Post-Standard,* 7 October 2001.

37. Robert Wells Jr., "Blocking Settlement of Indian Land Claims," editorial letter, *New York Times,* 9 April 1981.

38. Wayne King, "Bradley Offers Bill to Return Land to Sioux," *New York Times,* 11 March 1987.

39. "Petition to the President of the United States," in *The Oneida Land Claims: A Legal History,* by George C. Shattuck (Syracuse, N.Y.: Syracuse University Press, 1991), p. 205.

40. John H. Kennedy, "Appeals Court Rejects Indian Land Claim," *Boston Globe,* 2 November 1998.

41. Susan Lampert Smith, "Ho-Chunk Land Returned in Kickapoo Valley," *Wisconsin State Journal,* 29 October 1997.

42. James Odato, "Land Disputes Divide Residents, Tribes," *timesunion.com,* 24 October 1999, <www.timesunion.com> (accessed July 2002).

43. Joel Siegel, "Circling the Wagons: Upstaters Fighting Cayuga Indian Land Claims," *New York Daily News,* 16 September 1999.

44. Dianna Hunt, "Eyeing Gambling, Schramm Backs Indian Land Claim," *Houston Chronicle,* 11 March 1994.

45. Egan, "Indian Tribe."

46. "Land Claims by Indians in New York."

47. Brodeur, *Restitution,* p. 56.

48. Schneider, "Roots in Land Go Deep."

49. King, "Bradley Offers Bill."

50. Bordewich, *Killing the White Man's Indian,* p. 222.

51. Edward Lazarus, "Same Black Hills, More White Justice: Senator Daschle's Provision Granting Barrick Gold Company Immunity from Liability," *FindLaw's*

Writ, 24 January 2002, <writ.news.findlaw.com/lazarus/20020124.html> (accessed July 2002).

52. Richard E. Hart, ed., *Zunis and the Courts: A Struggle for Sovereign Land Rights* (Lawrence: University Press of Kansas, 1995), p. 234.

53. Hart, *Zunis and the Courts*, p. 317.

QUESTIONS

1) Why did the Taos Pueblo get their land back in 1970 but not the Sioux in 1980?
2) Should the Sioux have taken the $106 million judgment in 1980? Why? Why not?
3) What is the position of individual property owners in these claims? Is it legitimate?
4) Should a state resident be forced to make changes based on documents signed two hundred years earlier?
5) Do you agree with the following statement? "There really is a very strong moral principle here, and that is whether the United States is good for its word." If so, why? If not, why not?
6) What is the most compelling reason to support land claims? And why?
7) What is the most compelling reason not to support land claims? And why?
8) Which case best illustrates the complexity of the land claims process and why?
9) Write an essay on recent events in the New York State cases. How have the courts addressed the legal issues involved in the claims?
10) What is the place of Indian sovereignty in the claims process? What is at stake for Indians and non-Indians alike?
11) Consider the role of sacred sites in the claims process. What do they have to tell us about the reasons Native Americans spend decades, or even more than a century, fighting for their claims?
12) Research the outcome of the Seneca Nation land claim. To what extent were gambling issues connected with the land claim and the state's handling of it?
13) In what other ways does casino gambling intersect with the land claims process?
14) Research the land claims case of the Alabama-Coushatta tribes of Texas. In what ways is this case similar to and different from the ones discussed in this chapter?
15) Research a land claims case that developed in your state. Hold a mock trial on the merits of those who support it and those who oppose it, drawing on the arguments outlined in this chapter.

RESOURCE GUIDE

Suggested Readings

Adams, Jim. "Critical State Races: Clinton vs. Lazio." *Indian Country Today*, 1 November 2000.

Bordewich, Fergus M. *Killing the White Man's Indian: Reinventing Native Americans at the End of the Twentieth Century.* New York: Anchor Books, 1996.

Brodeur, Paul. *Restitution: The Land Claims of the Mashpee, Passamaquoddy, and Penobscot Indians of New England.* Boston: Northeastern University Press, 1985.

Campisi, Jack. "New York–Oneida Treaty of 1795: A Finding of Fact." *American Indian Law Review* (summer 1976).

———. "The Trade and Intercourse Acts: Land Claims on the Eastern Seaboard." In *Irredeemable America: The Indians' Estate and Land Claims,* edited by Imre Sutton. Albuquerque: University of New Mexico Press, 1985.

Chen, David W. "Battle over Iroquois Land Claims Escalates." *New York Times,* 16 May 2000.

Cheyfitz, Eric. "The Navajo-Hopi Land Dispute: A Brief History." *Interventions: International Journal of Postcolonial Studies* 2, no. 2 (2000).

Christie, John C., Jr. "The Catawba Indian Land Claim: A Giant among Indian Land Claims." *American Indian Culture and Research Journal* 24 (winter 2000).

Churchill, Ward. "Charades, Anyone? The ICC in Context." *American Indian Culture and Research Journal* 24 (winter 2000).

Gage, Beverly. "Indian Country, NY." *The Nation,* 27 November 2000.

"Gold in the Hills: Indian Land Claims." *The Economist,* 23 July 1994.

Gordon-McCutchan, R. C. *The Taos Indians and the Battle for Blue Lake.* Sante Fe: Red Crane Books, 1991.

Hart, E. Richard. "The Couer d'Alene Tribe's Claim to Lake Coeur d'Alene." *American Indian Culture and Research Journal* 24 (winter 2000).

———. "Zuni Claims: An Expert Witness' Reflections." *American Indian Culture and Research Journal* 24 (winter 2000).

———, ed. *Zunis and the Courts: A Struggle for Sovereign Land Rights.* Lawrence: University Press of Kansas, 1995.

Herbert, Bob. "Justice, 200 Years Later." *New York Times,* 26 November 2001.

Iverson, Peter. *"We Are Still Here": American Indians in the Twentieth Century.* Wheeling, Ill.: Harlan Davidson, 1998.

King, Wayne. "Bradley Offers Bill to Return Land to Sioux." *New York Times,* 11 March 1987.

Kuiper, Dean. "Return of the Native: As Native Americans Wage Legal Battles to Regain Their Land, Property Owners Go on the Warpath." *Omni,* September 1990.

Lazarus, Edward. *Black Hills/White Justice: The Sioux Nation vs. the United States, 1775 to the Present.* New York: HarperCollins, 1991.

———. "Same Black Hills, More White Justice: Senator Daschle's Provision Granting Barrick Gold Company Immunity from Liability." 24 January 2002. <writ.news.findlaw.com/lazarus/20020124.html> (accessed July 2002).

Lieder, Michael, and Jake Page. *Wild Justice: The People of Geronimo vs. the United States.* New York: Random House, 1997.

Lurie, Nancy O. "The Indian Claims Commission." *Annals of the American Academy of Political and Social Science* 436 (1978).

Nelson, Katherine F. "Resolving Native American Land Claims and the Eleventh Amendment: Changing the Balance of Power." *Villanova Law Review* (1994).

Porter, Robert B. "Apologies to the Iroquois Are Not Enough." *New York Times,* 27 May 2000.

Rosenthal, Harvey D. *Their Day in Court: A History of the Indian Claims Commission.* New York: Garland, 1990.

Rosier, Paul C. "Indian Claims Commission." In *Dictionary of American History* 4. Ed. Stanley L. Kutler. New York: Charles Scribner's Sons, 2003.

Scully, Diana. Maine Indian Tribal-State Commission. "Maine Indian Land Claims Case." *Passamaquoddy Tribe at Pleasant Point.* 14 February 1995. <www.wabanaki.com/land%20Claims%Settlement.htm> (accessed July 2002).

Shattuck, George C. *The Oneida Land Claims: A Legal History.* Syracuse, N.Y.: Syracuse University Press, 1991.

Sutton, Imre, ed. *Irredeemable America: The Indians' Estate and Land Claims.* Albuquerque: University of New Mexico Press, 1985.

———. "Not All Aboriginal Territory Is Truly Irredeemable." *American Indian Culture and Research Journal* 24 (winter 2000).

Vecscey, Christopher, and William Starna, eds. *Iroquois Land Claims.* Syracuse, N.Y.: Syracuse University Press, 1991.

Wilkinson, Charles, et al. "The Indian Claims Commission." In *Indian Self-Rule: First-Hand Accounts of Indian-White Relations from Roosevelt to Reagan,* edited by Kenneth Philp. Logan, Utah: Utah State University, 1995.

Young, John. "United Nations Official Hears Black Hills Claim." *Indian Country Today,* 21 September 1994.

Videos

In the Spirit of Crazy Horse. "Frontline," Public Broadcasting Service. 60 min., Parillas Productions, 1990. An excellent video that discusses the place of the Black Hills in the Sioux Nation's history and culture and the Sioux's search for its return.

"Whose Land Is It Anyway?" 12 min. Segment on *60 Minutes.* 23 May 1999. CBS Television. Segment on the Oneida land claim.

Web Sites

"Cayuga Award." *Indian Law Resource Center.* <www.indianlaw.org/Cayuga_award_dec.pdf>. Text of the Cayuga land claim decision.

"Cayuga Nation Decision." *Indian Law Resource Center.* <www.indianlaw.org/cayuga.htm>. Information on the Cayuga land claim.

Indian Law Resource Center. <www.indianlaw.org/land_rights.htm>. General site on land rights and eastern United States land claims.

Native American Rights Fund. <www.narf.org>.

Navajo-Hopi Long Land Dispute. <www.kstrom.net/isk/maps/az/navhopi.html>. Information on the Navajo-Hopi land dispute.

Oneida Nation Land Claims Information. <www.oneida-nation.net/landclaims.html>.

Upstate Citizens for Equality, Inc. <www.madisoncountyny.com/uce/index.htm>.

"U.S. Code Collection: Chapter 19—Indian Land Claims Settlements." *Legal Information Institute.* <www4.law.cornell.edu/uscode/25/ch19.html>. Indian land claims settlements legal site.

U.S. Senate Committee on Indian Affairs. <indian.senate.gov>. Includes historical and current hearings on Indian affairs.

<www.newsaic.com/caseindianland.html>. Utica NY Observer-Dispatch series on the Oneida land claims.

4

REPATRIATION OF ANCESTRAL REMAINS AND SACRED OBJECTS

A NATIVE AMERICAN IN SCOTLAND

In 1992 an American lawyer visited the Kelvingrove Museum in Glasgow, Scotland. He noticed in one of its exhibits a bloodied shirt, punctured by bullet holes, that had been worn by a Lakota Sioux, whose practice of the Ghost Dance ended with his death at the infamous Wounded Knee massacre of 1890 in which the U.S. Seventh Cavalry killed nearly three hundred Sioux men, women, and children. His discovery of the "Ghost Dance shirt" set off a battle by Lakota Sioux elders to repatriate the shirt, that is, return the object to its land of origin, in this case the Sioux reservation of South Dakota. After tribal elders visited the museum to negotiate the shirt's return, the Glasgow City Council voted to repatriate it to the Sioux people. Marcella Le Beau, a leader of the Wounded Knee Survivors Association, was overjoyed by the decision and thanked the city of Glasgow. "It's like a great thanksgiving and I want to cry. I thank you very, very much." Not all Glasgow residents were pleased with the decision. The head of the museum's curatorial services defended museums' "dignified and honourable" role in exhibiting cultural artifacts like the Ghost Dance shirt. He noted that "all museums in Britain have legal ownership of their artifacts and it is up to them whether they return them." He feared that the decision "opens the floodgates" to more repatriation requests.[1]

The Scottish museum case was just one of the 1990s, which saw legal and moral challenges to what Native Americans considered to be "imperial archaeology," the imprisonment of Indian physical remains and sacred objects like shirts, pottery, statues, and other elements of a culture's ritual practices and ceremonies in non-Indian museums that resulted from Americans' conquest and control of Indian America during the nineteenth and twentieth centuries. The dimensions of this contemporary Native American issue are varied—involving ethics, law, politics, religion, and science—and like the other issues explored in this volume, it is of great importance and interest to Indians and non-Indians alike.

HISTORICAL BACKGROUND

As white settlers, soldiers, and scientists fanned out across America in the nineteenth century, they came across or actively searched for Indian burial sites, which contained an array of cultural artifacts such as pots, arrowheads, and clothes; skeletal remains; and the sacred objects used in Indian ceremonies, including those used in the funeral ceremony itself, called *funerary objects*. *Body snatching*, as many Native Americans call it, became regularized in the mid-1800s when Samuel Morton recruited people to raid Indian gravesites for body parts so that Morton, practicing a pseudoscience called *phrenology*, could test his theory that skull size revealed the intellectual capacity of a race. In 1859 the U.S. surgeon general ordered the U.S. Army to ship to the Army Medical Museum in Washington, D.C., bodies of Indians killed in battle or found in gravesites for an "Indian Crania Study." In one particularly troubling case, six Pawnee scouts loyal to the United States Army were killed by a separate army unit despite their official discharge papers. The surgeon general asked that the Pawnee's heads be sawed off and sent to Washington to help test his theory that Indians were intellectually inferior to whites. Such artifacts and objects ended up in museums or private collections across the country and overseas, displayed like trophies by some collectors, while the skeletal remains, like those of the Pawnee scouts and other Indians chosen for research purposes, found their way to museums like the Smithsonian Institution in Washington, D.C., whose collection of burial remains grew to include those of some eighteen thousand five hundred Native Americans. The Smithsonian and other museums and research institutions collectively owned between six hundred thousand and two million funerary objects and bones, many of which were simply held in boxes in basements and warehouses, unopened and unused, forgotten.

The practice of "robbing" Indian graves for remains and objects continues to this day, fueled by high prices paid for cultural artifacts arising from both Americans' and Europeans' fascination with the legacies of Native America. The Federal Bureau of Investigation cited the rising value of Indian objects as a factor in the increase in numbers of both looters, who obtain artifacts illegally for profit, and relic hunters, who locate cultural objects for either hobby or profit. The *FBI Law Enforcement Bulletin* estimated in 1997 that "German and Japanese collectors alone buy approximately $20 million worth of Native American artifacts yearly."[2] A pot from the American Southwest can bring as much as $400,000. As a result, looters and relic hunters have plundered thousands of Indian gravesites across the country.

Schaghticoke Indian tribe archaeologist Lucienne Lavin, left, tribal historian Paulette Crone-Morange, center, and tribal chief Richard Velky, right, at tribal headquarters in Monroe, Connecticut, with some of the baskets made by their ancestors that they have been able to recover. The tribe faces difficulty recovering tribal artifacts as interest in Native American artifacts increases, along with the prices. (AP/Wide World Photos)

Native Americans objected to these grave-robbing practices from the beginning, feeling that the theft of remains and objects stripped Indians of their dignity, their past, and their identity. In the 1970s, they began to contest non-Indians' ownership of Indian remains and objects and initiated a campaign for their repatriation to the tribe of their origin. Articles in Native American publications like *American Indian Journal* and *American Indian Law Review* began to argue that the issue was one of religious freedom. This campaign was part of a larger campaign for self-determination. Reclaiming one's literal past, like reclaiming land use rights promised in treaties, became a cornerstone of this campaign.

In the face of this increasing pressure, federal officials moved to institute respect for Native American religious practices. In 1978 Congress passed the American Indian Religious Freedom Act, requiring federal agencies to work to "protect and preserve Native American religious cultural rights and practices," which included guaranteeing "access to sites, use and possession of sacred objects, and the freedom to worship through ceremonials and traditional rites."[3] Congress applied these principles a year later by passing the Archaeological Resources Protection Act (ARPA), declaring that investigation of archaeological sites on federal property could not be undertaken without a permit and in some cases without the consent of the tribe affiliated with the site. Although ARPA did nothing to reverse the flow of Indian objects and remains back to their people, it did create a moral imperative for the proper treatment of them and established criminal penalties for what Congress called "uncontrolled excavations and pillage."[4] A looter of a Cherokee site in Tennessee was later convicted and given a prison sentence; many looters were assessed civil penalties.

In the 1980s, tribal leaders began to push for a different result than just protection from future grave robbing. Wanting repatriation—the return of objects and ancestral remains—they went to Congress to appeal for federal help. In 1987, Northern Cheyenne spiritual leader Bill Tall Bull asked a Senate committee, "How would you feel if your grandmother's grave were opened, the contents were shipped back east to be boxed and warehoused with 31,000 others...and itinerant pot-hunters were allowed to ransack her house in search of 'artifacts' with the blessing of the U.S. government? It is uncivilized...savage...inhuman.... It is un-Christian."[5] In three prominent cases of the 1980s, Pawnee battled the Nebraska State Historical Society for the return of their ancestors' bones, the Iroquois won their 22-year fight to reclaim 12 ceremonial wampum belts held in a New York museum, and the Zunis of New Mexico sought the return of their "War Gods," known as *Ahayuda,* carved wooden statues that serve an important role in sacred ceremonies; Andy Warhol and Paul Klee each owned a War God, which could sell for as much as $100,000. In the Pawnee case, the federal government had forced the Pawnee out of their homes in Nebraska and relocated them to Oklahoma in the mid-1800s, resulting in a massive looting of ancestral remains, according to Walter Echo-Hawk, an attorney for the Native American Rights Fund (NARF), which successfully sued for the return of burial remains. The NARF lawsuits led to the passage of Nebraska state reparations laws, which helped to fuel the debate over a national law, as did Stanford University's 1989 agreement to repatriate the skeletal remains of nearly five hundred and fifty Ohlone-Costanoan Indians to their northern California descendants. The agreement was the culmination of a five-year effort by the Ohlone-Costanoan people to reclaim their ancestors' bones, which had been held in Stanford laboratories for years. Although the negotiations were "respectful," a Stanford University administrator said, "Anyone who believes that resolution of these [repatriation] issues is easy hasn't really thought about them."[6]

Indeed, as these repatriation campaigns became increasingly contentious and public, Congress stepped in to provide Native Americans with a legal mechanism to back their claims to ownership of bones and artifacts. In 1989 it passed the National Museum of the American Indian Act (NMAIA), which served two main purposes. One, it directed the creation of a central national institution (combining the Smithsonian's disparate holdings, including the massive collections of the Heye Museum in New York City) for the exhibition and research of Native American artifacts to "give all Americans the opportunity to learn of the cultural legacy, historic grandeur, and contemporary culture of Native Americans."[7] And two, it required the Smithsonian Institution, which had resisted repatriation efforts, to "inventory the Indian human remains and funerary objects" of its collections, determine their origins, and, if evidence supported it, "expeditiously return" both the remains and funerary objects "to the descendants or tribe."[8] NARF attorney Walter Echo-Hawk hailed the decision as "the beginning of the end of [Indians'] spiritual nightmare."[9]

A year later Congress passed into law the landmark Native American Graves Protection and Repatriation Act (NAGPRA), partly inspired, perhaps, by the nation's own search for the remains of veterans in Vietnam. NAGPRA, which Echo-Hawk helped design, established new codes for protecting Indian gravesites by raising civil and criminal penalties for the "illegal trafficking" of Native American remains and artifacts. And it addressed the process of repatriation along the lines of the NMAIA. NAGPRA required a federal agency or a museum receiving federal funding to first produce an inventory of its "human remains," "funerary objects," "sacred objects" ("ceremonial objects which are needed by traditional Native American religious leaders for the practice of traditional Native American religious"), and items of "cultural patrimony," defined as objects "having ongoing historical, traditional, or cultural importance, central to the Native American group or culture itself."[10] Second, the act required museums and agencies to notify tribal groups if their inventory contained remains or objects that were "culturally affiliated" with those groups and to arrange for their "expeditious" repatriation. NAGPRA gave museums and federal agencies five years to complete the analysis and inventory process. In the process, the National Park Service, which helped to oversee the project, developed a federal register of inventoried items. NAGPRA also made explicit that repatriation rested on the notion of "cultural affiliation," which meant that an Indian group could reclaim remains or objects only if direct cultural links to them had been established and if the Indian group requested their return.

NAGPRA provided the mechanics for the inventory and repatriation of hundreds of thousands of Indian remains and objects. The act's implementation created a series of problems, however, as it required delicate negotiations, time, and money. Museums felt swamped by the prospects of cataloging their holdings, Indian communities faced expensive trips to museums to identify possible remains, and non–federally recognized tribes felt left out. For example, the Phoebe Hearst Museum of Anthropology at the University of California-Berkeley faced the task of inventorying more than two hundred fifty thousand items and ten thousand bone sets. In addition to traveling to view such collections, tribal officials faced the prospect of storing the remains or objects, which could entail building new facilities. In California, a number of small tribal communities had no leverage in requesting the return of artifacts or remains because NAGPRA applied only to federally recognized tribes; given that 80 percent of the Hearst's holdings came from California, this lack of status proved especially frustrating to California Indians. Another problem entailed dual claims, in which two or more Indian nations claimed artifacts or remains as theirs, requiring further analysis. In addition, because NAGPRA applied only to those institutions that received federal funding, a number of smaller museums decided to unload their artifacts to private owners in anticipation of losing them to a new wave of federal repatriation laws or tribal lawsuits.

Some of these problems were addressed on the federal and state level. Most museums were granted an extension beyond the original five-year period. A 1997 NAGPRA amendment establishing fines for noncompliance created new incentives; as of 1999, nearly ten thousand human remains and roughly three hundred thousand artifacts had been repatriated. The National Park Service gave grants to some tribal communities to facilitate the repatriation process. California Indians were buoyed by the repatriation and reburial of the brain of Ishi, the last member of the Yahi tribe, in August 2000, after it had been held in the Smithsonian for 83 years; Ishi symbolized the end of a traditional way of life as well as California Indians' victimization. And in October 2001, the California legislature passed the California Native American Graves Protection and Repatriation Act to further the repatriation of items to California tribes. But the fundamental problem has remained: Native Americans want the remains and cultural artifacts back; scientists and some museum officials don't want to return them. We turn to a recent case that illustrates the bumpy topography of the repatriation debate.

FRAMING THE ISSUE

The Kennewick Man case highlights the strengths and the weaknesses of NAGPRA and the general explosiveness of the repatriation issue. In July 1996 two college students watching a boat race on the banks of the Columbia River uncovered a human skull, near Kennewick, Washington. Intrigued, James Chatters, a local anthropologist, returned to the site and uncovered the other skeletal remains. At first Chatters thought it was a Caucasian male, perhaps an early trader operating in the Pacific Northwest. But stuck in the pelvic bone was a spear point, complicating the picture. Chatters sent a piece of the bone to a laboratory, which determined through radiocarbon dating that the skeleton was between 9,300 and 9,500 years old. News of the find created great excitement among anthropologists and archaeologists, who were eager to examine a complete skeleton to learn more about prehistoric North American peoples, particularly because the skull had caucasoid fea-

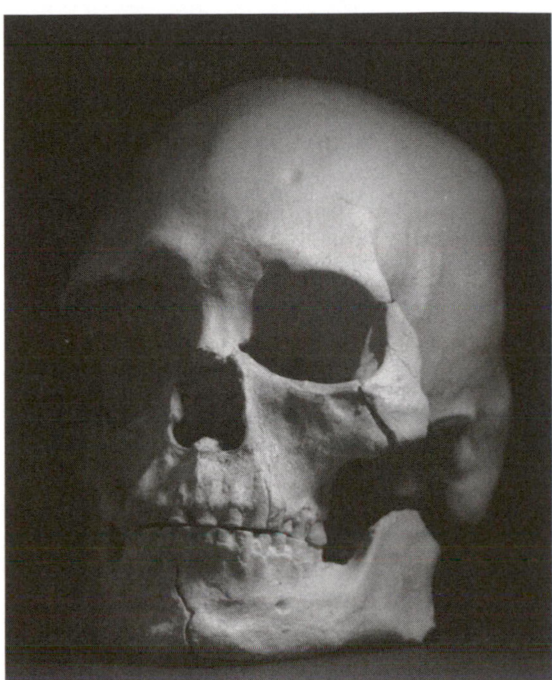

Plastic casting of a controversial 9,200-year-old skull from the bones known as Kennewick Man in Richland, Washington. (AP/Wide World Photos)

tures that did not appear to accord with those of Native Americans. The prevailing theory among scientists is that Native Americans evolved from Asian peoples, with whom they share genetic and physical similarities, who migrated from Siberia to Alaska across a strip of land called Beringia, what is now the Bering Strait, roughly twelve thousand years ago.

However, because the skeleton was found on federal land, leaders of Indian communities in the area claimed it as one of theirs, and using NAGPRA asked that the bones not be examined but reburied according to tribal customs. The U.S. Army Corps of Engineers impounded the skeleton to accord with NAGPRA, setting off a custody battle that has lasted for more than five years. Three main groups filed claims for the remains. Five tribes of the Pacific Northwest—the Umatilla, Yakima, Nez Perce, Colville, and Wanapum—exercised their rights under NAGPRA to claim the skeleton. In response, eight archaeologists and anthropologists filed suit in federal court to retain the right to examine the remains, claiming that the bones should not be repatriated and buried because their cultural origin was in doubt. A third group was the Asatru Folk Assembly, a group of Americans who claim the remains as one of their Norse ancestors. The five tribes and the scientists battled it out in court until September 2000, when Interior Secretary Bruce Babbitt concluded that study of the bones had provided evidence that the man was related to local tribal groups. The scientists appealed the decision. The case continues as of July 2002.

The Kennewick Man case captures the religious, spiritual, legal, and ethical issues at the heart of the repatriation debate. Native Americans saw the scientific community once again using invasive techniques to probe the bones of their ancestors while trying to minimize the long history of Indian peoples in North America; scientists wanted the opportunity to learn more about early settlers and possibly revise the Asian-migration theory, which many Native Americans did not accept. In this chapter, we consider some of these dimensions of the repatriation issue and try to answer a vexing question—*Who owns the past?*

OPPONENTS OF REPATRIATION

Even before NAGPRA became law in 1990, scientists, museum officials, and art dealers expressed concern about the effects of repatriation campaigns. Resistance began in the late 1960s when Indian activists began to claim ownership of ancestral remains and sacred objects. But scientists were increasingly put on the defensive when the calls for repatriation laws got louder in the late 1980s. As one anthropologist put it in 1989, "We are doing important work that benefits all mankind, and we're portrayed as grave robbers."[11] Dealers of Indian art also felt threatened by pending legislation. James Reid, president of the Antique Tribal Art Dealers Association, testified before Congress as it debated NAGPRA in 1990 that he opposed the idea that "the state should seek to amend the rights of private or public ownership of items that have been in non-tribal hands for many years, [that] may have been given as gifts [or] sold or traded from institutions or tribes or by individuals apparently in good faith. . . ."[12] Congress subsequently excluded private owners from following NAGPRA provisions. NAGPRA, however, did create a new set of rules for museum officials and for anthropologists and archaeologists.

NAGPRA created a burden for museums, large and small. While the Smithsonian Institution contained tens of thousands of remains and objects, it had professional staff that could devote their time to repatriation issues. Smaller museums had limited staff and budgets to contend with the time-consuming process. For example, the Milwaukee Public Museum held thousands of objects and the remains of fifteen hundred individuals. The cost of processing these items rose dramatically after NAGPRA and at a time of budget cuts. Museum president William Moynihan noted that the museum supported NAGPRA, which had engendered a "new and productive relationship with Native American groups," but he contended that his institution had received no federal funding to help implement a federal mandate.[13]

Repatriation created an identity crisis for museum officials—specifically, it has raised questions about their ownership and stewardship of valuable and important cultural artifacts. In 1970, in one of the earliest battles, officials of a

New York State museum that had possessed 12 ceremonial wampum belts from the Iroquois people since 1898 resisted their repatriation on the grounds that it would set a precedent that "could destroy the concept of museums and libraries being collectors of anything."[14] Anthropologists have pointed out in their defense that some Indians sold artifacts, either their own or those tribally owned, for profit or to allow important ritual objects to survive. While NAGPRA has not resulted in a massive transfer of Indian objects from non-Indian museums to Indian museums, as some feared, administrators have resisted returning objects unless they are deemed important for burial practices. Robert Archibald, director of the Missouri Historical Society, believes in maintaining a museum's role in exhibiting Native American culture, though he has made an effort to exhibit Indian artifacts in a culturally appropriate manner. He argues, "I don't think museums own things—in a legal sense they do, but in an ethical sense we're trustees. It can come down to an argument of whose stuff it is...."[15] An official of the Field Museum of Natural History in Chicago expressed concern for sacred Nightway masks destined for return to the Navajo Nation as well as Indian artifacts in general. Museum vice president Jonathan Haas contended, "We may not be able to take care of things spiritually, but we can take care of them physically. And we worry what will become of (these things) when we give them back and they don't have a facility to take care of them. They may fall apart in two or three years."[16] Given that some tribes lack space for storing sacred objects and cultural artifacts, some museum officials fear that they could resurface on the black market, the result of theft by either non-Indians or Indians, and go to private collectors rather than to museums. The other side of this coin is that some repatriated objects will disappear forever, because that is what some tribes originally intended. For example, returned Zuni War Gods would be allowed to decay naturally, as tribal customs dictate. And all or most funereal objects will be reburied.

Some museum officials and scientists have concerns about the validity of repatriation claims. In the 1980s, officials of the Smithsonian Institution resisted calls for it to repatriate Indian remains, in part because they believed that many of them could not be positively identified as having a cultural affiliation with a living Native American group, what they called a "clear biological or cultural link."[17] Those not clearly linked should remain available for study; otherwise, officials argued, "compulsory internment is an irretrievable loss of material of significant scientific and educational value."[18] Several cases have proved problematic and have created conflict between Indian nations. The Navajo Nation has claimed ownership of all cultural objects found on its huge reservation, but neighboring tribes like the Hopi, Zuni, and Pueblo believe that such a blanket claim precludes a proper investigation of objects that may be culturally affiliated with related tribes who occupied the land before the Navajo, especially the Anasazi cliff dwellers. Harvard University's Peabody Museum, which has the second-largest collection of Indian remains, found itself in the middle of a dispute between Wampanoag and Narragansett tribal leaders claiming ownership of the same group of ancestral bones and sacred objects. A similar case divided the Pequot and Mohegan nations of Connecticut, though they settled the issue by holding a joint reburial ceremony.

Impact on Scientists

Repatriation has also created an identity crisis for anthropologists and archaeologists, who have various reasons for opposing repatriation, one of which is professional survival. As Virginia Morell noted in a 1994 article published in *Science,* a magazine that has followed repatriation closely, "Hundreds of scientists who depend upon this material (bones and artifacts) will be cut off from their research data, and North American anthropology and archeology will be changed forever."[19] UCLA anthropologist Clement Meighan believes repatriation has had a "chilling effect on research," resulting in "intimidated teachers who are afraid to show a picture of a burial to their classes.... There is an increasing loss to American archeology and of course to the Indians whose history is dependent on it."[20] In response, more than six hundred archaeologists organized in the early 1990s to form the American Committee for Preservation of Archaeological Collections, which publicizes the valuable contributions the discipline offers science and society. Anthropologists have also published articles explaining their profession and justifying their work. For example, Patricia Landau and D. Gentry Steele's essay "Why Anthropologists Study Human Remains" appeared in a special issue of *American Indian Quarterly* devoted to the topic of repatriation. The authors write of anthropologists studying diseases such as rheumatoid arthritis through bones as well as investigating human history, believing that "all ancient peoples are the ancestors of modern peoples."[21] Some archaeologists and anthropologists are hurt by the tone of repatriation activists and feel betrayed, since their professions have done so much to help preserve cultural artifacts. For example, Meighan contends, "That part of American history that is Indian history is largely the contribution of archeology; *all* of it prior to 1492 is the contribution of archeology."[22] Archaeologists have also done much to protect and preserve Native American sites and cemeteries, both by publicizing the extraordinary damage looters inflict on them and by promoting among Native Americans an anti-looting activism.

On a basic level, some of these scientists object to the protection of Native Americans' religious rights over those of science. They thus see federal intervention in the matter as a violation of the doctrine of separation of church and state, and they fear that repatriation will create other forms of religious infringement on their work. Scientists, like some museum administrators, also oppose NAGPRA because it allows Native Americans to make broad claims of ancestral relationships, which means that tribal communities can request bones that may actually predate their known history; anthropologists make it clear that they do not oppose the return of bones clearly identified as those of known individuals or from specific historical events like the Sand Creek and Wounded Knee massacres.

More important, the return of skeletal remains will render the bones unusable for scientific research, which means that the cessation of research projects could affect scientists' understanding of diseases and genetics and thus their ability to contribute knowledge for the public good. Curator Douglas Ubelaker of the Smithsonian Institution's anthropology department contended months before NAGPRA passed that "skeletons offer glimpses into diet and disease. And we are at the very threshold of major changes in chemical and DNA analysis that will allow a much clearer picture of past life."[23] Ubelaker believed that a middle ground could be established to allow scientists to continue their study in a manner deemed inoffensive to tribal officials. The reburial of remains also means that scientists will not be able to use future techniques to reevaluate old material. Jane Buikstra, a physical anthropologist, noted, "Once the material is gone, it is no longer available for restudy or for future studies using new techniques, nor can anyone check the original data for observer error—something that is fundamental to science."[24] Philip Walker, an archaeologist on the staff of the Society for American Archaeology's Task Force on Reburial and Repatriation, also considered the impact on society's understanding of Indian cultures. Several months after NAGPRA passed, he said, "I worry about Native American children generations from now if today we make decisions that will deny them information needed to understand the contributions their ancestors made."[25] Omaha Indians, while supportive of repatriation, did allow University of Nebraska scientists to spend one year examining the bones of their ancestors in the interests of learning about their past, a solution that Ubelaker might have supported. In the end they got their ancestral remains and knowledge of their tribal history as well.

But cases of collaboration have created a new set of problems for archaeologists and anthropologists. In one case, physical anthropologist Ethne Barnes had to get permission from the Cochiti-Pueblo and the Hopi for her study of skeletal remains in the Smithsonian. The Cochiti-Pueblo said no, but the Hopi said yes. However, the Hopi required her to share her research results with tribal officials before she published them, which she called "a kind of censorship."[26] Another anthropologist needed 18 months to get permissions from state, church, and tribal officials to conduct an excavation in California. Other scientists have seen their control over the research process change considerably and expect that some tribes will ask for research materials like field notes and photographs as well as demand that scientists get their permission before publishing their findings. The Hopi tribe has asked scientists to discontinue altogether the study of its ancestors, alarming curators and scientists alike, some of whom see the repatriation process as a form of book burning, a denial of knowledge.

The Kennewick Man Controversy

When the Kennewick Man controversy entered the courts, a judge compared the skeletal remains to "a book that [research scientists] can read, a history written in bone instead of on paper, just as the history of a region may be 'read' by observing layers of rock or ice, or the rings of a tree."[27] Scientists believed that a unique opportunity for understanding the history and the genetic makeup of North America's earliest inhabitants was lost when the U.S. Army Corps of Engineers prevented them from evaluating the 9,300-year-old skeletal remains using NAGPRA as its basis. William Lipe, president of the Society for American Archaeology, criticized NAGPRA for its shortcomings: "The law does not adequately take into account the fact that genes, culture traits and language are not inherited in neat tribal packages, but spread, contract and change fairly independently over time.... Nor did the law provide for scientific studies to address the interests that other tribes and the general public might have in the early peopling of the Americas."[28] Lipe noted that his organization supports Indians' right to reclaim ancestral remains. But in the case of the Kennewick Man, not enough evidence existed to support the five tribes' "cultural affiliation" with the 9,300-year-old bones; NAGPRA requires repatriation to be supported by evidence linking the remains with living tribal groups. A number of scientists do not believe that linkage is there and argue that further study could help determine the remains' affiliation. Anthropologist D. Gentry Steele, a party to the lawsuit that eight scientists filed to prevent the Kennewick Man's reburial, contended that affiliation was unlikely given the length of time involved. "The chances of finding someone living in the same vicinity today who is closely related to an individual who died that long ago are very remote. Populations move and disperse through time....We won't know who he is most closely related to until he is studied."[29]

Other critics of the case worry about what is lost with the reburial of the remains. Amy Danise, a Nevada anthropologist, understands Indians' objection to museums and their claims on skeletal remains. But she contends that in the case of ancient remains, science and human understanding suffers. "I don't want to deny [Native Americans] their rights, but on the other hand, the rights of scientists are being violated too. They are being denied their right to knowledge."[30] Archaeologist Robson Bonnichsen called the skeletal remains "terribly important to our understanding of America's biological and cultural heritage."[31] Anthropologist Joseph Powell believes research on the skeleton could yield "important clues about recent human evolution."[32]

The Kennewick Man controversy is just one of the cases that has alarmed archaeologists and anthropologists. Bonnichsen, head of the Center for the Study of the First Americans at Oregon State University, complained that "repatriation has taken on a life of its own and is about to put us out of business as a profession." He considers repatriation to be a "battle over who controls America's past."[33] Douglas Owsley, a physical anthropologist at the

Smithsonian Institution, is dismayed by the Kennewick Man case and others like it. He noted that the Shoshone-Bannock tribe of Idaho was given the right to rebury a 10,675-year-old skeleton in 1992 after only a brief study. "It was a tremendous loss to science and the American people. And I don't think it's what Congress intended when it enacted NAGPRA."[34] Washington State representative Donald Hastings agreed, announcing during the controversy his intention to introduce legislation to amend NAGPRA to create "more exacting standards of identification" in the case of ancient remains like those of the Kennewick Man.[35] Congress did not adopt the legislation, but the animus against NAGPRA's lack of specific standards regarding cultural affiliation continues to trouble scientists and their supporters, who see the potential for more "books" like the Kennewick Man to be closed before they are opened.

PROPONENTS OF REPATRIATION

It is important to note that all Native American communities do not have the same spiritual beliefs and cultural practices, and they have thus looked at NAGPRA and the repatriation issue in different ways. But what unites them in their respective repatriation campaigns is the idea that over time, pieces of their culture—whether it is skeletal remains or a ceremonial mask—have been taken from them, often by force or violence, and rendered inert under museum glass or in a dusty box in the storage room of a distant museum and prevented from serving their true function or, in the case of remains, resting in peace.

The Spiritual Foundation of Repatriation

Most Native Americans believe that cultural artifacts have spirits that are suffocating under glass or that their ancestral remains will not rest unless they are reburied with their people. Seneca Nation leader Peter Jemison criticized a museum's display of masks from the Iroquois False Face Society, arguing that they should be seen only in ceremonies. "We consider the masks alive," he explained. "I'm comfortable with the concept of these masks as my uncles."[36] Kurt Dongoske of the Hopi Cultural Preservation Office explains that for the Hopi, "reburial of human remains is the only acceptable mitigation measure for the disturbance of graves because of the Hopi concepts of death. Hopis believe that death initiates two distinct but inseparable journeys, i.e. the physical journey of the body as it returns to a oneness with the earth and the spiritual journey of the soul to a place where it finally resides. A disruption of human remains interrupts and obstructs the spiritual journey. This creates an imbalance within the spiritual world and hence the natural world."[37] Many Native Americans cite the disruption of the spiritual world as the cause of contemporary problems. James Riding In explains the Pawnee worldview by writing, "Wandering spirits often beset the living with psychological and health problems.... Equally critical to our perspective are cultural norms that stressed that those who tampered with the dead did so with profane, evil, or demented intentions. From this vantage point, the study of stolen remains constitutes abominable acts of sacrilege, desecration, and depravity."[38] Not all Indian nations want physical remains returned to them, however. The Navajo, for example, avoid contact with human remains and consider it spiritually dangerous to handle them. For other tribes, however, the return of ancestral bones is considered an important part of cultural regeneration. Sebastian LeBeau of the Cheyenne River Sioux escorted skeletal remains back to his reservation. He believes that "with each return there's a spiritual healing that occurs among our people. What's always been agreed upon is that these ancestors had to come home, that their use for scientific study was wrong."[39]

This intersection of science and religion has been the crux of the debate for prominent Native Americans like Vine Deloria Jr. and Gerald Vizenor. They have written passionately about the issue of repatriation, claiming that Western science has appropriated the bones of Native Americans for the benefit of a select few and in the process have trampled, literally, on Indian burial grounds and, figuratively, on Indians' religious beliefs and freedoms. Vizenor writes, "The bone robber barons, as some archaeologists would be apprehended, are academic neocolonialists and racial technocrats... [who] protect their 'rights' to advance science and careers on the backs of tribal bones."[40] Deloria agrees, arguing that Native Americans have "become the province (and property) of scholars to the extent that the bones of their dead can be disinterred with impunity to be displayed in museum cases or used in speculative scientific experiments."[41]

This attitude helps to explain the reaction of Pacific Northwest Indians to the discovery of the Kennewick Man in 1996, which sharpened Native Americans' belief that their religious rights as well as their oral traditions transcend those of outsiders. Armand Minthorn of the Umatilla tribe helped lead the effort by the five local tribes to repatriate and rebury the remains. Minthorn defended his position, arguing, "Sacred human remains are not artifacts. They are what they are—sacred—and they are our ancestral remains, and they need to be treated as such."[42] Minthorn in particular objected to scientists' claim that the Kennewick Man could not be "culturally affiliated" with the Umatilla or the other local tribes and to their contradictory claim that reburial would destroy his tribe's past. "Some scientists say that if this individual is not studied further we, as Indians, will be destroying evidence of our own history. We already know our history. It is passed on to us through our elders and through our religious practices."[43] Anthropologists who accept the validity of oral traditions, in part because they offer details of climatological conditions accepted by other scientists, have supported Minthorn's claim that the Umatilla have lived in the area for ten thousand years. Deloria considers scientists' resistance to the Kennewick Man repatriation a breach of the law. He asks, "How long are people going to sit by and allow a select group of self-proclaimed experts scream, 'science, science, science' and disrupt their lives and beliefs. NAGPRA has set the limits, and it is up to the people to follow the law, particularly since the law was approved by the mass of professional archaeologists [the Society for American Archaeology endorsed NAGPRA]."[44] Commenting on a case that is similar to the Kennewick Man, Mervin Wright Jr., the tribal chair of the Pyramid Lake Paiute of Nevada, contends, "It's a fundamental problem with science. Scientists feel they have the right to do anything they want to investigate [their theories], without respecting our traditions. They need to accept what we know: that we've always been here. They don't need to look at any skeletons to determine this."[45]

Native Americans involved in repatriation also resent what they see as a double standard in the treatment of their remains and sacred objects. As with issues like Indian-themed sports mascots and images, activists ask whether America would tolerate such treatment of other ethnic or racial groups. Native American journalist Karen Lincoln Michel, a member of Wisconsin's Ho-Chunk Nation, wrote in a 1999 article, "I can't help thinking how other churches would react to their religious paraphernalia being collected, catalogued and put on display with a hodgepodge of items from other cultures. It's not unusual to browse through a paltry collection and find a peace pipe encased next to a war club of an enemy tribe. Somehow I think the Vatican might frown upon seeing a chalice used by Pope Pius XII placed on a museum shelf next to a tea set once owned by Jackie O." Michel admonished readers of the *Milwaukee Journal Sentinel*, "Instead of staring at [sacred items] through the glass case, look at your reflection and ask if you would want your past on display."[46] Native American activists make this argument especially forcefully when it comes to skeletal remains. NARF attorney Walter Echo-Hawk campaigned to close a Pawnee burial mound that a farmer charged admission to view. Echo-Hawk contended in 1990, "Desecrate a white grave and you get jail. Desecrate an Indian grave and you get a PhD."[47] Echo-Hawk made a similar argument to a Senate committee on Indian affairs a year later, testifying that the hundreds of thousands of remains held by museums and universities provide evidence that federal and state laws "which so strongly protect the sanctity of the dead for other citizens and guarantee a decent burial for all citizens have never been extended to include Native Americans."[48] It is this kind of argument, as well as the emotional reaction Native Americans have when seeing the bones of ancestors in museums, that has changed the opinion of a number of museum officials and scientists. Smithsonian secretary Robert McCormick Adams noted in 1989 that it remained hard for him to oppose repatriation. "After some years dealing with Native Americans, their story takes on an anguish . . . and becomes a weight one cannot carry. As I read more about the atrocities, the tragedy takes on a horrible deepness. These are the crimes of the past we cannot afford to repress."[49] Repatriation is, according to the director of the Heard Museum in Phoenix, "a human rights issue. What's at stake is the right [of Native Americans] to exercise custody over their heritage."[50]

Not all Native Americans have exercised this right to custody or have opposed invasive scientific exploration of ancestral remains. As noted previously, when the University of Nebraska agreed to relinquish its claim to Omaha Indians' ancestral remains, tribal officials gave university scientists a year to study the bones. Tribal historian Dennis Hastings supported the use of Western science to help the Omaha understand their past, believing that the solution to the Omaha's problems would be found when "we try to build on the past. It's like a puzzle. First you see where the culture broke and fragmented. Then you try to build on it where people have been practicing it all along. Then people start to think in a healthy way about what they were in the past. If you can get each person to be proud of himself, then, little by little, you can get the whole tribe to become proud."[51] The return of ancestral remains and of cultural artifacts, particularly those that have great symbolic importance, has helped create what Hastings calls a "cultural renaissance." By reclaiming their Sacred Pole and a number of other artifacts formerly held by the Peabody Museum of Harvard University, the Omaha helped rebuild their spiritual infrastructure. W. Richard West, director of the Museum of the American Indian, also uses the word *renaissance* in discussing repatriation. Educated at Harvard and Stanford, the Cheyenne-Arapaho lawyer said in 1990, "Repatriation is the most potent political metaphor for cultural revival that is going on at this time. Political sovereignty and cultural sovereignty are linked inextricably, because the ultimate goal of political sovereignty is the protecting of a way of life."[52]

The battle over repatriation created new bonds of understanding both between and within Native American communities. In November 1995, nine bands of Apache gathered at an All-Apache Summit to address problems with the repatriation process. Museums had classified a number of objects as Apache but had failed to determine *which* tribe of Apache. The summit produced the All-Apache Culture Committee, whose mission was to "oversee and act as an advocate for traditional cultural preservation and the repatriation of Apache cultural items and property." According to Ramon Riley, a Tribal Heritage Program director, the meeting was very productive. "We all thought something like this would never happen. It gives us a tool to work together. Now we're united to fight this."[53]

In January 1999, repatriation also brought a sense of unity to the Iroquois, who were finally able to bring home several hundred ceremonial masks that had been held in the Smithsonian's Heye collection; tribal leaders had fought for their return since the late 1960s. Several Iroquois leaders noted the significance of the repatriation. Rick Hill of the Tuscarora Nation said, "The masks have another whole way of working with the people. We have people working together who previously wouldn't talk to each other over a whole variety of issues, and that's a good feeling." Chief Oren Lyons of the Onondaga Nation, which repatriated 60 masks, agreed with Hill, saying of the masks' return, "I think it's a unifying event. They belong to everybody no matter what; we always try to put all that [discord] aside when we have our ceremonies."[54] Lyons referred to the Iroquois' midwinter ceremonies, perhaps the most important social and spiritual gatherings of the year, which would be made more complete with the return of the masks. The unifying nature of repatriation was evident in June 2000 at the first national Native American Repatriation Summit, organized by Chickasaw and Choctaw representatives to find ways to improve the repatriation process. Said Chickasaw governor Bill Anoatubby, "Hopefully what will come out of this is a continuing effort on the part of the tribes to work together on issues that are cross-cutting and those areas where there is conflict.... It is very difficult to solve these problems alone." Dale Sherman, the NAGPRA coordinator for the National Congress of American Indians, agreed, saying that repatriation "is the one thing that can unite the tribes across the United States. An issue that all of us believe in so much—bring home the ancestors to our communities."[55]

Repatriation has also created better relations between Native Americans and some scientists and museum officials. When Stanford University agreed to repatriate its remains and objects to California tribes in 1989, archaeologist Barbara Bocek argued that the decision reflected "an awakening among archeologists to the fact that we're dealing with the remains of people who still have living descendants."[56] In many cases, museum officials have been stuck in the middle of repatriation debates. While museum administrators object to the workload, complexities, and costs associated with repatriation, many stress their support of the idea of the project. Thomas Livesay, director of the Museum of New Mexico, said that anthropologists criticized him for his support of repatriation. "I respect their positions," he said. "But the position of the museum was the ethical and spiritual concerns of the Indians outweigh those scientific concerns."[57] Interestingly, repatriation has provided new perspectives on anthropological investigations of Native American life. Anthony Klessert, director of the Navajo Nation Archaeological Department, argues that if tribal customs call for items to be reburied or to decompose naturally, as in the case of Zuni War Gods, "from an anthropological point of view, maybe that's what should happen. If the makers, the designers, the users of the item want them destroyed, that's the way it should be."[58]

The debates have also opened new vistas for how museums present Indian culture. The Heard Museum of Phoenix, according to director Martin Sullivan, has made an effort to "redefine our relationship in terms of partnership and an emphasis on living culture."[59] Sullivan sees his profession moving from one characterized by an ethics of conquest to one characterized by collaboration. The Heard now shows the work of contemporary Indian artists as well as exhibits historical artifacts to help tell stories of Indian culture rather than simply emphasize their aesthetic qualities. At most museums, Native Americans are now consulted on NAGPRA issues or pending exhibitions. According to Richard Stofle of the Arizona State Museum, "The museum's going to be a better place because Indian people and museum professionals have gotten together."[60] The repatriation issue has also put pressure on antiquities dealers like Sotheby's to reconsider the sale of sacred Indian items. In several cases Native American leaders have attended Sotheby auctions to discourage buyers from purchasing sacred objects. In others, supporters of Native Americans have purchased them for repatriation purposes. In 1991 Elizabeth Sackler, then president of the Arthur M. Sackler Foundation, bought three items at a Sotheby's auction on behalf of the Navajo and Hopi nations, who had protested the sale. Sackler, who is now president of the American Indian Ritual Object Repatriation Foundation, explained her actions by saying, "I would hope more people would become more sensitive to other cultures. These Indian cultures are not dead. It's important for the art world to distinguish between objects of art and sacred objects of living cultures. These masks are part of a spiritual, ceremonial life, now in 1991."[61]

Native American activists resent the attitude of non-Indian administrators and scientists who worry about the fate of objects and remains returned to native communities. Pemina Yellow Bird, who for years has sought the return of sacred objects to their tribal homes, angrily claims, "the fact that they won't return things unless tribes have repositories that meet current museum standards is another example of shoving the white man's paradigms down our throats. How do you think these ancient things got in their possession if Native people didn't know how to take care of them? And who are they to tell us how to take care of our own sacred objects?"[62] The search for ancestral remains and tribal artifacts coincided with Native Americans' commitment to build museums to present their own histories. By the late 1990s, nearly two hundred Native American museums had been opened, providing a place to exhibit tribal artifacts as well as an opportunity for continued research, provided that scientists follow tribal guidelines. Some Indian museums have consulted with national museums to strengthen their security and exhibition facilities. Other Indian nations, lacking funds or space, have appreciated how museums treat their artifacts, and in some cases they leave them in their care. Native Americans, reendowed with this valuable material and invested with the responsibility of protecting it, have also become more interested in the archaeological and anthropological professions to help manage future collections.

Whether Indians or non-Indians exhibit the history, repatriation has brought Native Americans into contact with their respective tribal pasts. The right to repatriate remains led the Pawnee to the skulls of the six beheaded Pawnee scouts, which had languished in the Smithsonian Institution for more than a century. The U.S. Army was notified and, appalled by the facts of the case, got involved in the repatriation process. Army generals met Pawnee leaders at the airport and arranged for a full military escort of the remains in their return to Nebraska. In another ignominious case of the 1860s, more than one hundred and fifty Cheyenne and Arapaho were slaughtered by Colorado state militia, which sent a number of the bodies to the Smithsonian for study, on orders of the U.S. Army. When Arapaho chiefs went to reclaim these remains in 1996 they noticed that the skulls were punctured by bullet holes, revealing the extreme violence of the killing. Sioux leaders also had a visceral reaction to seeing the remains of their ancestors, especially those killed in the Wounded Knee massacre of 1890. As Avis Little Eagle wrote in *Indian Country Today,* "Viewing the skeletal remains of infants, children, and women—some with their heads caved in or with bullet holes marring their skulls—has been the hardest thing for one Oglala spiritual leader."[63] But Roger Byrd, the Oglala repatriation officer, is excited about the project, which will bring home bows, pipes, medicine bundles, and other objects of cultural and spiritual significance. Reburial or burning ceremonies will allow the freed spirits to continue their journey and will help the Sioux grieve and thus move into the future. This goes back to the themes of unification and spiritual or cultural renaissance. Cecil Anton, an official of the Gila River Indian community near Phoenix, believes repatriation has given his people "a tremendous lift. The younger people that take part in the reburials, they have more of a sense of their culture.... It gives them a sense of where they came from."[64] By taking control of their past, Native Americans feel better prepared to face the future. Suzan Harjo, a former director of the National Congress of American Indians who helped push for the passage of NAGPRA, has been fighting the repatriation battle for three decades. In the late 1960s, "A Cheyenne elder told us our nations couldn't heal and couldn't regain our strength and we as individuals couldn't heal until we recovered our dead relatives from these places and our sacred objects, our living beings." Harjo praises the efforts of the U.S. government by calling NAGPRA "a courageous" piece of federal legislation, "but more importantly it legislates respect about and for the human remains and sacred items of our Nations."[65] The healing, then, goes both ways—for both Indian nations and the United States, whose policies helped to create the plaintive and compelling cries for repatriation from Native Americans across the country.

NOTES

1. Shirley English, "Wounded Knee Shirt Is Going Home to the Sioux," *Times* (London), 20 November 1998.

2. Robert D. Hicks, "Time Crime: Protecting the Past for Future Generations," *FBI Law Enforcement Bulletin* 66, no. 7, (July 1997): 2.

3. *American Indian Religious Freedom Act, U.S. Statutes at Large* 92 (1978): 469–70.

4. *Archeological Resources Protection Act, U.S. Statutes at Large* 93 (1979): 721–23.

5. Kara Swisher, "Artifacts, Bones Spark the Last of Indian Battles," *Los Angeles Times,* 8 October 1989.

6. Anne C. Roark, "Stanford Agrees to Return Indian Skeletal Remains," *Los Angeles Times,* 22 June 1989.

7. Quoted in Alvin Josephy, Jr., et al. eds. *Red Power: American Indians' Fight for Freedom*, 2d ed. (Lincoln: University of Nebraska, 1999), 229.

8. Quoted in *Red Power*, 230.

9. John Elson, "Returning Bones of Contention: A Bitter Debate over Spiritual Values and Scholarly Needs," *Time,* 25 September 1989, p. 61.

10. *Native American Graves Protection and Repatriation Act, U.S. Statutes at Large* 104 (1990): 3048, 3050–55, 3057.

11. Swisher, "Artifacts, Bones."

12. Robert K. Landers, "Is America Allowing Its Past to Be Stolen?" *The CQ Researcher: Editorial Research Reports* 1, no. 3 *Congressional Quarterly Inc.*, 1991, p. 5.

13. Frank Aukofer, "Museums Hurt by Law on Indian Remains," *Milwaukee Journal Sentinel,* 6 December 1995.

14. "Iroquois Are Seeking Return of Ancient Belts Locked in Museum," *New York Times,* 16 April 1970.

15. Tom Uhlenbrock, "Bones of Contention...Skeletal Remains and Sacred Objects Put Art Museums and Indians at Odds," *St. Louis Post-Dispatch,* 7 April 1991.

16. Quoted in *Red Power.*

17. "Smithsonian in Dispute over Indian Skeletons," *New York Times,* 14 February 1986.

18. "Indians Seek Burial of Smithsonian Skeletons," *New York Times,* 8 December 1987.

19. Virginia Morell, "An Anthropological Culture Shift," *Science,* 1 April 1994, p. 20.

20. Clement W. Meighan, "Some Scholars' Views on Reburial," in *Repatriation Reader: Who Owns American Indian Remains?* edited by Devon A. Mihesuah (Lincoln: University of Nebraska Press, 2000), p. 196.

21. Patricia Landau and D. Gentry Steele, "Why Anthropologists Study Human Remains," in Mihesuah, *Repatriation Reader*, p. 90.

22. Meighan, "Some Scholars' Views on Reburial," p. 195.

23. David Arnold, "Indian Artifacts: Where Do They Rightfully Belong?" *Boston Globe*, 2 April 1990.

24. Morell, "An Anthropological Culture Shift," p. 21.

25. Paul Boyer, "Who Owns the Past? New Law on the Return of Indian Remains Challenges Both Scientists and Tribal Communities," *Tribal College Journal of American Indian Higher Education,* 31 January 1991, p. 6.

26. Morell, "An Anthropological Culture Shift," p. 22.

27. David Hurst Thomas, *Skull Wars: Kennewick Man, Archaeology, and the Battle for Native American Identity* (New York: Basic Books, 2000).

28. Leslie Alan Horvitz, "Indians and Anthropologists Are Battling over Old Bones," *Insight on the News,* 18 November 1996, p. 40.

29. Virginia Morell, "Kennewick Man's Trials Continue," *Science,* 10 April 1998, p. 190.

30. Horvitz, "Indians and Anthropologists."

31. "Skull Wars," *Current Events* 100, 27 October 2000, p. 3.

32. Morell, "Kennewick Man's Trials Continue," p. 190.

33. Horvitz, "Indians and Anthropologists," p. 41.

34. Morell, "Kennewick Man's Trials Continue," p. 191.

35. "Should Scientists Be Allowed to 'Study' the Skeletons of Ancient American Indians?" panel discussion, *Insight on the News,* 22 December 1997, p. 24.

36. Mike Vogel, "Museums Join in Negotiations on Artifacts Indian Items Sought in Local Collections," *Buffalo News,* 27 November 1993.

37. Kurt Dongoske, "The Native American Graves Protection and Repatriation Act: A New Beginning, Not the End for Osteological Analysis: A Hopi Perspective," *American Indian Quarterly* 20, no. 2 (spring 1996), p. 293.

38. James Riding In, "Repatriation: A Pawnee's Perspective," in Mihesuah, *Repatriation Reader*, p. 109.

39. Dennis O'Brien, "The Repatriation of Indian Remains," *Baltimore Sun,* 12 September 1996.

40. Gerald Vizenor, *Crossbloods: Bone Courts, Bingo, and Other Reports* (Minneapolis: University of Minnesota Press, 1990), p. 67.

41. Vine Deloria Jr., "Sacred Lands and Religious Freedom," *Native American Rights Fund Legal Review* 16, no. 2 (summer 1991). <www.sacredland.org/vinetext.html>.

42. "Bones of Contention," *PBS Newshour with Jim Lehrer,* 19 June 2001.

43. Thomas, *Skull Wars*, p. 239.

44. Vine Deloria Jr., "Balancing Science, Culture. Do Scientists Have Rights to All Finds?" *Denver Post,* 29 November 1998.

45. Morell, "Kennewick Man's Trials Continue," p. 191.

46. Karen Lincoln Michel, "Let Her People—and Their History—Go," *Milwaukee Public Sentinel,* 14 November 1999.

47. Arnold, "Indian Artifacts."

48. Landers, "Is America Allowing Its Past to Be Stolen?," p. 38.

49. Swisher, "Artifacts, Bones."

50. Boyer, "Who Owns the Past?," p. 6.

51. Fergus M. Bordewich, *Killing the White Man's Indian: Reinventing Native Americans at the End of the Twentieth Century* (New York: Anchor Books, 1996), p. 169.

52. Bordewich, *Killing the White Man's Indian*, p. 171.

53. "Summit Brings Unity to Protection of Apache Culture," *Fort Apache Scout,* 10 November 1995.

54. Liz Urbanski Farrell, "Seven Sacred Masks Returned to Tuscarora," *Buffalo News,* 17 January 1999.

55. Mary Pierpont, "Tribes Hope to Find Answers to Repatriation Issues in Unity," *Indian Country Today,* 21 June 2000.

56. Roark, "Stanford Agrees to Return Indian Skeletal Remains."

57. Kim Cobb, "Return of the Native: Too Many Remains and Too Little Money," *Houston Chronicle,* 26 November 1995.

58. K. J. Killheffer, "Reburying the Past," *Omni,* (winter 1995): 33.

59. Ralph Blumenthal, "Making Peace with Museums to Celebrate Their Culture; Phoenix Points the Way to Full Indian Collaboration," *New York Times*, 13 May 1999.

60. Killheffer, "Reburying the Past," p. 36.

61. "Art Patron Explains Why Native American Masks Belong with Tribes," *Christian Science Monitor*, 12 June 1991.

62. Tallman, "Repatriation Demanded across the Country."

63. Avis Little Eagle, "OST [Oglala Sioux Tribe] Repatriating and Reburying Relatives," *Indian Country Today*, 23 February 1994.

64. Jesse Emspak, "Repatriation Battles," *The Progressive*, July 1995, p. 15.

65. Kallen M. Martin, "The Beginning of Respect: The U.S. Repatriation Law," *Native Americas*, 30 September 1997, p. 27.

QUESTIONS

1) Imagine you went to a museum and discovered the bones of your ancestors on exhibit. How would you feel and on what grounds would you claim ownership of them?
2) Is it appropriate to distinguish between the right of a museum to own human bones and its right to own objects?
3) Is it appropriate to distinguish between the right of a museum to own cultural artifacts like drums and masks and its right to own funereal objects, those used in burial ceremonies?
4) Should scientists be allowed to examine the skeletal remains of ancient American Indians like the Kennewick Man? Why or why not?
5) What are the principal points of debate in the Kennewick Man controversy for both sides?
6) What is the role of religion in this debate? How do both sides view it?
7) Can one compare the religious dimensions of this issue with those of the mascot issue? What are the common features of these two debates?
8) Compare Native American views on burial with those of your religion. Are there differences? Is there common ground?
9) What is the most compelling reason to accept repatriation?
10) What is the most compelling reason to oppose repatriation?
11) Does the federal government's support of repatriation violate the separation of church and state?
12) Write an essay on the Kennewick Man controversy. How was it resolved? What were the final arguments on both sides?
13) What is the most interesting repatriation case, and in what ways does it help you understand the Native American point of view?
14) Research the Zuni tribe's pursuit of their *Ahayuda*, or War Gods. What legal, ethical, and religious dimensions define this particular repatriation case?

15) Research the case of Ishi's brain, mentioned only briefly in this chapter. What were the reasons for his brain's being sent to the Smithsonian Institution? To what extent does this expropriation reflect a colonial mind-set?

16) Visit a local museum containing an Indian artifact. Research the process by which that artifact ended up in the museum. In doing so, interview the museum director to get his or her views on repatriation. Has she or he dealt with NAGPRA issues?

17) Research the history of repatriation in your state. How does this history add to your understanding of the issue? In addition, has grave robbing been a problem in your state? If so, how have the cases been resolved?

18) A skeleton is found in your community. Stage a mock debate similar to the one that arose over the Kennewick Man case by developing legal briefs representing a tribal claim of the remains and the arguments of scientists for its continued study.

RESOURCE GUIDE

Suggested Readings

American Indian Ritual Object Repatriation Foundation. *Mending the Circle: A Native American Repatriation Guide (Understanding and Implementing NAGPRA, the Official Smithsonian and Other Repatriation Policies).* New York: American Indian Ritual Object Repatriation Foundation, 1997.

Arden, Harvey. "Who Owns Our Past?" *National Geographic,* March 1989.

Arnold, David. "Indian Artifacts: Where Do They Rightfully Belong?" *Boston Globe,* 2 April 1990.

Biolsi, Thomas, and Larry J. Zimmerman, eds. *Indians and Anthropologists: Vine Deloria and the Critique of Anthropology.* Tucson: University of Arizona Press, 1997.

Blumenthal, Ralph. "Making Peace with Museums to Celebrate Their Culture; Phoenix Points the Way to Full Indian Collaboration." *New York Times,* 13 May 1999.

Bordewich, Fergus M. *Killing the White Man's Indian: Reinventing Native Americans at the End of the Twentieth Century.* New York: Anchor Books, 1996.

Bowman, Margaret B. "The Reburial of Native American Skeletal Remains: Approaches to the Resolution of a Conflict." *Harvard Environmental Law Review* 13, no. 1 (1989).

Cowley, Geoffrey, and Andrew Murr. "The Plunder of the Past." *Newsweek,* 26 June 1989.

Deloria, Vine, Jr. "Balancing Science, Culture. Do Scientists Have Rights to All Finds?" *Denver Post,* 29 November 1998.

———. *Red Earth, White Lies.* New York: Scribner, 1995.

Dongoske, Kurt. "The Native American Graves Protection and Repatriation Act: A New Beginning, Not the End for Osteological Analysis: A Hopi Perspective." *American Indian Quarterly* 20, no. 2 (spring 1996).

Echo-Hawk, Roger, and Walter R. Echo-Hawk. "Repatriation, Reburial, and Religious Rights." In *American Indians in American History, 1870–2001,* edited by Sterling Evans. Westport, Conn.: Praeger, 2002.

Echo-Hawk, Walter R. "Tribal Efforts to Protect against Mistreatment of Indian Dead: The Quest for Equal Protection of the Laws." *Native American Rights Fund Legal Review* 1 (winter 1988).

Elson, John. "Returning Bones of Contention: A Bitter Debate over Spiritual Values and Scholarly Needs." *Time,* 25 September 1989.

Fabian, Ann. "Bones of Contention." *Common-Place,* January 2001. Available online. <www.common-place.org/vol-01/no-02/kennewick/kennewick-3.shtml>.

Ferguson, T. J., Roger Anyon, and Edmund J. Ladd. "Repatriation at the Pueblo of Zuni: Diverse Solutions to Complex Problems." *American Indian Quarterly* 20, no. 2 (spring 1996).

Graber, Dorothy J. "Anna Lee Walter's Ghost Singer Links Native Diasporas in Time and Space." *Wicazo sa review: A Journal of Native American Studies* 15, no. 2 (2000).

Green, Rayna, and Nancy Marie Mitchell, eds. *American Indian Sacred Objects, Skeletal Remains, Repatriation and Reburial: A Resource Guide.* BIBLIO, Washington D.C.: Smithsonian Institution, 1992.

Grimes, Ronald L. "Desecration of the Dead: An Inter-Religious Controversy." *American Indian Quarterly* 10 (fall 1986).

Hurst Thomas, David. *Skull Wars: Kennewick Man, Archaeology, and the Battle for Native American Identity.* New York: Basic Books, 2000.

Killheffer, K. J. "Reburying the Past." *Omni,* winter 1995.

Layton, R., ed. *Conflict in the Archaeology of Living Traditions.* London: Routledge, 1989.

Little Eagle, Avis. "OST [Oglala Sioux Tribe] Repatriating and Reburying Relatives." *Indian Country Today,* 23 February 1994.

Martin, Kallen M. "The Beginning of Respect: The U.S. Repatriation Law." *Native Americas,* 30 September 1997.

McGuire, Randall H. "The Sanctity of the Grave: White Concepts and American Indian Burial." In *Conflict in the Archaeology of Living Traditions,* edited by R. Layton. London: Routledge, 1989.

Messenger, Phyllis M. *The Ethics of Collecting Cultural Property: Whose Culture, Whose Property?* Albuquerque: University of New Mexico Press, 1999.

Mihesuah, Devon A. *Repatriation Reader: Who Owns American Indian Remains?* Lincoln: University of Nebraska Press, 2000.

Monroe, Dan L. "The Politics of Repatriation." In *American Indian Studies: An Interdisciplinary Approach to Contemporary Issues,* edited by Dane Morrison. New York: Peter Lang, 1997.

Morell, Virginia. "An Anthropological Culture Shift." *Science,* 1 April 1994.

———. "Kennewick Man's Trials Continue." *Science,* 10 April 1998.

Pierpont, Mary. "Tribes Hope to Find Answers to Repatriation Issues in Unity." *Indian Country Today,* 21 June 2000.

Preston, Douglas. "The Lost Man." *New Yorker,* 16 June 1997. Essay on the Kennewick Man.

———. "Skeletons in Our Museums' Closets." *Harper's Magazine,* February 1989.

Ravesloot, John. "On the Treatment and Reburial of Human Remains." *American Indian Quarterly* 14 (winter 1990).

Repatriation: An Interdisciplinary Dialogue. Special issue of *American Indian Quarterly* 20 (spring 1996).

"Should Scientists Be Allowed to 'Study' the Skeletons of Ancient American Indians?" Panel discussion. *Insight on the News,* 22 December 1997.

Spotted Elk, Clara. "Skeletons in the Closet (Indian Bones Profanely Gather Dust in Museums)." *New York Times,* 8 March 1989.

Talbot, Steve. "Desecration and American Indian Religious Freedom." *Journal of Ethnic Studies* 12, no. 4 (1984).

Thomas, David Hurst. *Skull Wars: Kennewick Man, Archaeology, and the Battle for Native American Identity.* New York: Basic Books, 2000.

Thornton, Russell. "Who Owns Our Past?: The Repatriation of Native American Human Remains and Cultural Objects." In *Studying Native America: Problems and Prospects,* edited by Russell Thornton. Madison: University of Wisconsin Press, 1998.

Vizenor, Gerald. "Bone Courts: The Rights and Narrative Representation of Tribal Bones." *American Indian Quarterly* 10 (fall 1986).

———. *Crossbloods: Bone Courts, Bingo, and Other Reports.* Minneapolis: University of Minnesota Press, 1990.

Walters, Anna Lee. *Ghost Singer.* Albuquerque: University of New Mexico Press, 1988.

Zimmerman, Larry J. "Made Radical By My Own: An Archeologist Learns to Accept Reburial." In *Conflict in the Archaeology of Living Traditions,* edited by R. Layton. London: Routledge, 1989.

Videos

"Mystery of the First Americans." *NOVA.* 15 February 2000. Companion Web site: <www.pbs.org/wgbh/nova/first>.

Science or Sacrilege? The video "examines [NAGPRA's] underlying moral and political issues, the practical consequences, and the prospects for science in the post-NAGPRA world." For information, e-mail dbickley@uclink.berkeley.edu.

60 Minutes. CBS News. 25 October 1998. Segment devoted to the Kennewick Man controversy.

Web Sites

American Indian Ritual Object Repatriation Foundation. <www.repatriationfoundation.org>. A non–federally funded organization facilitating repatriation.

"Bones of Contention." *PBS Online.* 19 June 2001. <www.pbs.org/newshour/bb/science/jan-june01/kennewick_6–19.html>. Transcript of PBS show interviewing all the principals of the Kennewick Man debate.

Confederated Tribes of the Umatilla Indian Reservation. <www.umatilla.nsn.us>. Web site of the Umatilla tribe, which claims the Kennewick Man as an ancestor.

Friends of the Past. <www.friendsofpast.org/news.html>. Friends of the Past supports scientific exploration of the Kennewick Man and other remains.

"Kennewick Man." *National Park Service Archeology and Ethnography Program.* <www.cr.nps.gov/aad/kennewick>. National Park Service site on the Kennewick Man, with scientific data.

Kennewick Man Virtual Interpretive Center. <www.kennewick-man.com>. Site on the Kennewick Man controversy.

"National NAGPRA Database." *National Park Service.* <www.cast.uark.edu/other/nps/nagpra>. National Park Service site with good links to historical documents and to the Kennewick Man controversy.

Native American Graves Protection and Repatriation Act. National Park Service. 16 November 1990. <www.cast.uark.edu/other/nps/nagpra/DOCS/lgm003.html>. Text of NAGPRA.

Native American Repatriation and Reburial: A Bibliography. <www-sul.stanford.edu/depts/ssrg/native/appf.html>. Extensive bibliography compiled by Barbara Bocek, a Stanford University archaeologist.

"Repatriation Issues." *Society for American Archaeology.* <www.saa.org/Repatriation/index.html>. Repatriation issues section of the Society for American Archaeology.

"Repatriation Program, Department of Anthropology." *National Museum of Natural History, Smithsonian Institution.* <www.nmnh.si.edu/anthro/repatriation>.

5

NATIVE AMERICAN GAMING

GAMBLING IN THE UNITED STATES: A QUICK OVERVIEW

Gambling has a long history in America, beginning with Native Americans' pre-Columbian gambling practices and continuing with the advent of colonial society. Puritan settlements in New England initially banned dice and card games but gradually loosened their rules. In the Virginia Colony in the 1600s, settlers bet on horse races as well as cockfights. Financiers of the Virginia Colony used lotteries to help raise funds for their venture. By the time of the Revolutionary War, all 13 colonies had used lotteries for one purpose or another, raising funds for schools (including Harvard and Princeton), public works, churches, and even, in an effort that failed, for waging war against the British, which had attempted to regulate colonists' lotteries. Benjamin Franklin, for one, supported the use of lotteries for civic purposes. Lotteries, betting on horse racing, and dice and card games continued to be popular into the nineteenth century. But in Victorian America, in the late nineteenth century, gambling was frowned upon and became an illegal, underground practice; some states had to agree to ban casinos in order to gain statehood. This antigambling attitude changed during the Great Depression. Bingo became a way to raise revenue for stricken communities. In 1931, Massachusetts "decriminalized" bingo to help charitable groups raise funds to help the needy. Horse racing also became legal and popular again, especially in California. The new gambling culture also sought to stamp out illegal gambling, forcing organized crime syndicates to find new venues for their operations, particularly Las Vegas. In the 1930s, Las Vegas began its run as the most popular casino-gambling destination in the country, helped by Nevada's liberal laws and the crackdown on gaming elsewhere in the country. The presence of organized crime in Nevada turned many states against casino-type gaming, and until 1978 it was the only state in the country to offer such high-stakes games. In 1978, Atlantic City, New Jersey, was a run-down seaside resort town. Civic leaders and businesspersons including Donald Trump hoped that casino gambling would help Atlantic City restore its appeal and become once again a popular tourist destination; casino operators like Trump have done well on the boardwalk, though it remains to be seen whether gambling will boost the general fortunes of Atlantic City. Casino-type gambling was restricted to Nevada and Atlantic City until 1988, when Native American gambling began to change the face of the country's gambling world.

NATIVE AMERICAN GAMBLING

Native Americans had played games and engaged in sporting contests like foot races, canoe races, lacrosse, wrestling, and archery for centuries, before Europeans arrived with their own ideas about leisure sports. Native Americans also placed bets on their games and sporting events, just as Europeans did. Stories of Indian gambling are found in tribal oral histories and Native American literature, and archeological evidence supports its occurrence. For example, the Navajo played stick dice and arrow and moccasin games as well as gambled, informally, on foot and horse races. The Dakota played a hand game called "hitting the bones" *(hampa ape' achunjpi)* and other forms of gambling that were used for healing and decision-making purposes, among others. The Crow Indians' favorite gambling game was "hiding," a guessing game; the Crow also had dice games, usually played by women, and gambled on various athletic contests like shinny, or "ball-striking." Native American gambling took many forms in premodern times, just as it does today; it could be ceremonial, social, or charitable. Native Americans also incorporated non–Native American games like poker and monte into their rituals. The overarching theme of Native American gambling before the 1980s, however, was that it served a social purpose rather than a financial purpose—it was cultural rather than practical.

The modern era of Native American gambling began in Florida in 1979 when the Seminole Nation ignored a Florida state law capping gambling jackpots at $100 by running high-stakes bingo games that offered a top prize of $10,000. Florida officials attempted to shut down the operation, but the Seminole sued the state on the grounds that it was a sovereign nation, protected by the federal government. In 1981, the U.S. Fifth Circuit Court of Appeals ruled in *Seminole Tribe of Florida v. Butterworth* that because Florida permitted bingo games off the reservation it had no legal authority to prohibit or establish guidelines for them on Indian reservations. As a result, the Seminole expanded their operations, began earning millions of dollars in revenue, and inspired other Native American groups to do the same. Another important impact was that the case helped to articulate for many Indian activists, and introduced to many American citizens for the first time, the general terms of Indian sovereignty—what a federally recognized Indian community's rights were in relation to state laws and regulations. Indian nations enjoyed a particular suite of legal protections guaranteed by congressional acts and Supreme Court cases; they were considered "nations within the nation," answerable only to their tribal governments or to the federal government, with the exception of certain state criminal statutes.

Outside the Seminole reservation, bingo gambling became especially popular in southern California. Small tribal groups like the Morongo, the Rincon, the Viejas, and the Cabazon Band of Mission Indians set up bingo parlors in the 1980s. They too faced efforts by law enforcement officials to shut them down. In response, these California tribes filed suit to protect what they considered to be their sovereign right to stage bingo games. In February 1987, the U.S. Supreme Court addressed this question of Indian sovereignty in a landmark court case, *California v. Cabazon Band of Mission Indians.* The issues of the case were similar to the Seminole battle with Florida: California officials had attempted to prevent the Cabazon Indians from running a bingo enterprise on their reservation. After a series of court battles the decision was put in the hands of the Supreme Court, which ruled by a vote of six to three that California state regulatory measures infringed upon the rights of the tribal government; the Court noted that California itself encouraged its citizens on a daily basis to participate in its own state-run gambling enterprise, the state lottery. The bottom line for the Supreme Court was that federal and tribal interests took precedence over state-level attempts to ban or regulate Indian gambling enterprises.

The Court's decision set a legal precedent that created additional interest among Native American groups for establishing gaming operations. At the time of the Cabazon court ruling, Indian gaming, much of it bingo related, was already a multimillion-dollar industry, bringing in more than $100 million per year. A nonprofit organization, the National Indian Gaming Association, was created in 1985 to facilitate the growth of Native America's new economic weapon. This interest in gambling was largely influenced by necessity. During the 1980s, the Reagan administration had made drastic cuts in federal aid to Native American communities, exacerbating already entrenched poverty conditions. By 1989, median family incomes in Indian communities amounted to roughly $13,000 compared with nearly $34,000 in the rest of the country; more than 47 percent of Indian families lived below the poverty line compared with the national average of 11.5; and Native Americans' alcoholism and suicide rates were much higher than in other communities.[1] But facing an expanding number of high-stakes bingo operations on Indian reservations and reports of Indians being defrauded by whites and Indians alike, federal officials began to consider the need to provide some kind of governmental system to prevent organized crime infiltration, to protect Indians' interests, and to foster a standardized process by which Native Americans asserted their sovereignty in states with different legal cultures, many of them antagonistic to the concept of Indian sovereignty.

THE INDIAN GAMING REGULATORY ACT OF 1988

In October 1988, in response to the Cabazon case, to the spread of Indian gaming, and to the endemic poverty in Native America, Congress passed the Indian Gaming Regulatory Act (IGRA), a far-reaching piece of legislation that produced the statutory basis for the administration of Indian gaming businesses. The language of the act indicated that the legislation was designed to promote "tribal economic development, self-sufficiency, and strong tribal governments," shield them "from organized crime and other corrupting influences," and "ensure that the Indian tribe is the primary beneficiary of the gaming operation."[2] The impetus of IGRA thus came from two directions. One, Congress wanted to give Native American communities an opportunity for revenue generation at a time when many of them did not have reliable sources of income or a stable job base. And two, Congress wanted to bring order out of potential chaos by establishing various criteria for Indian gambling and a method by which tribal communities could negotiate with state governments to reach an acceptable compromise and mitigate against tribe-state legal warfare. To oversee this increasingly complex field of Native American gaming, IGRA created within the Department of the Interior its own organization, the National Indian Gaming Commission.

IGRA created three types of gaming, the criteria of which remain in effect today. "Class I gaming" referred to low-stakes games or "traditional" games of chance that did not involve large prizes and were part of tribal ceremonies or celebrations; only tribal representatives are permitted to regulate Class I games. "Class II gaming" covered any form of bingo (including electronic versions), related games like pull tabs, lotto, punch boards, and tip jars, as well as " nonbanking" card games like poker; Class II games are regulated by tribal officials, but they fall under the jurisdiction of IGRA and thus only federal guidelines apply. It was the Seminole and Cabazon court decisions that protected this form of tribal sovereignty from state intervention. "Class III gaming" dealt with all other forms of gambling games. The major component in IGRA is that which dealt with Class III gaming, or casino-type games such as roulette, lotteries, "banking" card games like blackjack, and craps. The principal difference between Class II and Class III games is that in Class III game gamblers bet against the house, or the business, rather than against other gamblers.

The most important aspect of IGRA was the provision stating that if the proposed form of Class III gaming was permitted by state law, then IGRA required state governments to negotiate with Indian nations "in good faith" to establish "compacts," essentially agreements permitting those state-approved casino-type games within a reservation's borders; the compacts created rules governing the kind of games permitted, articulated the standards that needed to be followed, determined appropriate reimbursements to the state, and defined the particular role of tribal and state officials in keeping tabs on operations. Importantly, IGRA guidelines stipulated that if states failed to negotiate "in good faith," after 180 days tribal officials could request a federal mediator to resolve the conflict; the mediator in turn could choose either the state's or the tribe's best offer. This provision was included in anticipation of state resistance to the expansion of Indian gaming.

IGRA had three main effects. One, it codified previous federal court rulings establishing Indian political sovereignty in the economic realm of gambling by prohibiting state intervention in Class I and Class II kinds of games. Two, it established criteria for the distribution of tribal gambling revenue to ensure that it went to further tribal self-sufficiency rather than enrich individuals, either Indian or white. Three, IGRA opened the door to state influence of Indian operation of Class III or casino-type games by requiring tribal groups to negotiate with state governments to establish compacts. Representatives of some state governments, influenced in part by heavy lobbying by Nevada gaming interests, had fought hard for this compact provision in order to retain some degree of control over the expansion of Indian gambling within their borders. There had been to this point a lot of tension between state governments and Indian governments, in part because some state officials refused to recognize the basic principle of Indian sovereignty that Congress had articulated and that the federal courts had upheld. Many tribal officials worried that this compact provision would undercut their ability to create and maintain businesses without state interference. By 1995, the U.S. Supreme Court had pending before it 10 lawsuits filed by tribes protesting state restrictions on casino games.

EARLY RESISTANCE TO INDIAN GAMING

During the early 1990s, several cases demonstrated the difficulty and limitations of the compact negotiation process as state governments sought to expand their regulatory control over Indian affairs by either holding up the process or condemning it altogether. In 1990, in a states' rights argument that goes back to the 1800s, the State of Mississippi opposed IGRA's provision requiring the negotiation of compacts, protesting that Congress lacked constitutional authority to require state governments to obey federal court rulings like that of *California v. Cabazon*. Officials in Arizona, Alabama, Florida, and Washington subsequently filed similar complaints. State governments boldly resisted federal assertions of Indian sovereignty. The most notable case of state resistance involved the Mashantucket Pequot of Connecticut. In the early 1970s, the tribe consisted of one elderly member living on 178 acres of protected federal land. Fearing a state takeover of the land and the end of the official tribe at the time of her death, Elizabeth George helped to reconstitute the Pequot Nation with the help of her grandson Richard Hayward, who engineered an economic recovery in the 1980s using the vehicle of bingo gambling. After the Cabazon decision, the Pequot began negotiating with the State of Connecticut to create a compact permitting them to stage Class III gaming, citing Connecticut's gambling revenue and policy of allowing charities to hold "Las Vegas Nights" as their legal basis; Connecticut collected more than $265 million in gambling revenue in the 1989 fiscal year. Claiming that the two kinds of gambling were different, and fearing an infiltration of organized crime, state officials refused to negotiate with the Pequot. After a series of lawsuits, a federal court of appeals compelled them to work with the Pequot to produce a compact governing the casino's operation, exercising the IGRA provision designed to prevent state governments from stonewalling. When presented with the option of signing a compact granting them the right to oversee the operation, an unusual right granted by the Pequot, the state again resisted, appealing to the U.S. Supreme Court. But on April 22, 1991, the Court refused to hear the case, in essence forcing Connecticut to adhere to federal law. The Pequot became fabulously wealthy during the 1990s, and today operate what they claim is the world's largest and most profitable casino. Connecticut also learned from its early legal battles and benefited from subsequent negotiations with the Pequot Nation. In return for the state's permission to operate slot machines, the Pequot agreed to give Connecticut annual payments of at least $100 million. The result was that the Pequot's casino, Foxwoods, inspired other Native American tribes to set up casinos, while other state governments dissected the long and tense legal drama that culminated in Foxwoods's creation.

Another important event in the early development of Native American gaming was the violent confrontation that erupted between antigambling and pro-gambling forces on the Akwesasne–St. Regis reservation during the spring of 1990. The reservation straddles the U.S.-Canadian border along the St. Lawrence River, with jurisdiction shared by New York State and Ontario provincial authorities. In 1984, a bingo hall opened on the reservation, setting off a debate on the place of gambling in Mohawk society that grew increasingly violent. By 1989, six casinos were in operation, and opponents of gambling, called "antis," began to protest by smashing slot machines and roulette tables and, in one case, burning down a casino. An armed militia called the Mohawk Sovereign Security Force, or Warrior Society, began to protect casinos with automatic weapons. In March 1990, gun battles between the two factions began; a month later, pro-gambling forces smashed through roadblocks that had been set up to deter gamblers and attacked a tribal police station. The violence culminated in May when two Mohawk were killed, one from each faction. The killings brought in Canadian and U.S. officials to mediate what amounted to a civil war between pro-gambling and antigam-

The Mashantucket Pequot Foxwoods Resort and Casino in Ledyard, Connecticut. (AP/Wide World Photos)

bling Mohawk forces that escalated into a battle for control of the reservation. It was also a clash of cultures between "traditional" Mohawk opposed to gambling and "bingo chiefs," tribal members focused on economic development. For the latter group, gambling was a replacement for traditional occupations like fishing and dairy farming, which had been hurt by pollution. For traditional Mohawk, the casinos would, as an antigambling spokeswoman put it, "kill the Mohawk people, our culture, our history. It would all die."[3]

The Pequot and the Mohawk cases serve as the two poles of the Native American gaming experience. Somewhere between the tragic violence of the Mohawk situation and the astonishing success of the Pequot lay the future of an economic development agenda that would have far-reaching consequences for Native American political culture, legal sovereignty, and cultural identity.

FRAMING THE ISSUE

In December 1993, the *Cornell Hotel and Restaurant Administration Quarterly* published an article titled "Gaming in the U.S.—A Ten-Year Comparison." The article addressed several important trends in American gaming, one of which was the growth of Native American gambling enterprises and revenue since the 1981 *Seminole Tribe of Florida v. Butterworth* court decision that helped to launch the modern era of tribal gambling operations. The reporter found that in 25 states (out of 34 with federally recognized Indian communities) "170 of the 314 recognized tribes in the United States currently offer gaming. In the last four years [since IGRA was passed] the number of tribes providing legalized gambling has grown at a compounded average rate of 15 percent a year." Revenue from Indian gaming in 1993 was roughly $6 billion. Gary Vallen, the author of the study, predicted that "it won't be long before gaming on reservations is as commonplace as amusement parks as a form of recreation." What was interesting about the article, beyond the data indicating rapid growth of gambling revenues for Native American communities, was the extent to which gambling around the country had also become ubiquitous and profitable; Vallen, a former analyst for a large casino company, wrote that since 1983 "the growth of legalized gambling in the United States has reached a feverish pitch."[4] With the exception of Hawaii and Utah, all states had one form of gambling or another. Riverboat gambling had become particularly attractive to states along the Mississippi River; for example, Tunica County in Mississippi, once one of the poorest in the country, had prospered due to a floating casino. The number of states offering casino-type gambling had risen from the original two of Nevada and New Jersey to 13. Most significantly, the combined take from state lotteries alone exceeded $20 billion per year, nearly four times the amount of all Native American gaming.

The reason for this explosion of gambling, and for what Vallen called "a new era of gaming morality," was twofold. The expansion of Indian gaming since 1983 had a great effect, creating a model for revenue generation that states envied and decided to copy. A related reason was that states also desperately needed the revenue. Vallen writes that in 1983 "budget shortfalls were the primary catalyst for states' introducing new forms of legalized gambling. The weak condition of the U.S. economy left many state governments with huge deficits and declining revenues."[5] Across the country, therefore, state governments, churches, and private charities, in addition to Native Americans, had become accepting of gambling operations and aggressive in using them to raise needed funds. The impetus for both tribal and state adoption of institutionalized gambling, therefore, was the same.

It is thus important to situate Native American gaming in this expanding national gambling political economy. In the 1990s and beyond, Native Americans were forced to adapt to a shifting political, and legislative landscape in order to preserve the hard-won court decisions and congressional acts supporting their sovereignty from the 1980s. Politicians' philosophical objections to Indian sovereignty were supplemented by economic objections as two key issues emerged: a battle for tax revenues and increasingly aggressive lobbying by casino and dog and horse track operators who feared that Indian gaming would encroach on their turf.

Three recent cases provide evidence of this complicated landscape, which we can consider before looking at the respective arguments for and against Native American gambling. Indian gaming revenues rose dramatically during the 1990s. In 2001, they amounted to close to $13 billion, generated by 340 Indian gambling facilities in 29 states. Aside from the Pequot, however, the gambling activity began to be centered in California, Minnesota, Arizona, and, in the future, New York. State governments watched as Connecticut began scoring big sums from the Foxwoods and the Mohegan Sun casinos, which put into state coffers nearly $300 million. Some state officials learned two lessons from the Connecticut case—that resistance can produce federal intervention and that negotiation can result in benefits for the state. The 11 gambling compacts that Wisconsin signed in 1993 had no provision for "revenue sharing." Five years later the renewed compacts did, offering Wisconsin a piece of the gambling pie. In another example, Minnesota garnered some concessions in approaching the negotiations "in good faith," earning promises from Minnesota's 11 gaming tribes to limit table games to blackjack and to establish minimum gambling ages. Other states' officials put up resistance in establishing compacts for Class III gambling operations, asking tribes to kick back to the state a percentage of revenues along the lines of arrangements in Connecticut and Wisconsin. Tribal officials opposed this aspect of the compact negotiations, arguing on one hand that it amounts to one sovereign government taxing another, though acknowledging on the other hand that such deals are necessary to secure "exclusivity" agreements, which grant tribes exclusive rights to certain kinds of gaming.

Complicating the equation was the assertion by various state legislatures and private businesses that the negotiation of compacts with tribal officials is a legislative prerogative; unilateral negotiations by governors have been contested in several states including New Mexico, whose Supreme Court sided with the legislature. So even if a governor supported Indian gaming as an economic boost to the state's economy or simply decided that it was a matter of federal law, legislative bodies have held up compact negotiations, in large measure because they have been influenced by other state businesses. In Arizona, three track operators filed suit to prevent Governor Jane Hull from unilaterally negotiating with Arizona's 17 gaming tribes. Arizona's original compacts, which expired after 10 years, had provided no financial benefits to the states and Governor Hull was intent on securing the kinds of incentives that Connecticut had earned; her proposals would have provided nearly $83 million to the state in the first year, and close to $1 billion over the term of the compact. In May 2002, the Arizona House of Representatives voted down Governor Hull's proposals for negotiating new compacts. Beginning in February 2002, legislators and voters had been bombarded with information from anti–Indian gaming forces such as the Coalition for Arizona, sponsored by the state's racetrack industry. Arizona's tribes, and some voters, have become alarmed by the connection between the state legislature and the track industry in light of disclosures that the chairman of the state Republican Party is also a lobbyist for a Phoenix dog track. Arizona voters decided the issue in November 2002 by passing Proposition 202, which ensured at least ten more years of tribal gaming.

The Arizona case and one in California make clear what is at stake with the expansion of Native American gaming—enormous sums of money. In 1998, the costliest ballot initiative in American political history, known as Prop. 5 (officially the Tribal Government Gaming and Self-Sufficiency Act), was waged to decide the fate of Indian gambling in California. More than $92 million was spent by both sides, $66 million of which came from Native American tribal groups who would have managed the new gambling operations under terms of IGRA compacts. Importantly, the bulk of the money spent by Prop. 5 opponents came not from California companies but from Nevada casinos, which stood to lose business to Indian gaming businesses if Prop. 5 passed. The Coalition against Unregulated Gambling, the largest group, was funded by the Bellagio (Mirage Resorts), the Sahara Hotel and Casino, Caesars III, and Circus Circus Enterprises, all of Las Vegas. In addition, Nevada casino interests gave significant contributions to the California attorney general, who had regulatory power over California gaming, and to California's legislative leaders. In adopting Prop. 5, voters gave thumbs up to casino-style gambling in their state. Prop. 5, however, was thrown out as unconstitutional by the California Supreme Court, prompting a new round of negotiations. Governor Gray Davis negotiated new compacts with 60 tribal groups, but a condition was that a constitutional amendment ballot initiative would be staged in 2000. Proposition IA was accepted by California voters by a 65 to 35 percent margin in March 2000; Nevada opponents elected not to campaign against the measure, learning from Prop. 5 that they would be outspent and that California voters wanted casino-type gambling in their state.

A similar dynamic developed in New York State. A coalition opposed to Governor George Pataki's signing of compacts with Native American groups to establish six new casinos sued in state court to block the compacts. On May 2, 2002, a state appeals court upheld an earlier ruling that forced Pataki to seek legislative approval for the compacts. The challenge to Pataki's compacts came from various groups, including the evangelical group New Yorkers for Constitutional Freedoms, state legislators, and other antigambling groups. What was especially interesting about the New York case was the visceral debate that erupted between antigambling forces in the state and Native American supporters of gambling across the country. An editorial in the *Wall Street Journal* (March 1, 2002) criticizing Pataki and Indian gaming in general aroused a firestorm of protest from various Native American groups. The Arizona and California cases were state and regional battles, respectively. The New York case broke new ground in that the issue became a national one.

The *Wall Street Journal* editorial, titled "Big Chief Pataki," implied that Pataki was pushing the six compacts to help his reelection chances by winning over unions and hard-hit communities near Buffalo and in the Catskills, where the casinos would be built. The editorial also listed a litany of ills associated with gambling. Political posturing aside, what especially alarmed and angered Native Americans was the language of the editorial—it called Pataki either "Chief Pataki" or "Great White Father Pataki," referred to union negotiations as "traded beads with," and implied that "white guys behind the curtain" would control the casinos.[6] The editorial generated a number of heated replies, including one in the *Times Herald-Record* titled "Is *The Wall Street Journal* Racist?" The most visceral response came from *Indian Country Today,* a newspaper funded by the Oneida Nation of New York, which had gambling interests of its own. Its March 5 editorial defended the integrity of Indian gaming and blasted the *Journal's* argument that "white guys behind the curtain" controlled Indian gambling as racist because it implied Indians could not manage their own businesses. It argued that the "name-calling is belittling and prejudicial.... The *Journal's* position on Indian gaming in New York State and nationally is part and parcel of a growing national backlash against Indians. It seeks to disparage and to castigate Indians with all the same stereotypical images, denying the real economic base of the issue and mangling the facts."[7]

In the sections that follow, we consider the arguments espoused by the *Wall Street Journal, Indian Country Today,* and the various constituencies affected by Indian gaming—legislators, governors, taxpayers, people in rural communities and big cities alike, and, of course, Native Americans. In the past decade the issue has become, as the recent New York, California, and Arizona cases indicate, a complicated and emotional one. Much is at stake—Indian sovereignty, state regulatory authority, tax revenues, and economic power, as well as cultural conceptions of Indianness that cross traditional boundaries of race and class.

OPPONENTS OF NATIVE AMERICAN GAMBLING

In its aforementioned editorial of March 1, 2002, the *Wall Street Journal* argued against the expansion of Indian gambling in New York State by citing a number of reasons, including organized crime and corruption, a casino's burden to local communities' roads and local services, a conflict of interest in the tribal recognition process, and the spread of gambling addiction, which had the potential for "wrecking lives and families." The editorial closed by concluding, "The history of Indian gaming is that, like the craps tables themselves, it promises more than it ever delivers.... Indian casinos have become a political fixers game that is bad social and economic policy."[8] A second editorial followed in the wake of criticism by Native Americans of the first. "Tribal Casinos a Rotten Deal for N.Y." (April 5, 2002) criticized Indians' efforts to regulate the $10 billion industry, arguing that "Indian gaming looks like a corruption scandal waiting to happen. It already is a political scandal."[9] Notably, the *Journal* failed to list one positive aspect of Indian gaming in its two editorials. Though its attack was aimed at Pataki and the

New York State question, the editorials were clearly making generalizations about all Indian gaming. The editorials, therefore, can be seen as a summary of various objections that have been floated by gambling opponents since tribal gambling exploded upon the American scene in the 1980s.

The editorials also prompt us to use two separate contexts in which to evaluate these objections. Given that gambling opportunities expanded greatly in the 1990s, it is important to consider that Indian gambling was attacked as part of a *general* trend in gambling in the United States and as a *particular* form of it. By the end of the 1990s, state and federal officials were finding evidence of the social costs of gambling, whether it was state lotteries, Indian casinos, or riverboat bingo. In 1998, the National Gambling Impact Study Commission recommended a national moratorium on gambling expansion, Indian and non-Indian, while further study of its consequences could be done. Gambling addiction became more prevalent (estimated at 0.77 percent of the general population, but between 1.5 and 5 percent for residents living close to casinos), which in turn created gambling debts that precipitated suicides and, in some locations, crime. Gamblers Anonymous chapters grew dramatically in Mississippi after it legalized gambling, and calls to Iowa's Gamblers Anonymous sites also rose considerably in the mid-1990s. Although most Indian nations have given generously to gambling addiction treatment centers and hotlines, a perception has arisen, given the heated debate over Indian gaming, that they have helped fuel the problems rather than solve them.

In 1998, Americans were spending more money on gambling than they were on theme parks, video games, music, sports, and movie tickets combined! As Governor Angus King of Maine put it, "I don't care what anybody says; when you have that much cash, it's not healthy.... It brings with it inevitable corruption." King had announced his opposition to a $500 million casino proposed by the Passamaquoddy and Penobscot tribes by arguing, "I think it takes money out of pockets of local people. It's not true economic development."[10] Two groups—Casinos No! and No Dice—formed in Maine to battle the Penobscot and Passamaquoddy's casino proposal. Members of the organizations were concerned that their small businesses would be overwhelmed by the large project. A resort owner wondered how existing restaurants and hotels could remain competitive with a casino that "would be giving away lodging, that would be giving away food, that would be giving away alcohol.... I am at a loss to find an up sign."[11] Opponents in Maine and elsewhere argue that casinos take money from one part of the economy like small resorts and restaurants rather than create new revenue or income. Economists call this impact the "substitution effect." A recent study of American gambling practices described the substitution effect: "casinos cannibalize funds used for saving, recreation, race track betting, charitable gambling, and state legalized lottery games."[12]

Given that state lottery proceeds and tax revenues are at stake, some critics fear that the success of some Indian gaming operations will spur state governments not to fight Indian gambling operations but to copy them. Challenging Indians' monopoly on casino gambling, bar owners, developers, and race track operators in some states have been demanding the right to install slot machines in their establishments to compete with Indian enterprises. Industry analyst Eugene Christiansen notes that "Indian gambling is goading state legislatures to authorize casino games and other forms of gambling. If the Indians have casinos and states can't tax them, there is a natural tendency for legislators to say 'Hell, we'll have our own casinos that we can tax.' "[13] At the moment, government officials seem inclined to focus on extracting concessions from Indian nations during the compact negotiation process rather than expanding their state's gambling offerings, which reflects an uncertainty about the value of gambling to society and the hard-won reality that federal law compels them to negotiate the compacts. But as Anne McCulloch argued in the journal *Publius,* "The inability to control or profit directly from gambling facilities located within state borders, especially in a time of fiscal constraint, may increase state opposition to Indian gaming."[14]

The disparagement and resentment of Indian sovereignty leads us back to the spring 2002 editorials of the *Wall Street Journal,* which many Native American writers thought expressed the racism that underlies some of the criticism of Indian gaming. One of the most prominent of the *Wall Street Journal's* objections was that Indian gaming would create corruption and crime. The *Journal* cited an FBI statement outlining the ways in which "the mob" infiltrates legitimate gambling operations: "They understand not only the mechanics of gambling, but also how the industry works: the labor unions, the equipment, the pawn shops, the trucking industry, the housekeeping services, all the collateral industries. They set up kickback schemes, extortion schemes, sweetheart contract schemes."[15] The fear, then, was that Indian gambling, especially if it was managed only by what some commentators considered to be naive tribal authorities, would allow the spread of this kind of crime and violence into American communities. This argument has been one of the most widely cited of antigambling forces. It first appeared during California's legal efforts to shut down high-stakes bingo operations on its small Indian reservations. In the 1987 *California v. Cabazon* decision that resulted, the Supreme Court was not swayed by California officials' argument that organized crime would infiltrate such operations. Connecticut officials made the same argument in opposing the Pequot's drive to establish casino-type gambling in the late 1980s. State attorney general Richard Blumenthal argued that Connecticut feared having to contend with the "potential criminal activity that has been associated with casino gambling in Las Vegas and Atlantic City."[16] Facing competition from the Pequot's Foxwoods casino, Donald Trump, a New York multimillionaire with control of Atlantic City gambling operations, testified to Congress in May 1993 that he believed

Indian gaming had been infiltrated by organized crime figures; he also claimed in an unsuccessful lawsuit that IGRA was unconstitutional and gave Native Americans an "unfair advantage" in setting up casino operations. In addition, Nevada gaming interests and some California law enforcement officials made a similar argument in opposing California's adoption of casino-style gambling in 1999 during the Prop. 5 debate.

Corruption and crime have visited Indian casinos, both as a result of the actions of organized crime figures as well as from what many critics of Indian gaming have focused on, "disorganized" crime like fraud and violence. Department of the Interior (DOI) investigations in the early 1990s uncovered theft, mismanagement, and fraud that cost casino tribes more than $12 million. Gaming tribes have been ripped off by unscrupulous leasing companies, casino managers or employees, and tribal officials themselves. DOI investigators, working with the Task Force on Indian Gaming in the U.S. Attorney's Office, convicted four leaders of Minnesota's White Earth tribe of bribery, election fraud, and embezzlement, leading to prison sentences and fines. The former chairman of the Keweenaw Bay tribe was sentenced to two years in jail for accepting a slot machine company's cash kickbacks. Seminole Nation officials suspended tribal chairman James Billie for his alleged misconduct in signing off on improper contracts, which earned the Seminole a $3 million fine. One of the Seminole's casino partners, JPW Consultants, was fined $3.4 million for operating a casino without the approval of the National Indian Gaming Association, the independent trade group of Indian casino operators. Associates of the firm's owner, Seminole police officials alleged, were organized crime figures. Violence has occurred during tribal power struggles over casino operations. In a casino community north of San Francisco, 10 members of the Elem Pomo Indian community were wounded in gun battles between factions that developed over the tribal chairman's alleged embezzlement of casino funds; after a cease-fire was negotiated, the casinos were closed. Violence on the Seneca reservation of New York has been linked to casino issues.

Although federal law enforcement officials have called such acts of corruption and violence rare, these few cases illustrate how Indian casinos have created the grounds for opponents' complaints. The cases also point to what critics call a lack of effective regulation of Indian gaming. In the early 1990s, journalists criticized the federal government's National Indian Gaming Commission (NIGC) for failing to establish an effective regulatory mechanism capable of investigating organized crime activity in Indian casinos. This theme has been carried through to the *Wall Street Journal* editorials of 2002, which repeated a previous argument made by *Boston Globe* reporters that the NIGC had a smaller budget and fewer staff member than New Jersey employed to monitor Atlantic City gaming operations. The *Journal* and *Globe* articles also asserted that lobbyists employed by the National Indian Gaming Association spent millions of dollars convincing NIGC members to keep its budget small in order to prevent undue federal control of the industry and sent hundreds of thousands of dollars in contributions to politicians supportive of Indian gaming rights to head off legislative changes to the Indian Gambling Regulatory Act.

A Backlash against Native Gaming

The rise of Native Americans' lobbying power has increased citizens' opposition to Indian gaming, which has found expression in critical newspaper editorials and in letters to the editors. It is here that the question of race has appeared. Criticism of Indians' advantages, derived from their sovereignty, appeared shortly after IGRA was put into effect. While attempting to be sympathetic to Native Americans' historical mistreatment and their need for assistance, commentators like William Hamilton defended states' rights in determining policies, complaining that state governors had to "circle their political wagons against a ploy by tribes to use their sovereign rights under treaties with the USA to offer higher gambling stakes than the state laws permit at non-Indian gaming establishments. Higher stakes mean greater crowds, and that gives Indian gaming a distinct advantage."[17] Hamilton, writing in 1990, complained that some Indian nations could buy land outside their reservation boundaries and establish casino operations on it, another way that Native Americans were gaining what Hamilton called an "unfair advantage." The theme of "unfair advantage" due to sovereignty is echoed in other complaints. Written in 2001, a letter to the editor of a Connecticut newspaper used the word *racism* to describe Indian gaming. The writer argued that IGRA "promoted racism" by "allowing a group of people to have special privileges and in some cases to become multimillionaires and pay no taxes because of their ancestry and the hardships their ancestors had to endure."[18] He contended that descendants of Europeans should have the same opportunity. The writer failed to mention the $335 million that the State of Connecticut reaped from Indian gaming in 2001, or that all Native Americans pay federal income tax; he was more concerned with the idea of privilege, that one group received all these "advantages."

The backlash against Native Americans has become heated especially in California, which has seen the greatest casino-building activity and the greatest rise in Indian political influence in the past decade, as well as the most active participation of voters who have supported Indian gaming through several ballot initiatives. An opinion piece in the *San Diego Union-Tribune* of May 2001 captured the various arguments that have built up against Indian gaming nations. The headline said it all: "Impact of Casinos; Overwhelming Infrastructures, Lawmakers." The editorial was concerned particularly with "how the state should deal with a powerful special interest whose large campaign contributions have co-opted the legislature," which had blocked efforts to regulate Indian gaming. Warning of "casino saturation," the writer argued, "rather than revel in their newfound political clout, the tribes should be concerned about the potential for a public backlash against splashy casinos in rural areas.... [T]here is nothing funny about the strain these casinos place on county roadways, water supplies and other resources.... It's one thing for Indian tribes to become more self-sufficient through the incremental creation of gaming casinos. It's quite another for these complexes to spread like crabgrass and overwhelm rural communities."[19] A subsequent editorial noted that after September 11, the fears of new building and new infrastructure problems had not materialized, but the sentiment is a general one—that Indians' political influence and gaming operations had reached a point of diminishing returns for some Californians.

THE VIEW FROM NATIVE AMERICA

Just as non-Indians have expressed concern about the impact of Indian casinos on the social fabric, so have Native Americans themselves. Native American intellectuals and writers have been thinking about the impact of gaming since it expanded in the 1980s. Gambling has featured prominently in recent Native American fiction such as Gerald Vizenor's *Heirs of Columbus* (1992) and Louise Erdrich's *Bingo Palace* (1993); Vizenor has also written about the subject in *Crossbloods: Bone Courts, Bingo, and Other Reports* (1990). Many of these accounts are ambivalent, expressing both an understanding of the impetus behind Indian casinos and reservations about their ultimate impact.

For the reasons listed earlier in this chapter, and those specific to the tribal experience, a number of Native Americans have not jumped on the casino bandwagon. Gambling as a social practice does not disturb "traditionalists," those Native Americans who continue to follow cultural traditions and resist the forces of assimilation. Although it would be inaccurate to say all traditionalists oppose casino-style gambling, many Native Americans, especially "traditionalists," do feel threatened by the overwhelming changes that casinos can bring to formerly isolated and insular communities. Southwest Indian nations like the Hopi and the Navajo have been especially resistant to the spread of gambling operations in their communities. The Hopi rejected gambling in a tribal vote. In 1994 and again in 1997, the Navajo, the country's largest Indian nation (which rests in Arizona, New Mexico, and Utah), rejected casino gambling in a tribal referendum. Edison Wauneka, a Navajo official opposed to gambling, said, "There is really nothing that can come from gaming besides money. While it can make a lot of money, at the same time it's going to hurt a lot of people."[20] Some Navajo were, perhaps, motivated to vote against tribal gaming because of Navajo oral history, which tells of the "Legend of the Great Gambler," who promised to destroy the Navajo after losing a high-stakes game. Navajo medicine man Alfred Yazzie thought that "maybe the Gambler was the white man or maybe he's coming back in the form of casinos."[21] Navajo and other Native American critics don't necessarily need oral history to argue against gambling. The brief civil war that erupted into violence on the Mohawk's St. Regis reservation in 1990 shows how gambling can divide communities; one Mohawk died trying to prevent gambling from affecting his people. It is also important to note that, given the forces of assimilation, a number of Native American Christians oppose casinos for reasons similar to those of traditionalists as well as those of non-Indians—casinos can reorient community values; disrupt a community's rhythm; bring crime, cars, and noise to the streets; and invite political dissension and corruption.

What has alarmed many Native Americans is the extent to which gambling has been stripped of its cultural meaning and purpose and instead institutionalized in an economic context that makes it difficult for tribal leaders, elders in particular, to mediate its impact. Some Lakota and Dakota see casinos simply as the latest in a string of evil influences that include alcohol, Western-style political systems, and mass culture. Sociology professor James Fenelon has studied the impact of gambling on the Standing Rock Nation's reservation in South Dakota and found that the casino has reoriented the notion of community and how it comes together. Casinos, with their restaurants and activities, have become a central meeting space, which means that some Native people spend more time with these activities than with traditional activities including religious observances and gatherings of both the family *(tiwaye)* and the already weakened extended relations *(tiyospaye)*.[22] Another impact of the casino in this context is that Native Americans also find cause to gamble, which can reduce hard-earned living wages or government aid. One Lakota Sioux told Fenelon, "in a casino, if you don't have much money, you lose it quickly. . . . The long-term effects are they [the Sioux] spend, lose their money on the wrong things (instead of spending it on family needs)." Family life, the core of Native American society, can, therefore, be adversely affected by the lure of the casino, its employment miles away, and its reordering of social space.

With so much money and political power at stake, some Indian communities have been beset by political infighting that has damaged tribal unity. Gambling for the Seminole, who started it all, has brought both prosperity and discord. One Seminole faction believed so strongly against gambling that it created a new nation, the Independent Traditional Seminole Nation of Florida. Friction has developed when tribal governments have refused to hold referendums on whether to allow casinos on tribal lands, usually because gambling opponents would win, thus creating a crisis of democracy in some communities. Bill Lawrence of the Red Lake Band of Chippewa has worked to expose corruption in Minnesota's tribal casino industry, complaining that tribal members face harassment from tribal officials who are secretive about gaming revenues and protective of their control of them. His newspaper, the *Native American Press/Ojibwe News,* was boycotted by tribal casinos, and his wife was fired from her job at a tribal school. One of his central concerns is that many tribal voters do not have mechanisms to make their officials account for expenditures and policies. "We have no accountability. We don't know where the money goes, and there's no way we can force our elected officials to account to us." Lawrence established the nonprofit Tribal Accountability Legal Rights Fund to "pierce the veil," or what he calls the perception that it is only non-Indians who exploit Indians.[23] At the same time, the gambling issue has also led to antigambling candidates winning elections; Michael Schindler was elected president of the Cattaraugus Seneca Nation of New York in part because he opposed casinos.

Native American critics of gambling point not only to intratribal conflict, that which happens between members of a particular Indian community, but also to intertribal conflict, tension that develops between different Indian nations. Several tribes have attempted to block their neighbor's casino plans; in one case, the Wyandot opposed the Wyandotte's casino proposal because it would have been built on their sacred burial ground. Senator Ben Nighthorse Campbell, a Colorado Republican, has worried that the expansion of Indian gaming will reach a "saturation point" that will result in a scenario where "tribe will be turning against tribe. In some communities where the casinos have made some Indians the new rich, a backlash has been created."[24] As noted earlier in the chapter, the backlash can extend not only to poor Indian nations but also to Americans at large who resent what they consider "unfair advantages." There are some Native Americans who believe that the explosive growth of Indian casinos has created a backlash against all Indians, whether they are members of casino tribes or not, that American Indians are now unfairly and inaccurately stereotyped as both rich and receiving federal aid. Thus, gambling has had or could have in the future a negative impact on other Native American issues like land claims, treaty rights, and the campaign to ban Indian sports mascots and images.

Some Native American critics simply argue that casino gambling is not a panacea, that it hasn't produced real social progress for most Native Americans. A 1997 report by the organization Native Americans in Philanthropy, titled "Survey of Grant Giving by American Indian Foundations and Organizations," found that gaming revenues had not lowered poverty levels among American Indians, but that despite the gambling boom 51 percent of Indians residing on reservations still lived below the poverty line, which represented an increase from the 45 percent of 1980. The two principal reasons for this failure, according to the report, were related. One, "the big success stories in gaming are the exceptions rather than the rule," and two, successful gaming tribes are not "structurally organized to be grantmakers—very few tribes have foundations" for distributing funds to poorer tribes.[25] One question for some analysts and tribal leaders, then, is whether Native Americans have an obligation to think intertribally, to share the wealth in the form of grants and investments.

Some critics are not opposed to operating casinos per se but are opposed to how they are managed and how their revenue is spent and invested. Tim Giago, a prominent Native American writer, argues that "instead of giving tribal members per capita monthly payments, Indian tribes could be using gaming profits to purchase more land and expand their reservation base. They could put the money into long-term investments.... Some are doing this; many are not." Giago has also become concerned about who controls the casinos—the tribal members or outside managers. He notes that in some operations tribal officials "have allowed [outside] casino managers to take control...to desecrate and insult the religious practices, traditions and culture of other Indian tribes."[26] As John Dyer, an Onondaga, put it, "There's nothing wrong with a nation running a casino. The problem becomes when the casino runs the nation."[27] Some Native Americans might disagree, saying that all casino influences are bad ones. But Giago's comments point to a central concern for some Native Americans: casinos are potential targets not for organized crime but for outsiders, outsiders' values, and outsiders' control of an economic process set up by Native Americans for the benefit of Native Americans. Self-determination will only result if that control remains firmly in Native American hands.

PROPONENTS OF INDIAN GAMING

During the 1980s, according to Frank Ducheneaux, the House of Representatives' legal counsel on Indian affairs, the "Reagan cuts devastated tribes." Federal funds for Native Americans were cut by 29 percent, devastating health care, housing construction, and job-training programs; when the Reagan administration ended the Concentrated Training and Employment Act program, roughly 18,000 Native Americans lost their jobs and, as a consequence, welfare rolls expanded. Thus, Ducheneaux argued, "Indians had to find alternative sources of funding."[28] For many Indian communities, gambling enterprises became an alternative source of funding. What is more American than starting a business? Creating economic organizations to ameliorate poverty conditions and reduce dependency made political sense because entrepreneurship dovetailed nicely with the spirit of the pro-business Reagan White House. Reagan himself had encouraged Native Americans to pull themselves up by their bootstraps. In 1983, he said, "This administration affirms the right of tribes to determine the best way to meet the needs of their members and to establish and run programs which best meet those needs."[29]

Native Americans across the country watched as the Seminole, California tribes, and the Pequot used bingo and then casino-style gambling to "meet the needs of their members," creating tribal income, employment opportunities, and political power. After the Supreme Court refused to hear the State of Connecticut's suit against the Mashantucket Pequot in April 1991, thus securing the Pequot's right to operate casino gambling, tribal chairman Richard Hayward celebrated, saying, "This is a tremendous victory for Indian tribes throughout the United States. It means that state governments must deal with us on equal terms as sovereign governments.... This decision will allow us to become self-sufficient and self-determining."[30] Hayward's statement captured a sentiment shared by many Native Americans. Winning and retaining the right to gamble, through the Supreme Court's Cabazon decision of 1987, Congress's passage of the Indian Gaming Regulatory Act in 1988, and the Pequot's legal victory in 1991, was not just about finding alternative sources of funding but about being given an opportunity to achieve self-sufficiency in the face of federal budget cuts, to become self-determining rather than dependent, and to protect sovereign powers in the face of antagonistic state governments and envious casino competitors.

As casino gambling became a multibillion-dollar industry, its proponents have had to work hard to defend its integrity in the face of criticism that it is underregulated and rife with corruption. At the same May 1993 congressional hearing in which Donald Trump alleged that organized crime had infiltrated Indian gaming, representatives of the FBI, the Internal Revenue Service, and the Department of Justice all testified to the contrary, saying that they had found no evidence of extensive organized crime influences in Indian gambling enterprises. Supporters of Indian gaming argued that the testimony of Trump and others like him was just a smokescreen to cover up issues of competition; in opposing the Pequot's offering of Class III games in Connecticut, Trump merely wanted to preserve the monopoly status of Atlantic City casino-type gambling. Indian gaming officials admit that crime and corruption has occurred, especially in the early 1990s when enforcement mechanisms were being set up. But they claim theirs is now a well-regulated industry due to extensive tribal regulations, state law enforcement assistance, and federal oversight provided by Department of Justice, IRS, and FBI personnel; gaming tribes spend close to $150 million for internal policing of their operations. Testifying before Congress in July 2001, Bruce Ohr, the chief of the Organized Crime and Racketeering Section in the Criminal Division of the Department of Justice (the Department), noted "isolated incidents of organized crime *attempting* [author's emphasis] to infiltrate Indian gaming," but said the Department investigated and successfully prosecuted those cases. Importantly, Ohr concluded that "Indian tribal gaming has proven to be a useful economic development tool for a number of tribes, who utilize gaming income to support a variety of essential services. While tribal gaming has become a lucrative industry and a potential target for organized crime, the Department has found no systematic attempts by organized crime groups to become involved in tribal gaming."[31] Defenders of the integrity of

Indian gaming argue that the *Boston Globe* and the *Wall Street Journal* have attacked Indian gaming on the basis of *attempted* or *potential* infiltration rather than on the state of affairs articulated by Bruce Ohr.

In addition, critics of the *Wall Street Journal* editorials of 2002 argue that lobbying is a fact of life for all big industries, Indian or non-Indian. As Mississippi Choctaw leader Philip Martin put it in response to criticism of Indian lobbying efforts, "I learned that from the white man. If you want support you are going to have to make friends."[32] In many ways, then, these political efforts to protect the industry are signs of its maturation and explain why it has engendered such fierce criticism. The industry is successful in part because it has mirrored both the political and the economic behavior of non-Indian-owned casino businesses. Native American leaders have complained that some white Americans just can't accept the idea of Native Americans achieving success and that once they do achieve it, someone wants to take it away. Racism, they say, underlies many of the arguments that have been made against Indian gaming.

How Native Americans Have Benefited from Indian Gaming

For Richard Hayward, his tribe's gambling enterprise has meant the rebirth of the Mashantucket Pequot Nation, its culture, and its sovereignty. In the first year after the court victory, the Pequot grossed more than $300 million. Today it grosses roughly $1 billion per year, creating employment for Pequot and non-Pequot alike and providing the State of Connecticut with more than $300 million in revenue per year; the estimated revenue in 2002 was $372 million. In addition, the Pequot have spread the wealth to some extent, donating funds to the Native American Rights Fund, and they have made Native American culture a centerpiece of the casino in the form of traditional powwows and feasts and the recently opened Mashantucket Pequot Museum and Research Center, a 308,000-square-foot complex that cost $193 million; the center hosts scholarly conferences, presents the history of the Pequot Nation, and exhibits Native American traditional crafts.

Given the paucity of federal support for some areas of Native American life, and the difficulties of attracting businesses to remote reservations, it is clear that gambling revenues are of great importance to many tribes. But the perception exists, largely because of the press attention paid to the wealthy members of the Pequot Nation, that Indian gambling has created a generation of reservation millionaires. The reality is quite different, for a number of reasons. Studies have shown that roughly 20 tribal casinos earn as much as half of all gaming revenue; many smaller casino operations, especially those situated in rural Native America, have struggled to create profits. And the post–9-11 economy has meant layoffs for some. As with many stereotypes of Native Americans, the one of wealthy casino owners has distorted the continuing struggle of most Native Americans to achieve a measure of control over their lives and secure a reasonable standard of living. The reality is that tribal gaming in large measure has been about the progress of the community rather than of the individual. As the executive director of the Minnesota Indian Gaming Association put it, most tribes "are using gaming revenues to lever their communities out of the black hole of despair and get a shot at the American dream. For most tribes, it's about building schools, homes, clinics and hospitals, repairing infrastructure, providing social services and revitalizing the culture and traditions that a century of poverty nearly killed."[33] Gaming for most Native Americans, then, is about getting the things that most Americans take for granted—educational and employment opportunities, access to good health care, and safe neighborhoods.

Gaming tribes distribute money based on criteria set by individual tribal codes and IGRA (Indian Gaming Regulatory Act) specifications. As noted earlier in the chapter, IGRA established criteria for tribal distribution of gambling revenue to ensure that it enriched communities rather than individuals. Section 11 of IGRA stipulated that revenue had to be used to fund tribal government programs or operations; to provide for the *general* welfare of the tribal community; to promote economic development; to donate to charitable groups; or to reduce dependency on local government administration. Beyond per capita distributions (distributing an equal and fixed amount of money to enrolled or certified tribal members), which for some tribes can amount to tens of thousands of dollars per member, tribal officials have invested gaming revenues in reservation infrastructure like community centers, law enforcement, libraries, hospitals, drug and alcohol treatment centers, and water and sewer systems. They have also invested heavily in the future. Roughly 10 percent of gaming revenues have gone to improve existing educational facilities and to build new schools, both K–12 and college institutions, to establish scholarship funds, and to expand curriculum development that emphasizes Indian culture and language. Fundamentally, casinos have provided employment opportunities, job training, and income. Estimates of job creation range from 200,000 to 500,000, many of which have gone to non-Indians. Although friction exists between the wealthy and not-so-wealthy, gaming tribes have in some cases made donations or grants to or invested in less fortunate or nongaming tribes. The Yavapai Apache Nation of Arizona donated to the Hualapai tribe two generators for its dialysis machines. California gaming tribes recently signed off on an agreement to give a portion of their profits to nongaming tribes. Wealthy gaming nations like the Pequots have provided grants to less fortunate tribal communities and to national organizations like the Native American Rights Fund.

Gaming money has led to an improvement in the quality of life on a number of reservations. Several examples will suffice. The Mohegan, the Pequot's Connecticut neighbors, have used their gaming proceeds from the Mohegan Sun casino to reclaim tribal artifacts, establish a college scholarship fund, and build a group facility for their elderly members. The Oklahoma Choctaw have funded scholarship programs, built community centers, and created health programs to deal with diabetes and arthritis. The Tohono O'odham Nation of

Arizona has created scholarships for 1,200 students; covered all of the fire department's budget; built a 60-bed nursing home, a $2.5 million kidney dialysis center, and 11 youth recreation facilities that cost $30 million; and funded Early Childhood Head Start programs to the tune of $8.2 million. The Tiguas' Speaking Rock casino, located near El Paso, Texas, has allowed them to cut unemployment from about 70 percent to 1 percent. Their high school graduation rate is now 98 percent. Tribal members benefit from a new community health center, a fitness center, a library, and a drug and alcohol treatment facility. The Tiguas may not be rich like the Pequot, but they have created an avenue for a new generation to go to college and a home to return to that will provide them with job opportunities. They are also no longer dependent on state or federal services. Despite all this success, or because of it some Native American activists say, Texas authorities recently forced the Tiguas to suspend their gaming operations; the Tiguas are appealing in federal court.

HOW NON-INDIANS HAVE BENEFITED FROM INDIAN GAMING

Many El Paso area residents, who have benefited from job creation and crime reduction near the Tiguas' casino, will be angry if the casino remains shut down; an estimated 2,200 non-Indian jobs would be lost, the loss of disposable income would affect local businesses, and the Tiguas would stop donating to local charities. Given the rising fortunes of some gaming tribes, officials have been generous to surrounding communities, spreading the prosperity beyond the boundaries of the reservation. Indian casinos have provided more than 100,000 jobs to non-Indians. For example, the Grand Ronde's Spirit Mountain Casino in Oregon created 1,200 jobs, 1,000 of which went to non-Indians, many of them unemployed, uninsured, or on welfare. The Pequot and Mohegan employ nearly 20,000 full- and part-time workers, most of them non-Indian. Rising incomes have also meant both additional tax revenues for state governments (from increased employment and revenue-sharing programs) and declining dependency on local charities and on state and federal aid programs; Connecticut shares its tax wealth in the form of grants to local communities. Indian gaming tribes have contributed to civic life outside their reservations. The Grande Ronde tribe purchased rescue helicopters for Portland, Oregon, hospitals and built a medical facility that also benefits non-Indians. The White Earth Nation of Minnesota contributed $148,000 to the local hospital, sponsored Special Olympics events at its Shooting Star Casino, and provided free lodging to the victims of a devastating 1997 flood. California tribes near San Diego contributed $2.4 million in 1995–96 to symphonies, community centers, and other civic institutions. In addition, gaming tribes have contributed to both local and national charities. For example, after the September 11 attacks devastated New York City, Native Americans across the country responded by sending several million dollars in assistance. In California, the Morongo Band of Mission Indians enabled a disaster team to fly to New York by donating $25,000, in addition to holding a special blood drive. The Choctaw of Oklahoma donated $20,000 and revenues from gas station and casino operations to disaster relief. The Tiguas of Texas contributed $100,000 to the victims' fund.

At the least, some Americans question what business it is of theirs to oppose Indian gaming. But for many reasons, polls show that many Americans support Indian gaming. A survey of California residents found that three of four Californians supported Indian casinos, for a variety of reasons that included "compensating past injustices (75 percent); helping tribes become self-sufficient (73 percent); boosting jobs and economic benefit (58 percent)."[34] Speaking to the first reason indicated, California governor Gray Davis opened his September 1999 announcement of signing compacts with 59 California Indian nations by saying, "In the 11th hour of the 20th century, we have sought to make right with the first Americans. Indians have not asked for much, only that they be treated with respect and dignity. It is my privilege as governor of 33 million people to extend that honor to them."[35] Depressed cities and regions of America have opened their arms to Indian casinos. Thinking of inner city revitalization, Mayor Anthony Masiello of Buffalo, New York, announced in May 2002, "Without equivocation, we welcome and support an Indian gaming casino in the core of the downtown business district. The city is anxious to work together with the Seneca Nation to enhance the ability of the casino to be profitable, while at the same time making our community a more attractive tourist and visitor venue."[36] State officials have seen success stories develop in their region, in part the result of their residents traveling out of state to New York and Connecticut casinos, and have begun to ask, especially as their tax revenues have dropped, "Why should we let Connecticut benefit from gaming revenue?" New York, Rhode Island, Massachusetts, and New Hampshire authorities have begun reviewing Native American casino applications. As the debate over the Penobscot and Passamaquoddy casino proposal evolved in Maine, a Maine state senator made the argument that "this is our window of opportunity. We either do it now or we don't do it, because the other states are moving in that direction, and there is a market for it. Once other states go forward with their plans, we'll never be able to do it."[37] Just as Native Americans have seen that "window of opportunity," and seized it, so too have city and state officials.

THE NEW BUFFALO: GAMBLING AS A MEANS TO A BRIGHTER FUTURE

In April 2002, the chairman of the National Indian Gaming Commission advised tribal leaders to diversify their economies to avoid becoming dependent on casinos. But many gaming tribes had already developed the attitude that gambling is not an end in and of itself but a means to an end, that of self-respect and self-sufficiency. The Oneida of Wisconsin, for example, have diversified their economy, using casino revenues to invest in an industrial park, a chain of convenience stores, a bank, and a printing company. The Oklahoma Choctaw have used casino funds to invest in various businesses, the most successful of which is the Choctaw Nation Travel Plaza, which in 1992 produced monthly revenues of $1.4 million. The Tohono O'odham created a $15 million credit pool to fund more than 150 business grant requests. The Pequot Nation has invested its millions in local businesses, including a printing facility, a historical inn, and several manufacturing sites. Others have invested in hotels, ski resorts, banks, cement factories, and energy facilities.

Gaming tribes have also invested casino revenues in the cultural rehabilitation of their communities, which extends to using architecture to reflect important religious or cultural symbols. A prominent example is the Oneida's use of casino funds to "revive and preserve the tribe's language and folklore: experts have been hired to produce a written form of the Oneida language, and the tribe has begun production of a compact disk on which elders tell ancestral tales in the Oneida language."[38] The Oneida have also used funds to build a new elementary school, designing it in the shape of a turtle, which in Oneida mythology is considered a sacred figure. The use of architecture to reinforce the historic and symbolic values of a tribal culture as well as the creation of language revitalization programs reflects the extent to which many gaming tribes are preserving their cultural heritage through casino operations rather than letting money or outsiders' values weaken it as some critics have claimed casinos do. Another form of strengthening tribal culture through casino income is the land purchase programs conducted by gaming tribes like the Pequot and the Wisconsin Oneida, who in 1995 spent $11 million to purchase land lost years before by treaty or coerced sale. In Washington State, the Squamish have added to their land base by purchasing acreage lost during a time when they had no leverage with outsiders.

With renewed emphasis on culture and language, with an enlarged land base on which to house residents and create businesses, and because of employment opportunities at casinos and related businesses, the casino dynamic has also produced what prominent Native American writer and activist Vine Deloria Jr. calls "recolonization," the demographic reconcentration of native communities and identity. The Pequot revitalization is the best-known story of tribal reunification. But similar stories based on a similar dynamic have occurred across the country, particularly in Wisconsin, home to a large Native American population. Wisconsin's urban Indians, some facing poor job prospects, discrimination, and crime, have found reservation life particularly attractive. According to recent census figures, the number of Native Americans living on Wisconsin reservations and trust lands increased 21.7 percent between 1990 and 2000, from 30,621 to 37,276. In addition, the number of Wisconsin residents who identified themselves as American

Indian or as part–American Indian rose considerably, reflecting both the prospects of getting economic benefits as tribal members and the renewed pride of being American Indian.

Nettie Kingsley, a researcher for the Ho-Chunk Nation's cultural preservation program, believes the movement back to the reservations and the embrace of Indian identity are related to image as well as opportunity. "All these years, we were held back by society, by people who didn't want us around. The stereotypical Indian person was a drunk on welfare. A lot of people used to be ashamed to be Native American." With casino expansion, she notes, "Our young people have a more hopeful attitude toward the future."[39] The Oneida Nation, near Green Bay, Wisconsin, has seen a membership increase of 18.2 percent since 1990. Bobbi Webster, the nation's director of public relations, said that "the gaming industry for the tribes has created an economy.... It's improved the quality of life."[40] But she also noted that of the nation's 3,000 employees, half of them are in gaming-related jobs and the others are teachers and day care workers, lawyers, health care workers, and farmers. It is these professional workers who help create a more functional and native-centered society rather than simply a gaming reservation. Many Native Americans have returned to their home reservations to contribute to the revitalization of their communities. Stephan Grochowski left her position as an attorney with the Legal Aid Society of Milwaukee to serve as a tribal judge on the Menominee reservation, where she was born. Grochowski said, "I think a lot of people who leave the reservation and go to school . . . they just want to come back and give the tribe the benefit of what they've learned. You have to give back. I believe that with all my heart."[41]

When Indian gaming took off in the early 1990s, one Native American casino executive called it the "new buffalo," signifying the multiple ways that gaming has provided resources to Native Americans. It has improved reservation infrastructures and raised living standards, provided much-needed jobs and experience running businesses, expanded the number of schools and scholarships, elevated the political capital of Native American leaders, and even improved relations with non-Indian communities through charitable contributions and revenue-sharing programs. Gaming has reduced what education professor Gregory Cajete, a Tewa from Santa Clara Pueblo, has called "ethnostress," a state of affairs that facilitates despair, destructive behavior, and divisiveness. Wayne Stein, who has surveyed Native American gaming tribes, found that "young Indian people point with pride to their nations' successes in using gaming ventures as an economic tool. The very ability of tribal leaders to successfully run a major business enterprise to their tribes' benefit seems to empower individual tribal members with a sense of success."[42] The collective mental health of tribal communities and hope for the future, then, are important intangible by-products of the gaming experience.

NOTES

1. Roger Dunstan, "Gambling in California," *California Research Bureau,* January 1997, <www.library.ca.gov/CRB/97/03/crb97003.html#toc> (accessed August 2002).

2. *Indian Gaming Regulatory Act, U.S. Statutes at Large* 102 (1988): 2467–69, 2472, 2476, <www4.law.cornell.edu/uscode/25/ch29.html> (accessed August 2002).

3. Peeter Kopvillem, "Tribal Warfare," *Maclean's* 103, 14 May 1990, p. 14.

4. Gary K. Vallen, "Gaming in the U.S.—A Ten-Year Comparison," *Cornell Hotel and Restaurant Administration Quarterly* 34, no. 6 (December 1993), p. 51.

5. Vallen, "Gaming in the U.S.," p. 52.

6. "Big Chief Pataki," *Wall Street Journal,* 1 March 2002.

7. "The Wall Street Journal Loses Respect," *Indian Country Today,* 5 March 2002.

8. "Big Chief Pataki."

9. "Tribal Casinos a Rotten Deal for N.Y.," *Wall Street Journal,* 5 April 2002.

10. A. J. Higgins and Sean Murphy, "Maine Eyes Tribes' Bid for Casino in Kittery," *Boston Globe,* 28 February 2002.

11. "Opponents of Kittery Casino Meet in York," *MaineToday.com,* 19 March 2002, <www.mainetoday.com> (accessed August 2002).

12. Marjorie G. Adams and Frank S. Turner, "State Governments Elude Ethics and Concern for Public Image as They Compete for the Casino Gambling Dollar," *Business and Management Practices* 9, no. 1 (2001), p. 701.

13. Neal Lawrence, "Gambling on a New Life: Indian Gaming Is Not Such a Sure Bet; Despite Its Success, Opposition Abounds," *Midwest Today,* January 1995. <www.midtod.com/highlights/gambling.phtml> (accessed August 2002).

14. Anne Merline McCulloch, "The Politics of Indian Gaming: Tribe/State Relations and American Federalism," *Publius* 24, no. 3 (summer 1994), p. 21.

15. *Los Angeles Times* article, quoted in "Tribal Casinos a Rotten Deal for N.Y."

16. Judith Gaines, "Indians Gain in Ruling on Casino Tribal Rights Upheld," *Boston Globe,* 28 April 1991.

17. William Hamilton, "Indian Gaming Has Unfair Advantage," *USA Today,* 3 August 1990.

18. William Sowik, "Indian Casino Law Promotes Racism," *Hartford Courant,* 7 August 2001.

19. "Impact of Casinos; Overwhelming Infrastructures, Lawmakers," *San Diego Union-Tribune,* 27 May 2001.

20. Sean Paige, "Gambling on the Future," *Insight on the News* 13, no. 47, 22 December 1997, p. 8.

21. Paige, "Gambling on the Future," p. 8.

22. James V. Fenelon, "Dual Sovereignty of Native Nations, the United States, and Traditionalsists." In *Humboldt Journal of Social Relations* 27, no. 1, p. 12 in the outline version: <csbs.csusb.edu/sociology/societypage/HJSR%20Dual%20Sovereign%20final2.pdf> (accessed June 2002).

23. Paige, "Gambling on the Future," p. 10.

24. Paige, "Gambling on the Future," p. 10.

25. "Indian Gaming and Indian Poverty," *Native Americas Magazine,* 18 February 1997, <www.hartford-hwp.com/archives/41/067.html> (accessed August 2002).

26. Lawrence, "Gambling on a New Life.."

27. Quoted in *Raising the Stakes,* video (Wisdom Tree Productions, 1996).

28. David Segal, "Dances with Sharks: Why the Indian Gaming Experiment's Going Wrong," *Washington Monthly* 24, no. 3 (March 1992), p. 28.

29. Ronald Reagan, *Public Papers of the Presidents of the United States: Ronald Reagan,* vol. 1 (Washington, D.C.: Government Printing Office, 1983), p. 97.

30. Nick Ravo, "High Court Clears Way for Indian Casino," *New York Times,* 23 April 1991.

31. "Statement of Bruce G. Ohr, Chief, Organized Crime and Racketeering Section, Criminal Division, Department of Justice, Presented to the Senate Committee on Indian Affairs Oversight Hearing on the Indian Gaming Regulatory Act, Wednesday, July 25, 2001," *U.S. Department of Justice, Office of Tribal Justice,* <www.usdoj.gov/otj/statementbrucegohr.htm> (accessed August 2002).

32. Sean P. Murphy, "Indian Casinos Spend to Limit US Oversight," *Boston Globe,* 12 March 2001.

33. John McCarthy, "Minnesota Gaming Officials Stunned by *The Wall Street Journal's* Spin," *Indian Country Today,* 27 May 2002.

34. Chet Barfield, "3 in 4 Californians Back Tribal Casinos," *San Diego Union-Tribune,* 1 August 2001.

35. "Governor Davis Signs Historic Tribal Gaming Compact with Agua Caliente Band," Office of the Governor press release no. 99:227, 14 September 1999, <www.ca.gov/s/governor/l99227914.html> (accessed August 2002).

36. Lou Michel, "City, Business Leaders Welcome Senecas," *Buffalo News,* 19 May 2002.

37. Higgins and Murphy, "Maine Eyes Tribes' Bid for Casino in Kittery."

38. Christopher Miller, "Coyote's Game: Indian Casinos and the Indian Presence in Contemporary America," in *American Indians in American History, 1870–2001: A Companion Reader,* ed. Sterling Evans (Westport, Conn.: Praeger, 2002), p. 205.

39. Mike Johnson, "Heading Back Home; Casinos, Jobs Lure Indians Back to Better Lives on Reservations," *Milwaukee Journal Sentinel,* 30 April 2001.

40. Johnson, "Heading Back Home."

41. Johnson, "Heading Back Home."

42. Wayne Stein, "American Indians and Gambling: Economic and Social Impacts," in *American Indian Studies: An Interdisciplinary Approach to Contemporary Issues,* ed. Dane Morrison (New York: Peter Lang, 1997), p. 163.

QUESTIONS

1) Is there a difference between gambling and gaming? Does one have negative connotations and the other not?
2) On what grounds do Donald Trump and other white casino owners have the right to criticize Native American gambling operations?
3) Compare Native American gambling with other "American" gambling operations. What are the essential differences?
4) How do Native Americans see gambling fitting into their worldview?
5) What are the risks associated with a community's acceptance of gambling?

6) How would you feel if your school staged a casino gambling night, typically called a Monte Carlo night, to raise funds for school operations or a charity?
7) Can one support some forms of gaming by making a distinction between different kinds of gambling, say between Class II and Class III games?
8) Write a research paper on the New York State gambling cases. Develop pro and con arguments on the issues.
9) Investigate whether Native American gambling operations exist in your state or a neighboring state. Select teams to debate the pros and cons of this operation based on evidence collected from tribal and state agencies.
10) Should state governments be able to tax Native American gambling revenue?
11) If your school depended on gaming revenues to pay for classroom materials, school band instruments, and equipment for sports teams, how would you feel if outsiders told you that your school gaming program was wrong? How would you respond to that criticism?
12) Do you think wealthier gaming tribes should help out poorer tribes?
13) Do you think poorer nongaming tribes would accept money from wealthy gaming tribes?
14) Is it racist, as one critic contended, to give Native Americans advantages other Americans do not have?
15) What is the most important reason to oppose Indian gaming?
16) What is the most important reason to support Indian gaming?

RESOURCE GUIDE

Suggested Readings

Adams, Marjorie G., and Frank S. Turner. "State Governments Elude Ethics and Concern for Public Image as They Compete for the Casino Gambling Dollar." *Business and Management Practices* 9, no. 1 (2001).

"American Indian Opinion: Indian Gaming, Good or Bad for Reservations and Local Communities?" *Indian Country Today*, 16 August 2000.

Anders, Gary. "Indian Gaming: Financial and Regulatory Issues." *Annals of the American Academy of Political and Social Science* 556 (March 1998).

Anders, Gary, and Donald Siegel. "The Impact of Indian Casinos on State Lotteries: A Case Study of Arizona." *Public Finance Review* 29, no. 2 (March 2001).

Anders, Gary, et al. "Does Indian Casino Gambling Reduce State Revenues? Evidence from Arizona." *Contemporary Economic Policy* 16, no. 3 (July 1998).

Baker, James N. "Gambling on the Reservation." *Newsweek*, 17 February 1992.

Barfield, Chet. "3 in 4 Californians Back Tribal Casinos." *San Diego Union-Tribune*, 1 August 2001.

Bennett, Thomas, Jr. *The Casino Gambling Industry and Its Psychological Meaning for Individuals Living on an American Indian Reservation*. Minneapolis: Minnesota School of Professional Psychology, 1999.

Berkery, Peter M., Jr. "Supreme Court Resolves Split over Indian Gambling Taxes." *Accounting Today*, 7 January 2002.

"Big Chief Pataki." Editorial. *Wall Street Journal,* 1 March 2002.

Buck, Claudia, et al. "A Ballot Mouthful." *California Journal* (April 2000). Ballot propositions in California in March 2000.

Byrne, Ed, and David Townsend. "*Claims Casino*": *A Report on State-Indian Relations in New York State.* Albany: The Assembly, State of New York, 1995.

Cordeiro, Eduardo E. "The Economics of Bingo: Factors Influencing the Success of Bingo Operations on American Indian Reservations." In *What Can Tribes Do? Strategies and Institutions in American Indian Economic Development,* edited by Stephen Cornell and Joseph Kalt. Los Angeles: University of California Los Angeles, 1992.

Dean, Stephanie. "Getting a Piece of the Action: Should the Federal Government Be Able to Tax Native American Gambling Revenue?" *Columbia Journal of Law and Social Problems* 32 (winter 1999).

Dunstan, Roger. "Gambling in California." *California Research Bureau.* January 1997. <www.library.ca.gov/CRB/97/03/crb97003.html#toc> (accessed August 2002).

Eisler, Kim Isaac. "Revenge of the Indians; Gambling Has Made the Once-Poor Pequots Rich, and Other Tribes Are Getting in on the High-Stakes Casino Action." *Washingtonian Magazine,* August 1993.

———. *Revenge of the Pequots: How a Small Native American Tribe Created the World's Most Profitable Casino.* New York: Simon and Schuster, 2001.

Erdrich, Louise. *Bingo Palace.* New York: Harper Perennial, 1993.

Flanagan, William G., and James Samuelson. "The New Buffalo—But Who Got the Meat?" *Forbes,* 8 September 1997.

Gabriel, Kathryn. *Gambler Way: Indian Gaming in Mythology, History, and Archaeology in North America.* Boulder, Colo.: Johnson Books, 1996.

Green, Rick. "Study: Indian Casinos an Economic Powerhouse." *Hartford Courant,* 20 May 2002.

"History of Tribal Gaming." *American Indian Gambling and Casino Information Center (Sponsored by the National Indian Gaming Association).* <www2.dgsys.com/~niga/index.html> (accessed August 2002).

"Indian Gaming and Indian Poverty." *Native Americas Magazine,* 18 February 1997.

Johnson, Mike. "Heading Back Home; Casinos, Jobs Lure Indians Back to Better Lives on Reservations." *Milwaukee Journal Sentinel,* 30 April 2001.

Jorgensen, Joseph G. "Gaming and Recent American Indian Economic Development." In *Indian Gaming: Who Wins?* edited by David Kamper and Angela Mullis. Los Angeles: UCLA American Indian Studies Center, 2000.

Kamper, David, and Angela Mullis, eds. *Indian Gaming: Who Wins?* Los Angeles: UCLA American Indian Studies Center, 2000.

Krepps, Jonathan, et al. *The National Evidence on the Socioeconomic Impacts of American Indian Gaming on Non-Indian Communities.* Cambridge: Harvard Project on American Indian Economic Development, 2000.

McCarthy, John. "Minnesota Gaming Officials Stunned by *The Wall Street Journal's* Spin." *Indian Country Today,* 27 May 2002.

McCulloch, Anne Merline. "The Politics of Indian Gaming: Tribe/State Relations and American Federalism." *Publius* 24 (summer 1994).

Miller, Christopher L. "Coyote's Game: Indian Casinos and the Indian Presence in Contemporary America." In *American Indians in American History, 1870–2001: A Companion Reader,* edited by Sterling Evans. Westport, Conn.: Praeger, 2002.

Northrup, Jim. *The Rez Road Follies: Canoes, Casinos, Computers, and Birch Bark Baskets.* Minneapolis: University of Minnesota Press, 1999.

Ohr, Bruce. "Statement of Bruce G. Ohr, Chief, Organized Crime and Racketeering Section, Criminal Division, Department of Justice, Presented to the Senate Committee on Indian Affairs Oversight Hearing on the Indian Gaming Regulatory Act, Wednesday, July 25, 2001." *U.S. Department of Justice, Office of Tribal Justice.* <www.usdoj.gov/otj/statementbrucegohr.htm> (accessed August 2002).

Peroff, Nicholas C. "Indian Gaming, Tribal Sovereignty, and American Indian Tribes as Complex Adaptive Systems." *American Indian Culture and Research Journal* 25, no. 3 (2001).

Schaeffer, E. G. *Indian Casino.* Bloomington, Ind.: 1st Books, 2001.

Schmidt, Robert, and William N. Thompson. *Not Exactly "A Fair Share": Revenue Sharing and Native American Casinos in Wisconsin.* Thiensville: Wisconsin Policy Research Institute, 2002.

Segal, David. "Dances with Sharks: Why the Indian Gaming Experiment's Going Wrong." *Washington Monthly,* March 1992.

Sowik, William. "Indian Casino Law Promotes Racism." *Hartford Courant,* 7 August 2001.

Spilde, Katherine A. "Educating Local Non-Indian Communities about Indian Nation Governmental Gaming: Messages and Methods." In *Indian Gaming: Who Wins?* edited by David Kamper and Angela Mullis. Los Angeles: UCLA American Indian Studies Center, 2000.

Stein, Wayne, J. "American Indians and Gambling: Economic and Social Impacts." In *American Indian Studies: An Interdisciplinary Approach to Contemporary Issues,* edited by Dane Morrison. New York: Peter Lang, 1997.

"Tribal Casinos a Rotten Deal for N.Y." Editorial. *Wall Street Journal,* 5 April 2002.

Useem, Jerry. "The Big Gamble: Have American Indians Found Their New Buffalo?" *Fortune,* 2 October 2000.

Vallen, Gary K. "Gaming in the U.S.—A Ten-Year Comparison." *Cornell Hotel and Restaurant Administration Quarterly* 34, no. 6 (December 1993).

Vinje, David L. "Native American Economic Development on Selected Reservations: A Comparative Analysis." *American Journal of Economics and Sociology* 55 (October 1996).

Vizenor, Gerald. *Crossbloods: Bone Courts, Bingo, and Other Reports.* Minneapolis: University of Minnesota Press, 1990.

———. "Gambling on Sovereignty." *American Indian Quarterly* 16, no. 3 (summer 1992).

———. *Heirs of Columbus.* Wesleyan, Conn.: Wesleyan University Press, 1992.

"The Wall Street Journal Loses Respect." *Indian Country Today,* 7 March 2002.

"The Wall Street Journal's Derivative Fiction." *Indian Country Today,* 12 April 2002.

Video

Raising the Stakes. Wisdom Tree Productions, 1996.

Web Sites

California Nevada Indian Gaming Association (CNIGA). <www.cniga.com>. CNIGA provides information on California and Nevada Indian gaming issues.

California's Modern Indian War. <www.geocities.com/CapitolHill/Lobby/4621/1native.html>. Covers the battle over Proposition 5.

Casinos: Is Gaming the "New Buffalo"? <www.kstrom.net/isk/games/gaming.html>. Various opinions and articles on the gaming issue.

Gaming in Arizona. <www.arizonarepublic.com/gaming>. Special site on the Arizona gambling controversy.

Indian Gaming Regulatory Act. 1988. *Legal Information Institute.* <www4.law.cornell.edu/uscode/25/ch29.html>. Text version of 1988 federal national Indian Gaming Regulatory Act.

"Indian Gaming Resources." *Tribal Law and Policy Institute.* <www.tribal-institute.org/lists/gaming.htm>.

National Gambling Impact Study Commission. <govinfo.library.unt.edu/ngisc/index.htm>. Federal report on gambling across the United States.

National Indian Gambling and Casino Information Center. Sponsored by the National Indian Gaming Association. <www2.dgsys.com/~niga/index.html>.

National Indian Gaming Association. <www.indiangaming.org>.

National Indian Gaming Commission (NIGC). <www.nigc.gov>. NIGC is an independent federal regulatory body.

6

THE CONFLICT BETWEEN ECONOMIC DEVELOPMENT AND ENVIRONMENTAL PROTECTION

The search for Native Americans' natural resources began to accelerate during World War II as the need for petroleum products precipitated an increase in exploratory drilling on Indian land, especially in the Great Plains. The demands of the Cold War also prompted the search for uranium reserves, which were soon found on several Indian reservations, notably on those of the Laguna Pueblo and Navajo. In addition, population growth in the West after World War II helped to fuel demand for Native Americans' coal, oil, and gas reserves. After the war, a new generation of Native American leaders began to work to strengthen tribal sovereignty and become less dependent on the federal government. The drive for autonomy included the important goal of making reservations appealing places to live and to work, places where tribal officials were at least fighting to create jobs and provide economic opportunity. Self-sufficiency was a powerful stimulus for some tribes, and during the 1960s and 1970s the promise of natural resource development enabled a number of tribes to begin thinking along those lines.

In the mid-1960s, the Bureau of Indian Affairs (BIA) negotiated coal-mining leases for the Northern Cheyenne, the Navaho, and the Hopi. But the BIA failed to get those Indian nations a fair deal for their coal, accepting offers of 12 cents per acre while similar non-Indian coal fields were generating bids of between $16 and $100 an acre, or 100 to 1,000 times higher. The oil crisis of the 1970s created great demand and thus higher prices for oil and coal, which exposed the problem of leasing on Indian reservations. The Peabody Coal Company, assisted by the BIA, misled the Navajo by claiming that nuclear power would soon make their coal reserves in the Black Mesa part of the reservation obsolete, thus making its low offer seem better than it was. It turned out that the lawyer acting for the Hopi Nation, whose territory was included in the Black Mesa coal area, represented the Peabody Coal Company. Both political and environmental issues complicated the economic issues. The strip mining of coal on the Navajo and Hopi reservations devastated the landscape and angered traditionalists who revered the land as sacred. The Black Mesa coal "rip-off" became a cause for concern for environmentalists and supporters of Indian rights. CBS, ABC, the *Washington Post,* and the *New York Times* covered the story and turned Black Mesa into a symbol for the exploitation of Indians and the devastation of the environment at a time when many Americans were coming to grips with national environmental problems.

Poor lease rates and environmental damage produced two main changes: Native Americans reevaluated their policies of natural resource development, and tribal leaders organized to prevent future abuses. The Navajo formed the Committee to Save Black Mesa, inviting tribal leaders from other coal-producing tribes to witness the damage done by strip mining and discuss the problem of leasing. The Northern Cheyenne were particularly interested in this intertribal communication, because they owned huge coalfields and themselves had been ripped off in the 1960s.

Facing stiff resistance from the Northern Cheyenne, energy companies offered $9 per acre, still below market rates. In late 1972, Consolidation Coal, or Consol, raised the stakes by offering the Northern Cheyenne a bonus of $35 an acre, a royalty of 25 cents per ton, and a $1.5 million community health center—an incredible offer to a community with 50 percent unemployment and the kind of health problems one finds in rural America. Consol also intended to build gasification plants on the reservation. Consol demanded an answer to its offer within 15 days, putting enormous pressure on tribal officials. A number of Cheyenne were concerned that Consol's plan would quickly overwhelm their community, as the company would use valuable water resources for the four gasification plants and build a town to house nearly 30,000 workers, 10 times the number of Cheyenne. The promise of nearly $500,000 per Cheyenne family failed to appeal to all tribal members, and the offer was rejected. One Cheyenne spoke for many of his fellow citizens when he noted that he would rather be poor on his land, with his own people, and protect the Cheyenne way of life than live rich on degraded land surrounded by strangers. Consol's offer made Northern Cheyenne officials understand exactly how valuable their coal was, and they moved to cancel all existing leases on the grounds that federal officials had failed to represent the tribe's interests. They also charged that in addition to providing below-market royalties, coal companies had broken a variety of federal environmental regulations.

Native American leaders believed that energy companies were not to be trusted, but they also blamed the Interior Department and the BIA for failing to represent their interests; for example, the BIA provided little or no geological data with which a tribe could increase its leverage in negotiations,

Jim Wilson, left, and Jim Balluta from Nondalton, Alaska, join thousands of Alaska natives, Native Americans, and non–Native Americans, as they march through downtown Anchorage in 2002 during the fifth annual We the People march. This year's theme, "The Next 10,000 Years," expresses care and concern for the earth's ecosystem for future generations. The march concludes with a rally, where Alaska natives and Native Americans address the crowd. The first rally was called in 1997 in response to the U.S. Supreme Court's Venetie decision, which denied sovereignty to Alaska natives. (AP/Wide World Photos)

and it failed to recommend certain kinds of leases that would produce bonuses if prices rose. The Northern Cheyenne's petition to cancel existing leases caused consternation among energy companies and federal officials. After lengthy negotiations, the Cheyenne contracts were nullified, new federal coal leases were signed, and the tribe received millions of dollars in compensation for lost revenue, legal costs, and environmental damage. Other tribes also put coal leasing on hold until it better reflected their interests. Cheyenne leader Allen Rowland captured the mood of energy-producing tribes by saying, "We don't negotiate with the companies until they tear those leases up in front of us and burn them. And we can start over on our terms, not theirs."[1]

NATIVE AMERICANS ORGANIZE

The Black Mesa and Northern Cheyenne leasing problems inspired 26 tribes of the northern plains to form the Native American Natural Resources

Development Federation (NANRDF) to establish fair prices and tribal controls "on their terms" and not those of the energy companies. The stakes were high. In 1975, Native Americans' natural resources included about 3 percent of the nation's total reserves of oil and natural gas, between 100 and 200 billion tons of coal or about 10 percent of the nation's coal reserves, and, perhaps most important, a high percentage of the country's uranium reserves. In 1975, the Council of Energy Resource Tribes (CERT) was formed by 25 oil-, gas-, and mineral-producing tribes, including the Blackfeet, Navajo, Hopi, and Laguna Pueblo, replacing NANRDF as the nation's most influential organization of Indian energy-producing nations. CERT had moderate goals: serve as a clearinghouse for information regarding issues of resource development and its environmental impact, find ways to use the resources on reservations rather than export them, and develop statistical pictures of what reservations actually held in terms of resources.

In 1977, Peter MacDonald, the chairman of CERT's board of directors as well as the chairman of the Navajo Nation, called CERT a "domestic OPEC," a term that created animosity toward Indian nations, as some Americans thought they were exploiting the energy crisis for financial gain. But the problem with this public perception, as with the gambling phenomenon, was that few tribes were getting rich. Some Native Americans considered such criticism racist, because Exxon, Mobil Oil, and other multinational oil companies did not fail to take advantage of high demand and restricted supply. Most tribes did not have sufficient resources to justify an embargo, but more important, Native Americans did not intend to exploit the oil crisis but to earn what was coming to them. MacDonald lived on the Navajo reservation and knew very well how poorly the Navajo had benefited from natural resource production. To keep CERT from developing a separatist mentality, however, federal officials gave the organization more funding. CERT moved its headquarters to Washington, D.C., to improve its lobbying capability, but it generated criticism from Native Americans for doing little but spending money. Some member tribes objected to CERT's support of uranium mining, while others questioned the value of its advice, which came in part from industry specialists. But since reforms were instituted in response to those criticisms, CERT has fought to give Native Americans a voice in a complex process involving issues of economics, environmental law, and national security.

As a result of CERT's lobbying, the Interior Department revised its leasing and royalty policies, and Congress passed two laws: the 1982 Indian Mineral Development Act, which expanded Native Americans' options in the development process, including forming energy corporations of their own, as the Jicarilla Apache did that year; and the 1983 Federal Oil and Gas Royalty Management Act, which improved to some degree the government's ability to calculate royalties owed to Indian tribes as well as to punish with civil and criminal penalties those companies that cheated. Government reports found that Native Americans lost nearly $5.8 billion because of inadequate accounting procedures and lax BIA enforcement. Tribal governments also sought to regulate energy companies by asserting their right to impose severance taxes on firms doing business within their borders. The energy companies sued, but despite their high-powered legal teams the Supreme Court ruled in *Merrion v. Jicarilla Apache Tribe* (1982) that tribes possessed "inherent power" to tax and threw out the companies' suit.

Tax revenue became important during the Reagan years, which, as noted in chapter 5, were difficult ones for many Indians. Reagan's budget cuts in the first few years of his administration cut federal funding for Indian programs from $3.5 billion to $2.5 billion. But Reagan also promoted economic development on reservations, and he offered the government's support for the development of Native Americans' resources. Native Americans and America, he said, "stand to gain from the prudent development and management of the vast coal, gas, uranium and other resources found on Indian lands."[2] But this kind of economic development had environmental consequences, as the Navajo and Pueblo cases demonstrate.

URANIUM MINING AND ITS CONSEQUENCES

Uranium mining became a dangerous activity on Indian lands, which produced much of the country's domestic supply through 380 uranium leases. Mining began on the Navajo and Pueblo reservations in the 1940s and 1950s as the Cold War evolved. By the time the first wave of mining leases ended in the 1970s, the damage to miners and the environment was clear, making Native Americans hesitant to accept new uranium mining leases. As a Navajo tribal council member put it, "No one ever told us of the danger in [uranium mining].... It was the only employment that was ever brought to our part of the reservation.... Then the mines closed. [Mining companies] went away. Now the people are dying."[3] Rates of cancer and respiratory ailments among Navajo miners were found to be very high; but nonminers also suffered health problems that continue to this day, including birth defects, because uranium tailings, by-products of the mining operation, found their way into community water supplies and even materials used for building reservation homes. On the Laguna Pueblo reservation in New Mexico, the Anaconda Copper Company earned roughly $600 million over the life of its lease, which led to the development of the world's largest uranium mine. Although the company provided employment to hundreds of Pueblo miners, it too left the reservation with contaminated water supplies and land. An investigation revealed that the company had used low-grade uranium ore to build roads leading off the reservation, furthering the irradiation of the Pueblo reservation. In negotiating the Navajo and Pueblo leases, the Bureau of Indian Affairs failed to secure provisions for company cleanup of the sites after the mining operations ceased. Federal inspectors found numerous violations in the mines themselves that added to Indian miners' health risks. Dr. Joseph

Wagoner of the National Institute for Occupational Safety and Health said conditions at the Navajo reservation "present serious medical and ethical questions about the responsibility of the [Kerr-McGee Corporation] and the federal government."[4]

After lengthy negotiations, Anaconda agreed to pay more than $43 million to rehabilitate Pueblo land and water, in part because it hoped to return for more mining. Navajo and Pueblo efforts to secure compensation for their miners culminated in July 2000, when President William Clinton signed into law the Radiation Exposure Compensation Act Amendments of 2000. The original Radiation Exposure Compensation Act of 1990 put the burden of proof on the miners, many of whom were forced to hire lawyers and negotiate with a hostile bureaucracy to get limited compensation. The 2000 act, which potentially benefited hundreds of thousands of non-Indian uranium workers as well, recognized workers who suffered as a result of mining uranium for the nation during the Cold War and offered financial compensation to widows or to those still living who needed operations. In announcing the program, Energy Secretary Bill Richardson said, "Justice for our nuclear workers is finally happening. The government for a change is on their side and not against them."[5]

Even as groups like the Navajo Uranium Radiation Victims Committee and Navajo Nations Dependents of Uranium Workers Committee fought to secure that justice for Native American uranium workers, energy companies once again sought to mine Navajo land for uranium. In the mid-1990s, the Texas-based company Hydro-Resources Incorporated proposed a new uranium-mining project near the Navajo community of Crownpoint. The project would not have used below-ground miners but a special "leaching" process that dissolves uranium underground before bringing it to the surface. The legacy of the Navajo experience with uranium mining has led to firm resistance from the Eastern Navajo Diné against Uranium Mining (ENDAUM), while other Navajo supported the project's creation of jobs, thus dividing the community and even families.

In early 1993, another mining controversy erupted in northern Wisconsin when the Exxon Corporation resumed its efforts to secure approval to build the Crandon zinc-copper sulfide mine (in conjunction with the Canadian company Rio Algom); local groups had stopped previous proposals since 1975. Native Americans living near the site opposed the Crandon Mine because of fears that groundwater supplies would be contaminated. The Crandon controversy has divided state and federal governments over the rights of Native American governments to regulate local environmental conditions. In 1995, the U.S. Environmental Protection Agency (EPA) gave the Mole Lake Chippewa the right to set tribal water quality standards, which gave the Chippewa the authority to regulate upstream mining operations. But the Wisconsin state government and its Department of Natural Resources opposed the granting of such sovereignty, sending the matter to the courts, which ruled in the Chippewa's favor. The case, however, is under appeal, and the Crandon Mine proposal is still under review.

FRAMING THE ISSUE

The dumping of both radioactive and hazardous wastes is another source of controversy and stress among Native Americans. In 1982, Congress passed the Nuclear Waste Policy Act (NWPA), which established an agenda for dealing with the ever-increasing amount of spent fuel rods and other radioactive wastes that nuclear power plants produce; the act required the Department of Energy to assume ownership of the spent fuel, which would stay radioactive for ten thousand years, by 1998. A 1987 amendment to the act funded the search for a community to accept monitored retrievable storage (MRS) facilities to hold, temporarily, radioactive materials until a permanent site at Yucca Mountain, Nevada, could be built. In the early 1990s, Native American reservations were targeted as potential sources of MRS facilities. In December 1992, U.S. nuclear waste negotiator David Leroy offered Native American communities $100,000 just to consider participation in the MRS program; additional payments would be forthcoming at each stage of the approval process. Initially 29 tribes expressed interest, but after political opposition developed, the number dropped to just a few. Mescalero Apache politicians were the first to receive the $100,000 grant, dividing the Apache people among pro-dump and anti-dump forces. When Congress abandoned the grants program, because of pressure from politicians opposed to the dumping of nuclear wastes in their states, the Apache negotiated with utility companies directly. The Skull Valley Goshute of Utah recently negotiated a contract with Private Fuel Storage, a utility consortium, to store spent nuclear fuel rods on their small reservation roughly forty miles from Salt Lake City. The prospect has generated great concern among Utah politicians, who sued in federal court to stop the project.

This effort by both the federal government and private utilities to find a place for nuclear wastes set off heated debates on a number of reservations, as did the effort by private companies to find a place for hazardous wastes on Native American land. In the early 1990s, companies began to negotiate with tribal officials to establish hazardous and solid waste dumps. Indian reservations were seen as attractive for a number of reasons, one being that local and state environmental regulations did not apply because in the late 1980s Congress had given tribal authorities the right to establish their own standards and regulations on development and to work directly with the EPA on negotiating contracts for siting hazardous waste dumps on Indian lands (the BIA rather than the EPA regulates municipal solid waste facilities). These private companies found Native Americans initially willing to consider building waste sites or incinerators. Opposition from environmental groups squelched many of the deals, but others are in the works.

In short, both ends of resource development—the mining of resources for the production of energy and the wastes that result—have become part of the economic calculus for Native Americans. Given the country's energy demands, Native Americans' supply of natural resources, and a tortured history of development of these resources, in addition to Native Americans' traditional respect for the land, it is not surprising that this issue is an explosive one. As with the other issues we have considered, this one does not just affect Native Americans. Non-Indians support both economic boosters and environmental defenders. State officials oppose the efforts of federal officials. Questions of patriotism, national security, tribal sovereignty, federal energy policy, and environmentalism make the issue a complicated one. The stakes are high for energy companies; for federal, state, and tribal governments; and, especially, for Native Americans. In August 1994, a Native American teenager was killed in what members of his community believe was retaliation for his family's opposition to a toxic sewage dump; a day later the home of another environmental activist was raked by gunfire. On the Navajo reservation, an environmental activist received death threats after a controversial tribal logging operation was shut down. The toxic legacy of uranium mining in the Southwest makes the production of natural resources a potentially fatal enterprise. It is natural, therefore, that economic development plans engender conflict and controversy.

PROPONENTS OF MINING AND WASTE STORAGE DEVELOPMENT PROJECTS

The Economic Impetus

Native Americans are, as the reader knows by now, a diverse group of people—culturally, socially, politically, and geographically. Many Native American communities have adapted economic production to their environment—offering tourists access to it, harvesting wild rice from it, and, as noted in chapter 2, creating profitable commercial salmon fishing operations from its bounty. Many tribes have used proceeds from casinos to diversify their economic ventures, as was seen in chapter 5. The Mescalero Apache built a ski resort and logging operation. The Santa Ana Pueblo tax utility companies that run pipelines across their reservation and manage a casino, a golf course, a flour mill, and other businesses. The Couer D'Alene of Idaho charge fees for houseboats and docks on their waterways. The Seneca sell gasoline and cigarettes on their reservation, a successful operation because they don't tax the products. Non-Indian companies have made an increasing number of deals with Native Americans, in part because casino revenue has given Native Americans venture capital to invest outside reservation boundaries and also because working with Native Americans provides non-Indian businesses access to minority enterprise contracts.

The development of natural resources, however, has polarized many Native American communities. Development projects like coal mining, oil and gas exploration, and waste storage have been highly controversial, especially for Indian communities that have not succeeded with casinos, ski resorts, or other ventures. Because some Native Americans live on isolated and sometimes desolate land, their options for economic development are limited. In some cases, such as the Navajo, cultural opposition precludes the casino-gaming option. In the case of the Goshute of Utah, state law prohibits gambling, reducing their economic options. Several high-profile cases, outlined in the following sections, give us insight into why some Native American leaders support either the extraction of natural resources through mining or the storage of hazardous or nuclear wastes.

Even environmental activists have noted the reasons why tribal officials pursue potentially dangerous projects like mining and waste storage. A spokesperson for the Indigenous Environmental Network, a leading pan-tribal environmental group, said, “I understand why [tribal officials] do it. Most of our tribal governments are in a survival mode. They're trying to provide housing, education, and health care, plus they're fighting alcoholism and drug abuse and still trying to get the U.S. government to recognize its treaties. They're looking for resources anywhere they can.”[6] Tribal officials feel great pressure to provide not just basic human services to their constituents but jobs, especially well-paying jobs. The possible return of nuclear mining to the Navajo Nation is testimony to the powerful temptation that large-scale development can offer a tribal community facing unemployment rates of 30 percent or higher. In the case of the proposed Crownpoint uranium mine, the Navajo who would benefit are allottees, owners of allotments of land for which Hydro Resources would pay for the right to lease. But other Navajo support the project because Hydro Resources hires workers and pays relatively well in comparison with other reservation jobs.

Peter MacDonald, the leader of the Navajo Nation and a founder of CERT in the late 1970s, argued that resource development and conservation could go hand in hand if a people stayed true to their traditional relationship with their land. “My people must go beyond subsistence and survival through economic development. In the future we must have self-sufficiency based on using our resources to serve future generations. This means we must be conservationists and find a balance of all life.”[7] Other tribal officials, like Crow Nation chairman Richard Real Bird, have promised to situate mining in areas not considered sacred by their people or severely restrict development in those areas. The Crow have both a high rate of poverty and one of the largest coal reserves in the world. Real Bird said that reclaiming control of how the land is used is the first step toward ameliorating “all these social problems that are associated with poverty,” which include alcoholism and despair.[8] He believed that development, if controlled by tribal officials sensitive to Crow cultural traditions, could result in meaningful economic benefits.

Nuclear Waste Storage

Both tribal and federal officials have made the stewardship argument in promoting nuclear waste storage. David Leroy, head of the Office of the Nuclear Waste Negotiator, championed Native Americans' storage of nuclear waste for several reasons, one of which was Native Americans' "cultural traditions and respect for the land." In speaking to the annual conference of the National Congress of American Indians, Leroy tried to persuade tribes to participate in the government's monitored retrievable storage (MRS) plan. Yakima Indian Nation leader Russell Jim made a similar argument in justifying the Yakima's acceptance of an MRS grant. At first glance their interest was unusual because tribal officials had opposed the nearby Hanford Nuclear Reservation, which has required a hugely expensive cleanup of military nuclear waste. But Jim, the Yakima's environmental restoration and waste management manager, supports storage of nuclear wastes in part because it may help with the cleanup of Hanford, which could lead to the restoration of Yakima sacred sites that Hanford contaminated. While non-Yakima supporters of the project have emphasized the potential economic impact for a tribe struggling with unemployment, Jim champions the environmental aspect of it, even as he admits that the MRS may not "be acceptable at any price to our people. But it is not our fault the environment is damaged in such a manner, and to do nothing about it may be just as wrong."[9] Jim asked only for the tribe to study the MRS option.

In December 1990, Eddie Brown, Assistant Secretary of the Interior for Indian Affairs, called the debate over Native American waste storage "a very explosive issue." Federal officials claim to be helpful in providing information to native communities considering various proposals but have otherwise taken a hands-off approach. According to Brown, "Waste operations are going to have to exist somewhere in the United States. Our job is not to run reservations or to tell reservations what they can or can't do."[10] When the U.S. government tried to create interest in the MRS program, several Indian nations considered its potential. The Yakima eventually abandoned the MRS option, as did the Tonkawa of Oklahoma, the Pauite-Shoshone of Oregon and Nevada, and a number of other native communities. The Mescalero Apache of New Mexico, however, pursued it with great vigor. The Mescalero had already established several economic ventures, including ski and golf resorts. But Mescalero Apache Tribal Council (MATC) president Wendell Chino considered nuclear storage "a business opportunity" worth considering because "people need the work." Chino highlighted three reasons to consider the MRS project in a letter to nuclear waste negotiator David Leroy. "First, because we were asked to consider it by the United States government; second, because there appears to be an opportunity to operate a MRS facility on a sound commercial basis; and third, because we can bring to such a program our strong traditional values that favor protecting the earth."[11]

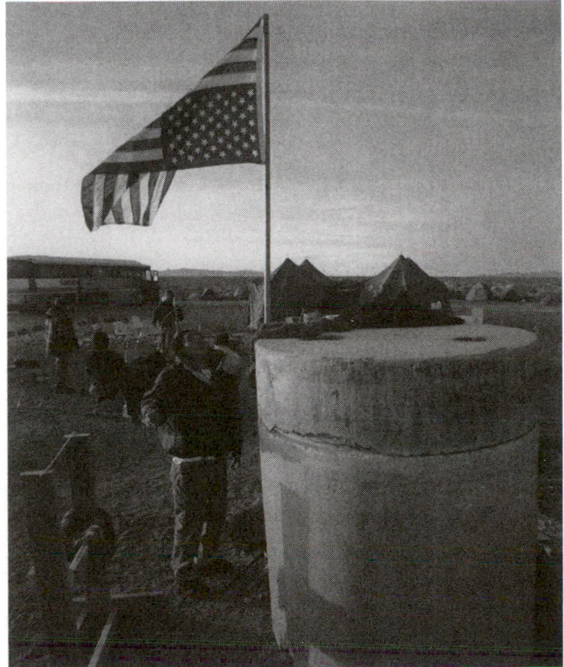

Newton Prentiss, a Kiowa from Carnegie, Oklahoma, unfurls an American flag that had become wrapped around its pole, flown upside down as a distress signal, at an Indian encampment at a proposed nuclear waste dump site in the Mojave Desert in Ward Valley, California, in 1998. The concrete cylinder caps a test well drilled years ago to test the groundwater. The Bureau of Land Management threatened to evict the Indians from the long-standing protest encampment. (AP/ Wide World Photos)

Chino's explanation captures several themes of the pro–waste storage argument: patriotism, economic opportunity, and environmental stewardship. Chino elaborated on his environmental perspective by telling Leroy, "If our assessment convinces us that [the facility] will be truly passive—nothing created, destroyed, changed or deposited in the earth—and if it's of a temporary nature, then we are prepared to consider moving ahead with a formal application to host such a project." Chino, like other tribal officials considering waste storage, defended his action on the basis of proceeding slowly and studying the potential. As he told the *Washington Post,* "We won't know until we have gone through the study whether to pursue it."[12] Fundamentally the MATC supported the project for economic reasons. Chino noted that it would require round-the-clock guards, technicians, and other professional jobs and would possibly reap between $15 and $25 million per year in revenues; he argued that "the storage of spent nuclear fuel is a 21st century industry with the attendant complement of high-tech, high-wage jobs not often available to Indian tribes."[13] MATC vice president Fred Peso echoed Chino's argument by calling the project "an economic opportunity that the Tribal Council needs to explore because it would diversity our tribal job base and place one more brick in the structure of economic self-sufficiency."[14] In addition, the project would require only 450 acres, one-thousandth of the reservation's acreage.

Under Chino's and Peso's guidance, the MATC went through the first two stages of the MRS permit process before applying for a $2.8 million final grant. In pursuing the project, the two leaders faced criticism from within the tribe and from New Mexico politicians opposed to nuclear waste storage in the state. Chino and Peso, as well as other tribal officials contending with similar criticism, decry what they see as a racist dimension of such opposition, which implies that the Apache don't know what they're doing. Peso defended the Apache in testimony to a congressional natural resources subcommittee: "You needn't worry whether the Mescalero Apache people are smart enough or capable enough to manage this project. We can be relied upon to protect our lands, ourselves and our neighbors."[15] Chino and Peso also felt betrayed when Congress, under pressure from Native American environmentalists and New Mexico representatives, killed funding for the MRS program before the tribe entered the $2.8 million stage. Peso told a reporter, "It's ironic that the state [of New Mexico] has enjoyed the benefit of nuclear projects," referring to New Mexico's long association with nuclear weapons development, which includes the atomic bomb's development at Los Alamos and ongoing nuclear testing at the Sandia Laboratory.[16]

Forced to pursue the project without federal funding, Apache leaders conducted private negotiations with a group of 33 utility companies. When the issue was put to a tribal vote in February 1995, the Apache people rejected the plan, 490 to 362. But tribal officials claimed that voters were not made aware of the economic benefits of the project and exercised a provision of the tribal constitution to petition for a second election. Amidst criticism that tribal officials unfairly influenced voters, the Apache then accepted the waste proposal in a second vote, 593 to 372. Chino's negotiations with the utility companies eventually broke down, influenced by the opposition that developed during the two tribal votes. According to Chino, there was "an ongoing inability by the parties to reach an understanding on critical issues related to the project."[17] Neither side elaborated on the reasons for the breakdown. Some utility companies backed out of the consortium as Apache opposition became more vocal. Given this opposition and the long-term environmental risks the project posed, the failed talks may well have had to do with Apache requests for guarantees that the waste would eventually be taken off the reservation if a permanent site such as Yucca Mountain was not built.

Watching the Mescalero Apache project develop and then dissolve were the Skull Valley Goshute of Utah, who picked up where the Apache left off. In 1997, tribal leaders signed an agreement with Private Fuel Storage, a private consortium of utility companies similar to the one that sought to use Apache land to store more than 44,000 tons of nuclear waste on the Goshute reservation for a period of 25 years; the waste, which would come from Minnesota, New York, and several other states, would be stored on roughly 840 of the reservation's 18,000 acres. Tribal officials supported the proposal for several reasons. One, it would create high-tech jobs, which could induce Goshute to return to the reservation. Tribal chairman Leon Bear argues that people left because of the Goshute's poor economic situation; less than 30 of 112 tribal members remain on Goshute land. "There's nothing there for them," he said.[18] Two, vice chairwoman Mary Allen notes that the land is not productive at the moment and should serve a purpose for the Goshute. Tribal officials tried to establish a casino on their reservation but the Utah legislature, influenced by a strong Mormon presence, prohibits gambling operations. Bear resents the implication that the waste site endangers Utah. Neighboring his reservation are army nerve gas and bomb testing ranges in addition to a facility stockpiling chemical weapons. Bear said that the federal government had already made that part of the state "an industrial waste zone." Given those risks, he believes the Goshute, as a sovereign nation, have the right to benefit from similar facilities. In addition, besides the jobs, Bear sees the millions of dollars in anticipated revenue funding a medical clinic, a police and fire station, and college scholarships for the next generation. The project, Bear believes, will help preserve the Goshute tribe, in part because the proposal includes funds for a tribal cultural center and programs to revive traditional language and crafts.

On July 23, 2002, President George W. Bush signed off on the $58 billion storage program at Yucca Mountain, Nevada. A week later a federal judge upheld the Goshute's sovereignty and thus their right to negotiate for the waste site, which would serve as a temporary resting place until the Yucca Mountain facility can be constructed. The final decision rests with the U.S. Nuclear Regulatory Commission (NRC), which was expected to reject or support the Goshute's storage proposal early in 2003. Antinuclear activists have traveled to the reservation to protest the Goshute waste site. Despite the recent court ruling, Utah's state and federal representatives have promised additional protests of their own as the NRC decision approaches. The terrorist attacks of September 11, 2001, have also complicated matters. The NRC recently conducted a new safety analysis of the proposed Goshute facility amid concerns that it could be vulnerable to infiltration by terrorist groups.

With America's energy demands increasing and world supplies vulnerable to political upheaval, the pressure on Native American communities to participate in the energy economy will no doubt increase as well. The Blackfeet of northwestern Montana began aggressively drilling for oil in the late 1990s. William Old Chief, chairman of the Blackfeet Tribal Business Council, believed that more Blackfeet citizens supported new drilling efforts than opposed them. He also resented outsiders telling the Blackfeet what to do with their lands. "We have the right to determine the destiny of our land, and no one knows its value or cares more about it than we do.... I can't overly stress how protective this council feels toward the land. These mountains are a source of spiritual strength."[19] Under the Bush administration, there has been renewed emphasis on exploring lands in the American West for oil and gas supplies. Some tribal leaders want to tap into this development agenda. In June 2001, several leaders of Great Plains Indian nations testified before a congressional Senate Indian Affairs Committee that they wanted federal aid to help attract oil and gas companies with tax incentives and feasibility studies. According to Tex Hall, chairman of North Dakota's Three Affiliated Tribes (the Mandan, Hidatsa, and Arikira Nation), Native Americans "want a paycheck" instead of a welfare check.[20] Hall has proposed that his tribe agree to an $81 million oil refinery to produce such paychecks. With poverty and unemployment part of the landscape of rural Native America, calls such as Hall's for communities to utilize their natural and human resources in large-scale development projects will continue.

OPPONENTS OF MINING AND WASTE STORAGE DEVELOPMENT PROJECTS

Native American Spiritual Traditions

Native Americans feel great ambivalence toward economic development. Jonathan Buffalo, a teacher on the Mesquaki Indian Settlement in Iowa, noted that "Indians are like people split in two. Economically, they have to get along with the outside world. Spiritually and culturally, they have to get along with themselves."[21] The effort to provide economic development through mining and waste storage has split many Indian communities because in the pursuit of such goals spiritual ties to the land have been threatened, damaged, or destroyed. As the aforementioned Northern Cheyenne case demonstrates, notions of monetary or economic progress do not always take precedence over spiritually based environmental concerns. As the cases outlined in subsequent paragraphs reveal, potentially destructive economic projects have engendered opposition on tribal, intertribal, and even intercommunity levels, creating effective campaigns to protect the environment and citizens' health.

For reasons of economic instability and environmental vulnerability, many Native Americans do not want to depend on extractive enterprises like coal and uranium mining. The fluctuating prices of oil and uranium, in addition to the environmental consequences of extracting them from reservation lands, have made reliance on natural resource production a risky business. For example, Navaho tribal budgets derived 94 percent of their revenue from mining in 1954 and 56 percent in 1981, the result of declining prices and slackening demand. A similar dynamic occurred on the Laguna Pueblo reservation in the late 1970s. The health problems of Navajo and Pueblo miners have alarmed Native Americans, as did two other notable cases. In the late 1970s, 3.5 million pounds of radioactive tailings were found on the Lakota reservation. On July 16, 1978, an accident near Churchrock, New Mexico, released nearly 100 million gallons of radioactive water into both Navajo and non-Navajo environments, which was a more serious environmental threat than that of Three Mile Island. Many Native Americans object to the storage of nuclear and hazardous wastes on reservation lands because of this history.

Opposition to environmentally dangerous projects has been driven by Native Americans' political consciousness and environmental and spiritual traditions, as well as a belief that other economic options more accurately accord with those traditions. William A. Young identified five main ecological themes of spiritual traditions: "Interconnectedness: We are all related; Reverence: All of life is spiritual; Mother Earth: The womb of life; Imbeddedness: We are the land and the land is us; Reciprocity: Living in harmony."[22] Prominent Native American intellectual Paula Gunn Allen describes the spiritual tradition when she writes that Native Americans do not see the land as "a means of survival, a setting for our affairs, a resource on which we draw.... It is rather a part of our being, dynamic, significant, real. It is ourself...in a sense more real than any conceptualization or abstraction about the nature of the human being can ever be."[23] Damage to the land can harm the spiritual ecology and physical health of a people. Many Navajo believe that when a person becomes ill it reflects an imbalance between the earth and its inhabitants. The physical illnesses and death that Navajo miners have suffered from uranium mining thus reflect the extent to which mining has damaged Native Americans' harmony with the earth. An Oneida activist, Kla Kindness, believes that drug and alcohol use "is due to the nature of the [mining] work: digging up mother earth is what it is, and there is some kind of mentality that develops from working in a destructive way."[24]

Some environmental activists, both Indian and non-Indian, see the issue as one of exploitation of isolated native communities, raising the argument that mining and waste storage constitute "environmental racism" and even "genocide." Lance Hughes of the group Native Americans for a Clean Environment says that "federal and corporate bureaucrats are using the old trick to go to 'Indian Country,' conveniently geographically removed from mainstream communities. The general public doesn't know anything about this move, and given the geographic and political segregation, they probably won't hear much about it."[25] Some Native American commentators connect the efforts of corporate America to dump waste on or mine toxic materials from their reservations as a form of ecocide that threatens human life. As the Women of All Red Nations warned in 1980, "To contaminate Indian water is an act of war more subtle than military aggression, yet no less deadly.... Water is life." Jill Bend agrees, arguing that "water is life but the corporations are killing it. It's a genocide of all the environment and all species of creatures."[26] Native American environmentalists may view threats to the earth and water from different perspectives, but they all agree that economic development that threatens the earth is not compatible with indigenous traditions of stewardship and use.

Resistance to Dumping and Mining Projects

In the early 1990s, a number of Native American communities—including the Kaw of Oklahoma, the Sioux in South Dakota, and the Choctaw of Mississippi—considered but ultimately rejected proposals to situate solid and hazardous waste landfills on their reservations. They did so for a number of reasons. Vocal opposition from citizens as well as tribal officials was the main cause. Clay Wesley, a Choctaw council member, spoke for many of his fellow Choctaw, saying, "We do not need hazardous waste on land that we want to leave to our children, their children, and their children's children."[27] Choctaw staged anti-dumping demonstrations to help kill the toxic waste project.

Waste opponents like Wesley have been helped by an emerging intertribal environmental movement that has brought native groups together. In July 1990, Native Americans from 23 tribal communities gathered on the Navajo reservation for the first "toxic powwow," a conference called Protecting Mother Earth—The Toxic Threat to Indian Land; the conference was organized by the Indigenous Environmental Network (IEN) and the Navajo group Citizens against Ruining Our Environment (CARE), assisted by the international group Greenpeace. Regular meetings have since been held by groups like the National Tribal Environmental Council (NTEC), which formed in 1991 to assist tribal communities in the protecting and preserving of their environment. NTEC organized the four-day National Tribal Conference on Environmental Management in May 1992 to bring disparate and isolated Native American groups together to find common ground as well as to help their leaders connect with federal officials of the BIA and EPA. NTEC administrator Roderick Ariwite argued that "some of the worst environmental problems in the country are on Indian reservations. Indians don't have the money to address the problems, and they don't have the technical expertise."[28] Ariwite championed intervention by federal agencies to offer protection from illegal dumping and to help with the cleanup of both non-Indian- and Indian-generated dump sites. Besides NTEC, a number of other native groups like the IEN have set up information networks providing environmental information, current regulations, and profiles on companies' histories of dealing with tribal officials to help Native Americans fight against proposed storage or mining projects. IEN coordinator Tom Goldtooth told *Environmental Action Magazine* that after the initial conferences, "Our campaign has switched to looking at the gap that's created when we don't have the resources states do to resolve environmental issues and when we aren't even getting equal treatment from the federal government.... At the same time, we want to create a push to develop tribal laws that apply our indigenous philosophy, which calls for protecting Mother Earth. Whatever we develop will be more stringent than federal regulations."[29]

Opponents of hazardous and nuclear waste dumping on reservations have been influenced by meetings such as the "toxic powwow" at which they became aware of previous cases of environmental damage. In the southwest, Mescalero Apache Rufina Marie Laws became aware of the Navajo's health problems and started Humans against Nuclear Waste Dumps to oppose her tribal council's nuclear waste storage proposal. With a nuclear dump on her reservation, she said, "It will be like the Navajo uranium mining problems with so many cancers."[30] Laws's organization quickly networked with other Native American groups facing similar battles. According to Laws, "As I met more people concerned with this issue, I realized that it takes on a much broader scope than just the Apache. We are giving support to other Native American groups across the country that are facing this issue.... This radioactive waste knows no boundaries, be they geographical, political or racial."[31]

Indeed, environmental issues have crossed racial boundaries in several prominent cases, largely because the stakes involved in mining and waste storage have created coalitions of white and Indian communities that in most cases have been at odds with each other over other issues, notably treaty rights and sovereignty. Two cases suffice. In 1978, William Janklow was elected governor of South Dakota, thanks in part to contributions from energy corporations. In his first week as governor, Janklow abolished the state's Department of Environmental Protection and issued a gag order prohibiting state employees from commenting on energy policies. White and Indian citizens in South Dakota banded together to form the Black Hills Alliance to fight Janklow-supported energy development projects, which included uranium mining in the Black Hills region, that would have threatened water sources and the general quality of life. In a more recent case, the controversy over the Crandon Mine in Wisconsin united local whites and Native Americans who sparred in the 1980s, sometimes violently, over treaty rights to fish walleye. White residents and business owners feared the destruction of fishing waters and tourism; the town of Nashville established a Web site called Nashvilleundersiege.com to gain publicity for its anti-mine efforts. Chippewa elder Frances Van Zile, a leading opponent of the Crandon Mine, argued that company officials "don't care about us. They don't care if we live or die. All they want is that copper and zinc."[32] Non-Indians came to adopt this position as well.

Non-Indian newspapers have also supported activists' efforts to fight dumping proposals. Editors of the *St. Louis Post-Dispatch* argued, "How insulting and demeaning to Indians and non-Indian-Americans alike that waste haulers would target reservations as sites for the disposal of the refuse of modern society. Their rejection should be a warning to all Americans that the solution to the solid-waste problem must come in a way that does not further degrade the environment.... The Indians could have let American society continue to escape the direct consequences of its wasteful ways, but they chose not to. They chose their lands over a fast buck—which they desperately need. For that, they deserve praise and thanks."[33] Carter Camp of the Ponca Nation of Oklahoma echoes this argument, calling on federal officials to help Native Americans resist the demands of "American cities to use reservations like ocean dumps for their overgrown waste problems."[34]

Non-Indian politicians also have claimed that companies ruthlessly exploit Native Americans because they believe tribal leaders don't have the expertise to fully understand the technical issues involved in waste storage. Senator Tom Daschle of South Dakota joined the Sioux's protest over a proposed landfill by arguing that "Indians are the least prepared to make the kind of sophisticated decisions that need to be made about these proposals."[35] Some Sioux may have seen this comment as paternalistic, but they welcomed the support of their congressional representative. Other non-Indian politicians have both personal and political reasons to oppose dumping on Indian lands that lie within their state boundaries. The Goshute Nation's proposed nuclear waste storage project immediately generated protests from Utah state officials and congressional representatives. Governor Michael O. Leavitt is especially sensitive to nuclear issues, as he grew up in a community affected by atmospheric nuclear tests: "I have seen with my eyes the effects of radioactive material. I had friends in childhood die, farmers lose herds of sheep only to be told by the Federal Government, it must have been something they ate."[36] In opposing the Mescalero Apache's MRS program, U.S. senator Jeff Bingaman expressed concern about the Apache's handling of the waste but also argued that New Mexico had done its share to store the country's nuclear waste; for example, Carlsbad, New Mexico, houses waste from nuclear weapons production. Virtually all of New Mexico's local, state, and federal politicians opposed the Mescalero Apache's MRS proposal. New Mexico attorney general Tom Udall contested the plan for environmental and political reasons, opposing the Apache's exercise of tribal sovereignty on the grounds that the stakes involved were too high: "The issue of sovereignty gets pretty murky when you're talking about doing something that has a direct and substantial impact on public safety.... What happens 39 years from now if there is no permanent site? The state ultimately may have to pick up the pieces."[37]

Grace Thorpe's lobbying effort through the National Environmental Coalition of Native Americans helped persuade New Mexico's congressional delegation to cut off funding for the MRS program. Thorpe, the daughter of the late great Sac and Fox athlete Jim Thorpe, has become a leading opponent of economic development that threatens environmental damage. In a statement to the National Congress of American Indians, which has been criticized for accepting grants from the Department of Energy to consider nuclear dumping projects, Thorpe contested the stewardship argument made by advocates of waste storage projects. "The nuclear waste issue is causing American Indians to make serious environmental and possibly genocidal decisions regarding the future of our people. It is wrong to say that it is natural that we, as Native Americans, should accept radioactive waste on our lands, as the U.S. Department of Energy has said. It is a perversion of our beliefs and an insult to our intelligence to say that we are 'natural stewards' of these wastes."[38] Thorpe is one of a number of what environmental activist Winona LaDuke calls "plain-old heroes," many of whom are women, who believe that Native Americans need to take a leadership role in protecting the environment and in particular opposing nuclear waste.[39] "We cannot shirk our responsibilities for protecting the land, for protecting the waters and for protecting the air.... Is making money the only criteria for success, is our health and our safety and the future generations of our people against deformities to be ignored?.... We, the Indian people, must set an example for the rest of the nation. We, the Indian people must tell the polluters in no uncertain terms that we will not tolerate nuclear waste on our lands *no matter how much money the nuclear industry offers us.*"[40]

Joseph Geronimo, the great-grandson of the famous Apache leader Geronimo, a symbol of nineteenth-century resistance to the American way of life, is also concerned about future generations. Displaying a tenacity that would make his great-grandfather proud, he explained his vote against the MRS plan proposed by the Mescalero Apache Tribal Council by saying, "Very few of us will be around 40 years from now. Our children will be stuck with it. And what would they get for it? Nothing? Our people have made the choice that their tradition and culture is the most important thing in the world, and Grandmother Earth is not for sale at any price."[41] The theme of protecting the earth for future generations dominates the arguments of environmental activists. Navajo Jane Yazzi voiced concern for future generations in protesting a proposed incinerator and dump on her reservation. As she considered the economic virtues of the project, she also "thought about the land and how we rely on it—that this dump would poison the water and the land. It's not just temporary, my children and grandchildren will have to live on this land forever."[42] The Navajo in particular are sensitive to projects that damage the earth, given the sickness and death that has resulted from nuclear and coal-mining projects. Opposition also comes from within the small Goshute tribe, currently facing the prospects of a nuclear waste facility. Margene Bullcreek has organized several protests against the proposal, arguing, "We don't know what will happen years from now. As a traditionalist, we respect Mother Earth. We are doing this for future generations and our children."[43]

Echoing the concern of other Native American citizens, Bullcreek thinks tribal officials did not allow all Goshute citizens to vote on the nuclear storage proposal. Environmentalist opponents have challenged tribal councils' dealings with the Department of Energy and private utility companies, saying that those deals are conducted without the knowledge of the tribe's voting members. The Mescalero Apache voted down the tribal council's MRS proposal only to see the council stage a second and successful referendum. Opponents claimed council leaders bribed voters to change their minds. Rufina Marie Laws, the leader of anti-dumping forces on the Apache reservation, said that her people "have been diabolically and deliberately excluded" from decision making that may obligate tribal members "to agreements and contracts without the input and consensus of the people."[44] Perceptions of voter manipulation come from non-Indians as well. Michael Mariotte, executive director of the Nuclear Information and Resource Service, followed the Apache referendums and argued that the consortium of utility companies seeking waste storage on the reservation was "overtly racist" because it exploited poor members of the community and tried to "buy itself an election it couldn't win in a fair vote."[45] The outcome of elections staged on reservations dealing with waste or mining issues will sometimes hinge upon the pro-dumping or anti-dumping position of the candidates. On the Sioux reservation, for example, opponents of a large garbage and toxic ash landfill waged their campaign with the slogan "A vote for an incumbent is a vote for out-of-state trash."[46]

The Search for Alternatives

Opposition to the Crownpoint Mine on the Navajo reservation has divided families and the community at large. Facing a landscape of "hundreds of wells and miles of pipe" near her home in the Crownpoint area of the reservation, Grace Tsosie, a 66-year-old Navajo, asked a compelling question: "Would you want this to happen in your community?"[47] A related argument is that with all the sacrifices Native Americans make, their communities don't benefit from the end result. Mining companies take resources off reservations, converting them elsewhere into electricity, which may or may not benefit the reservations that provide the raw materials or handle the waste that nuclear power generates. As the energy crisis hit America in the 1970s, Native Americans resisted pressure to solve it at their expense, not only because many of them considered mining to be environmentally and spiritually damaging but also because they were not affected by the crisis. As a young Hopi put it, "Don't tell me about an energy crisis. I don't even have electricity in my village."[48] The Council of Energy Resource Tribes, the principal Native

American organization focused on energy development, acknowledges the contradiction. A. David Lester, CERT's executive director, pointed out that in the year 2000, "Indian Tribes own significant energy and water resources that produce electric power for millions of other Americans. Tribes have borne a disproportionate share of the burden from energy development, yet are among those who benefit least from it."[49] A Department of Energy report (March 2000) supports Lester's claim: "Household energy availability and use on Indian lands are significantly below that of non-Indian households. In fact sizable Indian populations have no access to electricity at all. This perpetuates a low standard of living, as energy supply and economic well-being are closely linked."[50]

Navajo and Hopi, both of which face continued environmental damage from Peabody Western Coal Company projects, have been at odds over land claims and the issue of coal-mining leases. But the impact of mining on water supplies has brought the Hopi and Navajo together in the Black Mesa Water Coalition (BMWC), which opposes the use of Native American water supplies for industrial purposes. Both nations understand that their governments depend on mining revenue to fund other projects, and they don't call for the outright closure of the coal mines. But the threat to the water supply has raised important questions among activists. Said Roberto Nutlouis of the Indigenous Youth Coalition, "We need to stop financing the dominant society with resources from here" and "develop [resources] in a way that is sensitive to the culture of our people."[51] Members of the BMWC and other environmental groups like Citizens against Ruining Our Environment are calling on their councils to limit their exposure to corporate control and consider sustainable nonextractive energy production such as solar and wind power. Laurie Goodman, a Navajo member of CARE, testified at the World Uranium Hearing in Salzburg, Austria, in 1992, offering a compelling argument for spiritually sound and environmentally safe economic development: "Our people are being sacrificed to satisfy America's need for ever more energy. Native lands are sought for use as burial ground for hazardous and radioactive waste. As an organization we asked ourselves: Why are we allowing this to continue? Enough is enough! Why should we sacrifice our land, culture and future generations so that the dominant society can continue to live a lifestyle that demands and depletes our resources? Viable alternatives which are cleaner, safer and cheaper are available."[52] Goodman argued that solar and wind power and energy conservation projects could benefit both Indian and non-Indian societies.

Wind and Solar Power

Interest in renewable energy sources like wind and solar power started to grow in the early 1990s. In 1994, the Department of Energy began offering small grants to Native American communities to explore renewable energy projects; 33 small-scale projects were started, fueling interest in the program and in the prospects for energy sources other than coal and uranium. Indian lands offer some of the best territory for such projects. Just as important, such projects offer an alternative to extractive and thus environmentally damaging development, representing both business opportunity and a form of development that dovetails with as well as protects cultural traditions. Journalist Peter Asmus described the Hopi's perspective on solar power: "Some traditional Hopi . . . revere the spiritual power of the earth so greatly that they refuse to allow infrastructure such as power lines to scar the land. Photovoltaic (PV) panels offer a solution that satisfies both ancient cultural practices and future needs."[53] Several Hopi elders have started to use solar electricity. In addition, the Ute Mountain Ute of Colorado have adapted solar power to their businesses by using PV-powered pumps in their livestock operations.

Other native communities have begun to consider more environmentally friendly projects such as wind power, including a number of tribes that rejected waste dumping in the early 1990s. Along with the Otoe-Missouria tribe, the Kaw of Oklahoma have commissioned feasibility studies, supported by the Oklahoma Department of Commerce and the U.S. Department of Energy. The Spirit Lake Sioux of North Dakota recently installed a wind turbine to provide power for their casino.

The Department of Energy has provided grants to other tribes looking to use wind power. The Blackfeet of northwestern Montana have had much success with the development of their oil resources, but like other communities they fear that such extractive development will damage reservation lands. Blackfeet opposed to oil drilling have fought against projects in what they consider the sacred lands of the Badger–Two Medicine wilderness area. When tribal officials signed a 50-year oil and gas lease with a Canadian development company in 1997, the Blackfeet Nation became divided over the prospects of a massive drilling program. A number of Blackfeet protested the poor lease rates in the contract, while others demanded that the government conduct a proper environmental impact study before agreeing to drilling. Though oil has potential for providing tribal revenue, tribal officials are also interested in investigating wind power. Using a DOE grant, Blackfeet officials installed a small 100-kilowatt turbine, in part because it offered them an opportunity to assert control over development projects. Marty Wilde of the Blackfeet Community College extolled the potential of wind power but also called the project "a glowing example of how local people took the initiative. Historically, hustlers have promised the world [to the Blackfeet], only to let them down time and time again. This project could be a major morale boost that will allow the Blackfeet tribe to determine their own destiny."[54]

In September 2000, the Blackfeet became the first Native American community to establish a utility-scale wind power project when it signed an agreement with the SeaWest WindPower company; the Blackfeet I Wind Power Project would produce 22 megawatts, enough power to electrify more than 6,000 houses. According to Earl Old Person, chairman of the Blackfeet

Tribal Business Council, "This wind energy project will allow the Blackfeet Tribe to take advantage of one of our most plentiful natural resources on our Reservation."[55] Although the deal with SeaWest WindPower fell apart, many Blackfeet hope wind power will prove more profitable and thus help preserve and protect their lands for future generations to come. If that can be done, the Blackfeet and many other native communities may be able to heal that "split" to which Jonathan Buffalo referred, allowing Native Americans to engage economically with the outside world while maintaining important spiritual and cultural ties among themselves.

NOTES

1. Donald L. Fixico, *The Invasion of Indian Country in the Twentieth Century: American Capitalism and Tribal Natural Resources* (Niwot: University Press of Colorado, 1998), p. 147.

2. Ronald Reagan, *Public Papers of the Presidents of the United States: Ronald Reagan*, vol. 1 (Washington, D.C.: Government Printing Office, 1983), p. 98.

3. Peter Iverson, "*We Are Still Here*"*: American Indians in the Twentieth Century* (Wheeling, Ill.: Harlan Davidson, 1998), p. 168.

4. Ward Churchill, *Struggle for the Land: Indigenous Resistance to Genocide, Ecocide, and Expropriation in Contemporary America* (Monroe, Maine: Common Courage Press, 1993), p. 267.

5. "U.S. to Pay Workers for Radiation Exposure," *The Return of Navajo Boy*, 12 April 2000, <www.navajoboy.com/ARTUS.HTM> (accessed August 2002).

6. Bruce Selcraig, "Common Ground: Native Americans Join to Stop the Newest of the Indian Wars," *Sierra*, May–June 1994, p. 47.

7. Peter MacDonald, "Navajo Natural Resources," in *American Indian Environments: Ecological Issues in Native American History*, ed. Christopher Vecsey and Robert Venables (Syracuse, N.Y.: Syracuse University Press, 1980), pp. 168–70.

8. "Tribal Council Seeks Help with Development of Crow Reservation," *St. Louis Post-Dispatch*, 6 February 1989.

9. Elouise Schumacher, "Native Americans and N-Waste—Yakimas Take First Step toward Allowing Dump on Reservation," *Seattle Times*, 3 February 1992.

10. Bill Lambrecht, "Money Fights Land Purity for Indians' Consideration," *St. Louis Post-Dispatch*, 24 December 1990.

11. Thomas Lippman, "Tribe Considers Nuclear Dump; Application for Study Grant Is First under Energy Dept. Program," *Washington Post*, 21 October 1991.

12. Lippman, "Tribe Considers Nuclear Dump."

13. Randel Hanson, "Indian Burial Grounds for Nuclear Waste," *Multinational Monitor* 16, no. 9 (September 1995), pp. 4–5. <www.cwis.org/fwdp/Americas/nukewast.txt> (accessed June 2002).

14. David Einstein, "New Mexico Tribe Wants to Build Nuclear Waste Dump on Reservation," *San Francisco Chronicle*, 23 April 1994.

15. Rudy Abramson, "New Mexico Apaches Have a Hot Idea: Providing Nuclear Waste Storage," *Los Angeles Times*, 28 May 1994.

16. George Johnson, "Nuclear Waste Dump Gets Tribe's Approval in Re-Vote," *New York Times*, 11 March 1995.

17. Tom Meersman, "NSP's Talks on Nuclear Waste Break Off," *Minneapolis Star Tribune,* 19 April 1996.

18. Matthew Wald, "Tribe in Utah Fights for Nuclear Waste Dump," *New York Times,* 18 April 1999.

19. Frank Clifford, "Oil Field on Reservation Fuels Dispute," *Los Angeles Times,* 28 June 1999.

20. Brenda Norrell, "Oil Battle Focuses on Profits vs. Future Generations," *Indian Country Today,* 11 July 2001.

21. Dennis McDonald, "Indian People Just Want to be Themselves," *Education Week,* 2 August 1989, p. 1. <www.edweek.org> (accessed June 2002).

22. William A. Young, *Quest for Harmony: Native American Spiritual Traditions* (New York: Seven Bridges Press, 2002), p. 330.

23. Young, *Quest for Harmony,* p. 343.

24. Amanda Siestreem and Paul Rowley, "An Interview with Sayo': Kla Kindness: An Oneida Woman Talks about Mining," *Cultural Survival Quarterly* 25, no. 1 (2001), p. 2.

25. Hanson, "Indian Burial Grounds for Nuclear Waste," p. 1.

26. Daniel Brook, "Environmental Genocide: Native Americans and Toxic Waste," *American Journal of Economics and Sociology* 57, no. 1 (January 1998).

27. Bill Lambrecht, "Choctaw Rebellion Toxic Waste on Tribal Land Splits Tribe," *St. Louis Post-Dispatch,* 28 March 1991.

28. John Harmon, "Environmental Plight of Reservations Spurs Indians," *Atlanta Journal-Constitution,* 20 May 1992.

29. Barbara Ruben, "Tom Goldtooth: Holding the Government Accountable," *Environmental Action Magazine* 25, no. 3 (fall 1993), pp. 13–14.

30. Hanson, "The Mescalero Apache: Nuclear Waste and the Privatization of Genocide," *The Circle* 15, no. 8 (August 1994), p. 4.

31. Hanson, "The Mescalero Apache," p. 4.

32. Zoltan Grossman and Al Gedicks, "Native Resistance to Multinational Mining Corporations in Wisconsin," *Cultural Survival Quarterly* 25, no. 1 (spring 2001), p. 4. <www.wrpc.net/cs0301.html> (accessed June 2002).

33. "The Paiute Say No," editorial, *St. Louis Post-Dispatch,* 12 February 1991.

34. Bill Lambrecht, "Money Fights Land Purity for Indians' Consideration," *St. Louis Post-Dispatch,* 24 December 1990.

35. Lambrecht, "Money Fights Land Purity for Indians' Consideration."

36. Wald, "Tribe in Utah Fights for Nuclear Waste Dump."

37. Johnson, "Nuclear Waste Dump."

38. "Pauite-Shoshone Overwhelming [sic] Oppose Nuclear Storage at Ft. McDermitt," *The Circle,* (October 1994), p. 36.

39. Winona LaDuke, "Native Environmentalism," *Cultural Survival Quarterly* 17, no. 4 (1994), <www.indians.org/library/nate.html> (accessed September 2003).

40. Grace Thorpe, "No Nuclear Waste on Indian Land," in *Red Power: The American Indians' Fight for Freedom,* 2d ed., ed. Alvin M. Josephy Jr., Joane Nagel, and Troy Johnson (Lincoln: University of Nebraska Press, 1999), p. 163.

41. Hanson, "Indian Burial Grounds for Nuclear Waste," p. 4.

42. Quoted in Josephy Jr., Nagel, and Johnson, *Red Power,* p. 164.

43. "Leavitt Reiterates Opposition to Nuclear Waste Storage," *Ojibwe News,* 6 June 1997.

44. Hanson, "Indian Burial Grounds for Nuclear Waste," p. 4.

45. Meersman, "NSP's Talks on Nuclear Waste Break Off."

46. Linda Kanamine, "Tribes Take on Waste Industry," *USA Today,* 10 June 1991.

47. Chris Shuey, "Uranium Mining Plan Splits Navajo Communities in New Mexico," *The Workbook* 21 (summer 1996), <www.antenna.nl/wise/uranium/upcrp.html> (accessed August 2002).

48. Fixico, *The Invasion of Indian Country in the Twentieth Century,* p. 145.

49. Council for Energy Resource Tribes, "Indian Energy 2001: Energy Solutions," <www.certredearth.com/fall01/energy.shtml> (accessed August 2002).

50. Department of Energy, "Energy Consumption and Renewable Energy Development Potential on Indian Lands," April 2000, <www.eia.doe.gov/cneaf/solar.renewables/ilands/introduction.html> (accessed August 2002).

51. Brad Miller, "Draining the Life from the Land," *Earth Island Journal* 17 (autumn 2002), p. 28.

52. "Testimonies, Lectures, Conclusions: The World Uranium Hearing, Salzburg 1992," <www.ratical.com/radiation/WorldUraniumHearing/Index.html> (accessed August 2002).

53. Peter Asmus, "Landscapes of Power: Can Renewable Energy Help Native Americans Reclaim Their Resources," *Amicus Journal* 18, no. 4 (winter 1998), p. 13.

54. Asmus, "Landscapes of Power," p. 14.

55. "Blackfeet Indian Tribe to Build First Commercial Utility-Scale Wind Power Project on Tribal Lands," PR Newswire, 6 September 2000.

QUESTIONS

1) Suppose that uranium is discovered in your town, which is affected by high unemployment. Choose sides and debate the pros and cons of agreeing to a uranium-mining operation in your community.

2) Define *environmental racism.* Is environmental racism at work in the targeting of Native American lands for dumping of hazardous or radioactive materials? Compare this with examples of hazardous or toxic sites in poor neighborhoods across the country. Also, find out how wealthy communities deal with nuclear power stations or toxic sites near them in your state. Write a report for your classmates.

3) Compare the views of Wendell Chino, tribal leader of the Mescalero Apache, and those of Grace Thorpe, the environmental activist opposed to nuclear waste dumping. In what ways do the two differ? Is there common ground? Research a tribal controversy in your state and see what the consequences have been for tribal relations.

4) If your community uses electricity that is generated by a nuclear power plant, to what extent does that fact complicate your examination of the issue?

5) Research the outcome of the Goshute Nation's proposal to store nuclear wastes while Yucca Mountain is being built. What new dimensions of the issue emerge from this particular case? Trace the proposed route of transportation of the waste to Yucca Mountain. Consider the effects on people, animals, and the environment in the exposure radius. Write a position paper explaining why you approve

or disapprove of the Yucca Mountain plan; be sure to include ramifications of disaster situations.

6) Examine the debate over storing nuclear wastes at Yucca Mountain. To what extent are Native Americans' concerns a part of that debate?
7) Research the outcome of the Crandon Mine controversy in Wisconsin. To what extent has it created a diverse coalition of interests opposed to the mine? What are the principal arguments that coalition uses to oppose the mine?
8) What is the most compelling reason to oppose nuclear waste storage on Indian reservations?
9) What is the most compelling reason to support nuclear waste storage on Indian reservations?
10) Research the July 16, 1978, accident near Churchrock, New Mexico, in which nearly 100 million gallons of radioactive water were released into the Rio Puerco River and surrounding lands. Why was this incident not better publicized in comparison to the Three Mile Island accident? To what extent was "environmental racism" part of the equation?
11) Tex Hall, chairman of North Dakota's Three Affiliated Tribes, proposed in the summer of 2002 to build a large oil refinery on the Fort Berthold reservation in North Dakota. Contact tribal officials by phone, e-mail, or letter, and search through local and national newspapers to determine the status of the project and any opposition that has formed against it.
12) Research the state of alternative energy use on Indian reservations. Has wind power become an economically viable form of development? Discuss the pros and cons of wind power on Indian reservations and compare the dynamics of these cases with those of projects planned elsewhere in the United States, particularly near Cape Cod, Massachusetts.
13) Consider the arguments made by non-Indians, politicians in particular, both for and against mining and waste storage on Indian lands. Which arguments are the most compelling and which are the least supportable?
14) The Zuni are joining forces with other groups to stop strip mining in the Salt River Project, which threatens the Zuni Salt Lake. Explore this issue by looking at the coalition formed to stop the project. What is their common ground?
15) What is the status of the Blackfeet Nation oil lease with the K2 Energy Corporation of Calgary? To what extent were environmentalists able to stop or to change the oil-drilling program on the reservation?

RESOURCE GUIDE

Suggested Readings

Ali, Saleem, and Larissa Behrendt, eds. *Mining Indigenous Lands: Can Impacts and Benefits Be Reconciled*. Special issue of *Cultural Survival Quarterly* 25, no. 1 (2001).

Allen, Leslie. "Who Should Control Hazardous Waste on Native American Lands?" *Ecology Law Quarterly* 14, no. 1 (1987).

Ambler, Marjane. *Breaking the Iron Bonds: Indian Control of Energy Development.* Lawrence: University Press of Kansas, 1990.

Asmus, Peter. "Landscapes of Power: Can Renewable Energy Help Native Americans Reclaim Their Resources?" *Amicus Journal* 19, no. 4 (winter 1998).

Bauerlein, Monika. "Prairie Island Revisited: A Minnesota Reservation Fights for a Nuclear-Free Future." *Native Americas* 12, no. 12 (1995).

Beasley, Conger, Jr. "The Dirty History of Nuclear Power." *E* 5, no. 1 (February 1994).

Brook, Daniel. "Environmental Genocide: Native Americans and Toxic Waste." *American Journal of Economics and Sociology* 57, no. 1 (January 1998).

Brugge, Doug, Timothy Benally, and Esther Yazzie-Lewis. "Uranium Mining on Navajo Land." *Cultural Survival Quarterly* 25, no. 1 (2001).

Churchill, Ward. *Struggle for the Land: Indigenous Resistance to Genocide, Ecocide, and Expropriation in Contemporary America.* Monroe, Maine: Common Courage Press, 1993.

Churchill, Ward, and Winona LaDuke. "Native North America: The Political Economy of Radioactive Colonialism." In *The State of Native America: Genocide, Colonization, and Resistance*, edited by M. Annette Jaimes. Boston: South End Press, 1992.

Davis, Tony. "Apaches Split over Nuclear Waste." *High Country News,* 27 January 1992.

———. "Uranium Has Decimated Navajo Miners." *High Country News,* 18 June 1990.

Eichstaedt, Peter H. *If You Poison Us: Uranium and Native Americans.* Santa Fe: Red Crane Books, 1994.

Fixico, Donald L. *The Invasion of Indian Country in the Twentieth Century: American Capitalism and Tribal Natural Resources.* Niwot: University Press of Colorado, 1998.

Gedicks, Al. *The New Resource Wars: Native and Environmental Struggles against Multinational Corporations.* Boston: South End Press, 1993.

Grinde, Donald A., and Bruce E. Johansen. *Ecocide of Native America: Environmental Destruction of Indian Lands and Peoples.* Sante Fe: Clear Light, 1995.

Grossman, Zoltan. "Linking the Native Movement for Sovereignty and the Environmental Movement." *Z Magazine,* November 1995. <//cnie.org/NAE/docs/grossman.htm> (accessed August 2002).

Grossman, Zoltan, and Al Gedicks. "Native Resistance to Multinational Mining Corporations in Wisconsin." *Cultural Survival Quarterly* 25, no. 1 (2001).

Hernandez, Juan A. Avila. "How the Feds Are Pushing Nuclear Waste on Reservations." *Cultural Survival Quarterly* 17, no. 4 (1994).

Josephy, Alvin M., Jr., Joane Nagel, and Troy Johnson, eds. *Red Power: The American Indians' Fight for Freedom.* 2d ed. Lincoln: University of Nebraska Press, 1999.

LaDuke, Winona. "Native Environmentalism." *Cultural Survival Quarterly* 17, no. 4 (1994).

Lewis, David R. "Native American Environmental Issues." *American Indian Quarterly* 19, no. 3 (spring 1995).

MacDonald, Peter. "Navajo Natural Resources." In *American Indian Environments: Ecological Issues in Native American History,* edited by Christopher Vecsey and Robert Venables. Syracuse, N.Y.: Syracuse University Press, 1980.

Miller, Brad. "Draining the Life from the Land." *Earth Island Journal* 17, no. 3 (autumn 2002).

Nietschmann, Bernard, and William Le Bon. "Nuclear States and Fourth World Nations." *Cultural Survival Quarterly* 11, no. 4 (1988).

Ringholz, Raye C. *Uranium Frenzy: Boom and Bust on the Colorado Plateau.* New York: Norton, 1989.

Robinson, William Paul. "Uranium Production and Its Effects on Navajo Communities along the Rio Puerco in Western New Mexico." In *Race and the Incidence of Environmental Hazards,* edited by Bunyan Bryant and Paul Mohai. Boulder, Colo.: Westview Press, 1992.

Ruben, Barbara. "Grave Reservations: Waste Company Proposals Targeting Native American Lands Are Meeting with a Growing Pattern of Resistance." *Environmental Action Magazine* 23, no. 1 (July/August 1991).

———. "Protecting Mother Earth's Bottom Line." *Environmental Action Magazine* 25, no. 3 (fall 1993).

Shuey, Chris. "Uranium Mining Plan Splits Navajo Communities in New Mexico." *The Workbook* (Southwest Research and Information Center publication) 21, no. 2 (summer 1996).

"Testimonies, Lectures, Conclusions. The World Uranium Hearing, Salzburg 1992." <www.ratical.com/radiation/WorldUraniumHearing/Index.html> (accessed August 2002).

Thorpe, Grace. "No Nuclear Waste on Indian Land." In *Red Power: The American Indians' Fight for Freedom.* 2d ed. Edited by Alvin M. Josephy Jr., Joane Nagel, and Troy Johnson. Lincoln: University of Nebraska Press, 1999.

Tomsho, Robert. "Dumping Grounds: Indian Tribes Contend with Some of Worst of America's Pollution." *Wall Street Journal,* 29 November 1990.

Viers, Becky J. Miles. "Environmental Law: Uranium Mining on the Navajo Reservation." *American Indian Law Review* 7, no. 1 (1978).

Young, William A. *Quest for Harmony: Native American Spiritual Traditions.* New York: Seven Bridges Press, 2002.

Videos

Radioactive Reservations. 55 min. For information, see <www.alphacdc.com/necona/nufre.html>.

The Return of Navajo Boy. 52 min. For information, see <www.navajoboy.com>.

Wasteland. 15 min. For information, see <www.alphacdc.com/necona/nufre.html>.

Web Sites

Council of Energy Resource Tribes. <www.certredearth.com>.

Eastern Navajo Diné against Uranium Mining. <www.endaum.org>.

"Energy Consumption and Renewable Energy Development Potential on Indian Lands." April 2000. <www.eia.doe.gov/cneaf/solar.renewables/ilands/toc.html>. Department of Energy study of Native Americans' resources, including wind and solar power potential.

Hanford Nuclear Reservation. <www.hanford.gov/doe/inp/index.htm>. Department of Energy site on the Hanford Nuclear Reservation and its connection with four neighboring Native American communities.

"Indian Country Environmental Justice Clinic." *Vermont Law School.* <www.vermontlaw.edu/community/firstnations/icejc.cfm>. Description of the ICEJC and the First Nations environmental law program.

Indigenous Environmental Network. <www.ienearth.org>.

"Memories Come to Us in the Rain and the Wind." <www.inmotionmagazine.com/brugge.html>. Excerpts from the book *Memories Come to Us in the Rain and the Wind: Oral Histories and Photographs of Navajo Uranium Miners and Their Families.*

Midwest Treaty Network. <www.alphacdc.com/treaty/content.html>. Offers information on Wisconsin battles over the Crandon Mine.

National Environmental Coalition of Native Americans. <www.alphacdc.com/necona>. Grace Thorpe's antinuclear site.

National Tribal Environmental Council. <www.ntec.org>.

Native Americans and the Environment. <www.indians.org/library/all.html>. Sponsored by the American Indian Heritage Foundation.

Navajo Nation Environmental Protection Agency. <www.epa.gov/owm/mab/indian/navajo.htm>.

Navajo Uranium Radiation Victims. <www.sonic.net/~kerry/uranium.html>.

Prairie Island Coalition. <www.no-nukes.org/prairieisland/processing.html>. Coalition against nuclear power.

Region 9: Indian Programs. <www.epa.gov/region9/indian>. Environmental Protection Agency site on American Indian environmental issues.

The Return of Navajo Boy. <www.navajoboy.com>. Information on the Navajo radiation documentary.

Southwest Research and Information Center. <www.sric.org/index.html>. Central organization for environmental information and advocacy in the American Southwest.

INDEX

Navajo codetalkers, xi
Navajo-Hopi Land Settlement Act of 1974, 66

About the Author

PAUL C. ROSIER is Visiting Assistant Professor of History at Villanova University.